Citizen Designer

Perspectives on Design Responsibility

Edited by Steven Heller and Véronique Vienne

ALLWORTH PRESS
NEW YORK

School of
VISUAL ARTS

09 08 07 06 05
6 5 4 3 2

Published by Allworth Press
An imprint of Allworth Communications, Inc.
10 East 23rd Street, New York, NY 10010

Cover design by Milan Bozic,
James Victore Inc.

Page composition/typography by
SR Desktop Services, Ridge, NY

Library of Congress Cataloging-in-
Publication Data
Citizen designer : perspectives on design
responsibility / edited by Steven Heller
and Véronique Vienne.
        p.   cm.
Includes bibliographical references and
index.
    ISBN 1-58115-265-5 (pbk.)
    1. Design—Philosophy.   2. Design—
Social aspects.   3. Design—History—20th
century.   4. Designers—Interviews.
I. Heller, Steven.   II. Vienne, Veronique.

    NK1505.C54 2003
    745.4—dc21   2003004213

Printed in Canada

*This book is dedicated to
Milton Glaser,
for your wisdom.*

The editors would like to thank all of the contributors to this book. Their work on behalf of society is not to be underestimated.

Thanks also to our editors, for without them there would be no book: Nicole Potter, senior editor, Jessica Rozler, editorial assistant, and Tad Crawford, publisher.

James Victore's cover and interior design have given this content its appealing form. Thanks again to him and to Milan Bozic at James Victore Inc.

Contents

Introduction

Steven Heller

Milton Glaser often says, "Good design is good citizenship." But does this mean making good design is an indispensable obligation to the society and culture in which designers are citizens? Or does it suggest that design has inherent properties that when applied in a responsible manner contribute to a well-being that enhances everyone's life as a citizen?

For the answer we must also ask the question: What is good design? Is it rightness of form or aesthetic perfection? Is it flawless conception or intelligent usability? The converse, bad or poor design is design that doesn't work. So, is bad design bad citizenship? In fact, bad design is just plain mean while good design presumably serves many citizens.

Nonetheless, "goodness" is subjective and one can be a good (or great) designer without necessarily being a good citizen. But if good design (regardless of style or mannerism) adds value to society, by either pushing the cultural envelope or maintaining the status quo at a high level, then design and citizenship must go hand in hand.

Thomas Watson Jr. said, "Good design is good business." When the former IBM chairman and leading American corporate design patron proclaimed this in the fifties, business was the white knight of postwar American society. Yet during the subsequent years, good business has not always been good business, and good design has sometimes unwittingly supported bad companies. Business malfeasance is all too common these days. For example, having risen to the level of tragic-comedy, Enron's shenanigans were the apotheosis of corporate wrong-doing in the year 2002. During the process of spiraling into the abyss, Enron's design—specifically the Enron logo created by Paul Rand in 1996—became the MGM (Money Grabbing Mongrels) lion of greed and corruption. Rand's mark was created to bond Enron's workforce to the corporate culture while branding the company's positive assets on the nation's consciousness. In the modernist tradition, graphic design was employed to foster professionalism, and in this instance Enron's mark helped unify the chaos of its sprawling business. At the time, there was no hint that Enron's leaders would defraud employees or investors; in fact, just the opposite. As a new energy conglomerate it assured jobs for thousands and services to millions. Good design underscored the promise of good business, and, by extension, good citizenship. But when Enron started to rot from the inside the logo became an icon of decay.

So, what is the responsibility of a designer when design is impeccable but the client is tainted? Being accountable to some moral standard is the key. A designer must be professionally, culturally, and socially responsible for the impact his or her design has on the citizenry. Indeed, every good citizen must understand that his or her respective actions will have reactions. All individual acts, including the creation and manufacture of design for a client, exert impact on others. But Rand could not foresee Enron's gross betrayal. And even if large corporations are sometimes suspect, why should he or any designer refuse to work for Enron or any similar establishment? A designer cannot afford to hire investigators to compile dossiers about whether a business is savory or not. Yet certain benchmarks must apply, such as knowing what, in fact, a company does and how it does it. And if a designer has any doubts, plenty of public records exist that provide for informed decisions. However, each designer must address this aspect of good citizenship as he or she sees fit.

Two years ago, when Milton Glaser was illustrating Dante's Purgatory, he become interested in the "Road to Hell" and developed a little questionnaire to see where he stood in terms of his own willingness to lie. Beginning with fairly minor misdemeanors, the following twelve steps increase to some major indiscretions.

1. Designing a package to look bigger on the shelf.
2. Designing an ad for a slow, boring film to make it seem like a light-hearted comedy.
3. Designing a crest for a new vineyard to suggest that it has been in business for a long time.
4. Designing a jacket for a book whose sexual content you find personally repellent.
5. Designing a medal using steel from the World Trade Center to be sold as a profit-making souvenir of September 11.
6. Designing an advertising campaign for a company with a history of known discrimination in minority hiring.
7. Designing a package for children whose contents you know are low in nutrition value and high in sugar content.
8. Designing a line of T-shirts for a manufacturer that employs child labor.

9. Designing a promotion for a diet product that you know doesn't work.
10. Designing an ad for a political candidate whose policies you believe would be harmful to the general public.
11. Designing a brochure for an SUV that turned over frequently in emergency conditions and was known to have killed 150 people.
12. Designing an ad for a product whose frequent use could result in the user's death.

A dozen additional steps of varied consequence could be added, but Glaser's list addresses a significant range of contentious issues. Designers are called upon to make routine decisions regarding scale, color, image, etc.—things that may seem insignificant but will inevitably affect behavior in some way. An elegant logo can legitimize the illegitimate; a beautiful package can spike up the sales of an inferior product; an appealing trade character can convince kids that something dangerous is essential. The graphic designer is as accountable as the marketing and publicity departments for the propagation of a message or idea.

Talented designers are predisposed to create good-looking work. We are taught to marry type and image into pleasing and effective compositions that attract the eye and excite the senses. Do this well, we're told, and good jobs are plentiful; do it poorly and we'll produce junk mail for the rest of our lives. However, to be what in this book we call a "citizen designer" requires more than talent. As Glaser notes, the key is to ask questions, for the answers will result in responsible decisions. Without responsibility, talent is too easily wasted on waste.

This book examines and critiques through essays and interviews three areas in which designers practice and in which responsibility to oneself and society is essential. Sections on Social Responsibility, Professional Responsibility, and Artistic Responsibility offer insight into how our peers view their practices as dependent on moral codes. The final part, Raves and Rants, is a soapbox, pure and simple. Our goal in editing this book is not to offer dogmatic decrees or sanctimonious screeds but to address the concern that the design field, like society as a whole, is built on the foundation of . . . well, you fill in the blank.

Part I
Social Responsibility

Good Citizenship
Design as a Social and Political Force
Katherine McCoy

This decade finds us in a crisis of values in the United States. Our increasingly multicultural society is experiencing a breakdown in shared values—national values, tribal values, personal values, even family values—consensual motivating values that create a common sense of purpose in a community.

The question is: How can a heterogeneous society develop shared values and yet encourage cultural diversity and personal freedom? Designers and design education are part of the problem and can be part of the answer. We cannot afford to be passive anymore. Designers must be good citizens and participate in the shaping of our government and society. As designers, we could use our particular talents and skills to encourage others to wake up and participate as well.

Before the U.S. congratulates itself too much on the demise of Communism, we must remember that our American capitalist democracy is not what it used to be, either. Much of our stagnation comes from this breakdown of values. Entrepreneurial energy and an optimistic work ethic have deteriorated into individual self-interest, complacency, corporate greed, and resentment between ethnic groups and economic classes. Our traditional common American purpose is fading— that sense of building something new where individuals could progress through participating in a system that provided opportunity. Consumerism and materialism now seem to be the only ties that bind. The one group that seems to be bound by more than this is the Far Right; but their bond is regressive, a desire to force fundamentalist prescriptive values on the rest of us.

In the Reagan-Bush era we were told it was all O.K., that we could spend and consume with no price tag attached. During this period, graphic designers enjoyed the spoils of artificial prosperity with the same passive hedonism as the rest of the country. Now we are beginning to realize it was not all O.K. The earth is being poisoned, its resources depleted, and the U.S. has gone from a creditor to a debtor nation. Our self-absorption and lack of activism has left a void filled by minority single-issue groups aggressively pushing their concerns.

There are serious threats to our civil liberties in the United States from both fundamentalist censorship of the Right and political correctness from the Left. We have seen the dismemberment of artistic freedom at the National Endowment for the Arts in recent years, and aggressive attempts to censor public schools' teaching—from Darwin to Hemingway to safe sex—continue. A conservative Congress continues to push for content restrictions on Internet discourse. And as graphic designers specializing in visual communications, the content of our communications could be seriously curtailed if we do not defend our freedom of expression.

But even more troubling is our field's own self-censorship. How many graphic designers today would feel a loss if their freedom of expression were handcuffed? Most of our colleagues never exercise their right to communicate on public issues or potentially controversial content. Remove our freedom of speech and graphic designers might never notice. We have trained a profession that feels political or social concerns are either extraneous to our work, or inappropriate.

Thinking back to 1968, the atmosphere at Unimark International during my first year of work typified this problem. Unimark (an idealistic international design office with Massimo Vignelli and Jay Doblin as vice presidents and Herbert Bayer on the board) was dedicated to the ideal of the rationally objective professional. The graphic designer was to be the neutral transmitter of the client's messages. Clarity and objectivity were the goal. During that year, the designers I worked with, save one notable exception, were all remarkably disinterested in the social and political upheavals taking place around us. Vietnam was escalating with body counts touted on every evening newscast; the New Left rioted before the Democratic National Convention in Chicago; Martin Luther King and Robert Kennedy were assassinated; and Detroit was still smoking from its riots just down the street from our office. Yet hardly a word was spoken on these subjects. We were encouraged to wear white lab coats, perhaps so the messy external environment would not contaminate our surgically clean detachment.

These white lab coats make an excellent metaphor for the apolitical designer, cherishing the myth of universal, value-free design—that design is a clinical process akin to chemistry, scientifically pure and neutral, conducted in a sterile laboratory environment with precisely predictable results. Yet Lawrence and Oppenheimer and a thousand other examples teach us that even chemists and physicists must have a contextual view of their work in the socio-political world around them.

During that time, I became increasingly interested in the social idealism of the times: the Civil Rights movement, the anti-Vietnam peace movement, the antimaterialism and social experimentation of the New Left, and radical feminism. Yet it was very difficult to relate these new ideas to the design that I was practicing and the communication process that I loved so much. Or perhaps the difficulty was not the values of design so much as the values of the design community. About all I could connect with was designing and sending (to appalled family members) an anti-Vietnam, feminist Christmas card and silk-screening T-shirts with a geometricized "Swiss" version of the feminist symbol. Meanwhile, we continued to serve the corporate and advertising worlds with highly "professional" design solutions.

The implication of the word "professional" as we use it is indicative of the problem here. How often do we hear, "Act like a professional" or, "I'm a professional, I can handle it?" Being a professional means to put aside one's personal reactions regardless of the situation and to carry on. Prostitutes, practitioners of the so-called oldest profession, must maintain an extreme of cool objectivity about this most intimate of human activities, highly disciplining their personal responses to deliver an impartial and consistent product to their clients.

This ideal of the dispassionate professional distances us from ethical and political values. Think of the words used to describe the disciplined, objective professional, whether it be scientist, doctor, or lawyer: "impartial," "dispassionate," "disinterested." These become pejorative terms in a difficult world crying for compassion, interest, concern, commitment, and involvement. Disinterest is appropriate for a neutral arbitrator but not for an advocate. In fact, design education most often trains students to think of themselves as passive arbitrators of the message between the client/sender and audience/receiver, rather than as advocates for the message content or the audience. Here is the challenge: how to achieve the objectivity and consistency of professionalism without stripping oneself of personal convictions.

Our concept of graphic design professionalism has been largely shaped, and generally for the better, by the legacy of twentieth-century modernism as it has come to us through the Bauhaus and Swiss lineages. However, there are several dominant aspects of this modernist ethic that have done much to distance designers from their cultural milieu. The ideals, forms, methods, and mythology of modernism are a large part of this problem of detachment, including the paradigms of universal form, abstraction, self-referentialism, value-free design, rationality, and objectivity.

Objective rationalism, particularly that of the Bauhaus, provided a much needed antidote to the sentimentality and gratuitous eclecticism found in nineteenth-century mass production, visual communications, and architecture. Linked to functionalism, objective analysis formed the basis of problem-solving methods to generate functional design solutions to improve the quality of daily life. Expanded more recently to include systems design, this attitude has done much to elevate the quality of design thinking.

Linked to the ideal of the objective, clear-sighted designer is the ideal of value-free universal forms. Perhaps a reaction to the frequent political upheavals between European nations, especially World War I, early-modern designers hoped to find internationalist design forms and attitudes that would cross those national, ethnic, and class barriers that had caused such strife. In addition, a universal design—one design for all—would be appropriate for the classless mass society of industrial workers envisioned by early-twentieth-century social reformers.

But passing years and different national contexts have brought different results from the application of these modernist design paradigms. The myth of objectivity unfortunately does much to disengage the designer from compassionate concerns. Strongly held personal convictions would seem to be inappropriate for the cool-headed, objective professional. Functionalism is narrowly defined in measurable utilitarian terms. Too often this means serving the client's definition of function—generally profits—over other concerns, including safety, the environment, and social/cultural/political impacts. Universalism has brought us the homogenized proper corporate style based mainly on Helvetica and the grid, ignoring the power and potential of regional, idiosyncratic, personal, or culturally specific stylistic vocabularies. And the ideal of value-free design is a dangerous myth. In fact, all design solutions carry a bias, either explicit or implicit. The more honest designs acknowledge their biases openly rather than manipulate their audiences with assurances of universal "truth" and purity.

Abstraction, modernism's revolutionary contribution to the visual language of art and design, further distances both designer and audience from involvement. Stripped of imagery, self-referential abstraction is largely devoid of symbols and disconnected from experience in the surrounding world, cool and low on emotion. Abstraction is predictable in application—polite, inoffensive, and not too meaningful—thereby providing a safe vocabulary for corporate materials. Imagery, on the other hand, is richly loaded with symbolic, encoded meaning, often ambiguous and capable of arousing the entire range of human emotions. Imagery is difficult to control, even dangerous or controversial—often leading to unintended personal interpretations on the part of the audience—but also poetic, powerful, and potentially eloquent.

The modernist of agenda has conspired to promote an attitude of apoliticism among American designers, design educators, and students, building on the pragmatic American tendency to avoid political dialectics. American designers consistently take European theories and strip them of their political content. Of the various strains of modernism, many of which were socially concerned or politically revolutionary, American design either chose those most devoid of political content or stripped the theories of their original political idealism.

More recently we have seen a strong interest in French literary theory. But its original element of French contemporary Marxism has been largely ignored in the U.S., perhaps rightly so. The American political environment is far different from the European; European political dialectics may not be appropriate to us. Yet we cannot assume that no political theory is needed to ground our work—all designers need an appropriate framework to evaluate and assess the impacts of their work within its social/ethical/political milieu. Perhaps this evaluative framework is different for each individual, dependent on the values of each, reflecting our strong tradition of American individualism.

Designers must break out of the obedient, neutral, servant-to-industry mentality, an orientation that was particularly strong in the Reagan-Thatcher-Bush years, and continues to dominate design management and strategic design. Yes, we are problem-solvers responding to the needs of clients. But we must consider the problems we take on. Should one help sell tobacco and alcohol, or design a Presidential memorial library for a man who reads only pulp cowboy novels? Does society really benefit from a strategic plan for plastic housewares or fast-food? The answers may be more subtle than a yes or no. But one thing is clear: Design is not a neutral, value-free process. A design has no more integrity than its purpose or subject matter. Garbage in, garbage out. The most rarefied design solution can never surpass the quality of its content.

A dangerous assumption is that corporate work of innocuous content is devoid of political bias. The vast majority of student design projects deal with corporate needs, placing a heavy priority on the corporate economic sector of our society. Commerce is where we are investing our assets of time, budgets, skills, and creativity. This is a decisive vote for economics over other potential concerns, including social, educational, cultural, spiritual, and political needs. This is a political statement in itself both in education and practice.

Postwar American art has greatly ignored societal issues as well. The self-reference of abstract expressionism and minimalism has been largely divorced from external conditions. Pop art embraced materialism more than it critiqued it. The more recent postmodernist ironic parodies have been full of duplicity and offer no program as antidote to the appalling paradigms they deconstruct. But the past several years have brought a new involvement by artists in the socio-political environment around them. A recent book, *The Reenchantment of Art*, advocates a second postmodernism, a reconstruction that moves beyond the detachment of modernism and deconstruction. Suzi Gablik, the author, calls for an end to the alienation of artists and aesthetics from social values in a new interrelational, audience-oriented art.

There are signs that this is happening. Issue-oriented art has been spreading like wildfire among graduate students in the fine arts. At Cranbrook and a number of other design programs, fine arts students are attending graphic design critiques, eager to learn design methods for reaching their audiences. Fashion advertising is beginning to occasionally embrace issues. Perhaps humanistic content is good for sales: witness Esprit, Benetton, Moschino. That these clients are prepared to make social advocacy part of their message is evidence of a need and receptivity in their audiences. But are many graphic designers prepared to deal with this type of content? Graphic design is a powerful tool, capable of informing, publicizing, and propagandizing social, environmental, and political messages as well as commercial ones.

How does compassionate design shape a practice? The occasional pro bono piece as a relief from business as usual is not the answer here. The choice of clients or content is crucial. The most fortunate can find a worthy cause in need of a designer with the funds to pay for professional design services. Unfortunately, good causes often seem to have the least resources in our present economic system. Is it possible to shape a practice around non-business clients or introduce social content into commercial work? The compassionate designer must strategize an ethical practice and be an informed, involved citizen in a Jeffersonian participatory democracy, agile and flexible, prepared to turn the tools of visual communications toward a broad spectrum of needs.

How does one educate graphic design students with an understanding of design as a social and political force? Can a political consciousness be trained? Can an educator teach values? The answer is probably no in the simplistic sense. However, the field of education has a well-developed area referred to as "values clarification" that offers many possibilities for graphic design educators. Too often we take individuals with eighteen years of experience and strip them of their values, rather than cultivate them for effective application in design practice.

In teaching, these issues must be raised from the beginning for the design student. This is not something to spring on the advanced student after their attitudes have been fixed on neutrality. At the core of this issue is the content of the projects we assign from the very first introductory exercise. Most introductory graphic design courses are based on abstract formal exercises inherited from the Bauhaus and the classic Basel school projects. The detachment problem begins here. These projects either deal with completely abstract form—point, line, and plane, for instance—or they remove imagery from context. The graphic translation projects, so effective in training a keen formal sense, unfortunately use a process of abstractional analysis, thereby stripping imagery of its encoded symbolism. (I have to admit to being guilty of this in my assignments in past years.) Divorcing design form from content or context is a lesson in passivity, implying that graphic form is something separate and unrelated to subjective values or even ideas. The first principle is that all graphic projects must have content.

The type of content in each assignment is crucial. It is disheartening to see the vast number of undergraduate projects dedicated to selling goods and services in the marketplace devoid of any mission beyond business success. Undoubtedly all students need experience in this type of message and purpose. But cannot projects cover a broad mix of content, including issues beyond business? Cultural, social, and political subjects make excellent communications challenges for student designers.

Project assignments can require content developed by the student dealing with public and personal social, political, and economic issues and current events. The responsibility for developing content is a crucial one; it counteracts the passive design role in which one unquestioningly accepts client-dictated copy. On a practical level, we know how frequently all designers modify and improve client copywriting; many graphic designers become quite good writers and editors, so closely is our function allied to writing. In a larger sense, however, self-developed content and copy promotes two important attitudes in a design student. One is the ability to develop personal content and subject matter, executed independently of client assignments, where the reward is the expression of personal concerns. Secondly, the challenge to develop subject matter stimulates the design student to determine what matters on a personal level. A process of values clarification must go on in the student before a subject or subject-matter position can be chosen. And the breadth of concerns chosen as subjects by fellow students exposes each student to a wider range of possibilities.

The critique process for issue-oriented work can be a very effective forum for values clarification. This is particularly true of group critiques in which all students are encouraged to participate, rather than the authoritarian traditionalist crit in which the faculty do all the talking. In evaluating the success or failure of a piece of graphic communications, each critic must address the subject matter and understand the design student's stated intentions before weighing a piece's success. This expands the critique discussion beyond the usual and necessary topics of graphic method, form, and technique. Tolerance as well as objectivity are required of each critique participant, in that they must accept and understand the student's intended message before evaluating the piece.

For instance, two fundamentalist Christian students recently brought their religiously oriented work to Cranbrook graphic design crits during a two-semester period. It was a challenge—and a lesson in tolerance—for the other students to put aside their personal religious (or nonreligious) convictions in order to give these students and their work a fair critique from a level playing field. It was quite remarkable—and refreshing—to find us all discussing spirituality as legitimate subject matter. This has held true for many other subjects from the universe of issues facing our culture today, including local and global environmental issues, animal rights, homelessness, feminism, and reproductive choice.

The point here is content. As design educators, we cast projects almost as a scientist designs a laboratory experiment. The formula and the variables conspire to slant the results in one direction or another. The project assignment and the project critique are powerful tools that teach far more than explicit goals, and carry strong implicit messages about design and designers' roles.

Design history also offers a rich resource for understanding the relationship of form and content to socio-political contexts. We all know how often works from art and design history are venerated (and imitated) in an atmosphere divorced from their original context. By exploring the accompanying cultural/social/political histories, students can see the contextual interdependencies and make analogies to their present time.

Am I advocating the production of a generation of designers preoccupied with political activism, a kind of reborn sixties mentality? I think rather what I have in mind is nurturing a crop of active citizens—informed, concerned participants in society who happen to be graphic designers. We must stop inadvertently training our students to ignore their convictions and be passive economic servants. Instead, we must help them to clarify their personal values and to give them the tools to recognize when it is appropriate to act on them. I do think this is possible. We still need objectivity, but this includes the objectivity to know when to invoke personal biases and when to set them aside. Too often our graduates and their work emerge as charming mannequins, voiceless mouthpieces for the messages of ventriloquist clients. Let us instead give designers their voices so they may participate and contribute more fully in the world around them.

Originally presented as a talk at the Design Renaissance International Conference, Glasgow, Scotland, September 4, 1993, and then at the American Institute of Graphic Arts National Conference, Seattle, Washington, September 29, 1995.

Socially Responsible Advertising
Altruism or Exploitation?
Judith Schwartz

Consider this: Your breakfast cereal has the American Cancer Society logo on its box. Does this mean your cereal will reduce the chance of your getting cancer? Sixty percent of consumers think so. The American Heart Association logo is on 700 products from sixty different companies but it's not on your product. Do you think the product doesn't meet AHA standards? The American Heart Association allows manufacturers to put the AHA logo on products for a one-time "contribution" of $2,500 plus $650 per year.[1] They give out exclusivity agreements so that no other companies with similar products can get the logo. Still, these charities claim they don't make product endorsements even though evidence shows otherwise.

"Cause-related marketing" is a creative strategy that ties a company and its products to a social issue or cause with the goal of improving a weak public image and boosting sales, while providing benefits to a worthwhile charity. Cause marketing is the fastest growing form of sponsorship. In 2000, American businesses spent over $700 million on ads and events espousing their commitment to social concerns, $575 million more than in 1990.[2] A Roper Starch Worldwide poll has concluded that cause marketing influences consumers, their perception of brands, and their purchasing decisions.

Socially conscious advertising has affected mainstream corporations as well as companies who are known for their "grassroots values." Corporations seem to have one goal in common—to increase their profits through advertising. Many go one step further—their cause becomes their mission statement. For example, Kenneth Cole is known for its involvement in AIDS awareness. Causes chosen for advertising campaigns tend to be based on universally accepted, noncontroversial issues, since the more popular the cause, the higher the profit. For example, the most visible marketing trends of the nineties were those focused on wildlife and nature. Some other "hot" causes that bring in high market shares are women's and children's issues, literacy, homelessness, human rights, AIDS, drug prevention, mental and physical disabilities, and racial harmony.

When asked what she would do with her million dollars in the final round, Tina Wesson, the winner of the 2001 game show *Survivor*, said she would put money into a fund and donate the yearly interest to a worthy cause. It is possible that this influenced voting in her favor. Marketing social responsibility plays to people's emotions and hearts and has caused controversy, negative criticism, and charges of exploitation.

There are those who feel that this type of marketing is in a company's self-interest, while others feel that it is a sincere effort to "do good." Ann E. Kaplan, research director of Giving U.S.A., which tracks contributions, says, "Companies by their nature are not philanthropic. They are giving to advance their business interests."[3] On the other hand, Carol Cone of Cone Communications, a strategic marketing firm in Boston, disagrees: "A good cause-marketing undertaking is a win-win proposition for both parties."[4] Recent research by Cone Communications has found that nearly two-thirds of American consumers report that they would be likely to switch brands or retailers to one associated with a good cause.

Niche Marketers

Certain companies are at the highest level of corporate conscience; their consumers recognize their brands as being sympathetic to various humanitarian causes. These companies create this niche for themselves. Their company executives are products of the counterculture and the baby boom generation; they set up their businesses to reflect their grassroots values and convictions and tend to be idealists. Examples of companies that fall into this category are Ben & Jerry's, The Body Shop, Working Assets, and Tom's of Maine. Their products and advertising strategies all coincide with their brands' ethics.

Ben & Jerry's

In addition to ice cream, Ben & Jerry's is best known for bringing sixties values to today's business world. They give a percentage of their pretax profits to charity and support social causes, such as rain forest preservation, the peace movement, and helping minorities and the disadvantaged.

Lesa Ukman, president of International Events Group, a Chicago-based research firm that tracks sponsorships, called Ben & Jerry's "the quintessential cause marketer." "They've created their own niche, doing things that are radical instead of chic. Instead of supporting a children's hospital, they supported peace,"[5] she said. In the eighties Ben & Jerry's introduced a product called "peace pops" as part of a campaign advocating massive reductions in the military budget.

On the other hand, there has been lots of bad press when it comes to Ben & Jerry's. Investigative journalist Jon Entine, formerly of *Prime Time Live*, wrote, "This is all about campaigns to create a marketing image for the company. General Motors sells sex to sell their cars, Ben & Jerry's sells idealism to market their ice cream. Ultimately it's exploitative."[6]

Ben & Jerry's Rainforest Crunch was meant to raise the consciousness of consumers about the destruction of tropical rain forests. The label read, "Money from these nuts will help Brazilian forest peoples start a nut-shelling cooperative." In actuality, Ben & Jerry's purchased less than 5 percent of their nuts from the "nut-shelling cooperative" and soon they completely stopped buying nuts from the co-op. However, the label remained on ice cream containers claiming that the nuts came from a co-op of "forest peoples" in Brazil, when they were actually being harvested by non-Indian Brazilians. This wasn't resolved until Jon Entine did an exposé in 1994.

It's not hard to be cynical about Ben & Jerry's, as CEO Jerry Greenfield is fully aware: "It's natural when a company is trying to do good things that people will be skeptical. They've been trained by business to think that business is just about self-interest."[7] Jerry claims the press have always idealized what they were trying to do, and have blown the mistakes out of proportion. In spite of all of the criticism, Ben & Jerry's have built a franchise spread across fifteen countries. In 1999, they donated 7.5 percent of their pretax dollars, amounting to approximately $1,120,000. Their net sales were $237 million.

The Body Shop

The Body Shop is known for beauty products that use natural ingredients. The company was founded espousing strong ethical principles and is a symbol of corporate responsibility. As founder Anita Roddick puts it, "Profits are an integral part of the business, but you do something more, beyond your own accumulation of material wealth. You do something more which spiritually enhances you or educates you."[8]

The Body Shop has sponsored everything from tree-planting programs to a save the whales campaign with the environmental group Green Peace. They have been active in a crusade to stop the testing of cosmetics on animals as well as being involved in a number of human rights issues through Amnesty International. The Body Shop's advertising campaigns are geared toward women, who form 90 percent of their target market.

This being said, there have been many exposés that have been detrimental to the Body Shop's reputation. In 1992, an NBC documentary questioned the company's policy on animal testing and their sincerity toward environmental and social issues. Anita Roddick sued for libel and won more than $400,000 in damages.

In 1994, Jon Entine wrote an article in *Business Ethics* magazine called "Shattered Image," revealing that "The Body Shop sells expensive mediocre products filled with petrochemicals (according to *Consumer Reports* and other independent journals); has a history of penurious charitable contributions; misrepresents its ethical trading practices; and struggles with troubled employee and franchisee relationships across the world."[9] After these charges of exploitation, The Body Shop's stocks plunged.

Later, an independent research group concluded that Entine's charges were "broadly unfair,"[10] though other independent research published corroborates many of Entine's conclusions. After keeping a low profile in the United States, in 1995 The Body Shop experimented with print and radio ads geared toward issues such as self-esteem in women, and in 1996, for the first time, the company increased their U.S. promotional budget by 75 percent to $7 million and selected Goodby, Silverstein & Partners, San Francisco, to handle their account.

Passion Branders

Carol Cone, of Cone Communications, calls companies with a long-term commitment to a cause "passion branders." They not only raise money, but are deeply involved in their causes."[11] McDonald's is an example of a long-time passion brander. Ray Kroc, founder of McDonald's, was one of cause marketing's first advocates. "He created a corporate ethos that still stresses things like local scholarships, environmental clean-up programs, and Ronald McDonald House, where families of hospitalized children can stay while a child is being treated."[12] McDonald's charities have helped hundreds of organizations dedicated to helping children.

Avon

Joanne Mazurski, director of Worldwide Communications for Avon Products, says, "Passion branding goes beyond a marketing program. It becomes an umbrella for the kind of company you are and the kind of relationship you have with your consumers and sales reps."[13] Avon's Breast Cancer Awareness crusade is the largest corporate supporter of breast health programs in America. The creative strategy "Take The Pledge," which has raised over $100 million worldwide, was designed to educate women about breast cancer and to provide more low-income, minority, and older women access to early-detection services. The crusade was promoted through Avon catalogues, television spots, and consumer ads in major women's magazines.

Breast cancer coalitions have expressed concerns that more money should be spent on research and less on corporate images.

Reebok

Reebok is a passion brander that has extended its corporate commitment to a controversial issue—human rights. It began in 1988 with sponsorship of a musical tour featuring pop artists, including Sting and Bruce Springsteen, to raise funds for Amnesty International. The artists wore Reebok athletic shoes on stage and the company incorporated the human rights theme into its "Reebok Let UBU" advertising. Reebok's Web site portrays the company as a promoter of human rights in the Third World. However, they have been criticized for hypocritically employing Indonesian workers for twenty-five cents an hour. Reebok's contract work overseas is being scrutinized for allowing poor conditions. "The company's contracting factories in Southern China are riddled with wage, hour, and health violations, and Reebok continues to exploit child labor in Pakistan, despite a public pledge to put an end to the practice."[14]

Many other clothing and shoe companies have been accused of similar contradictions. Nike has been the target of many boycotts, repeated media investigations, and international protest. Nike's award-winning "Let Me Play" campaign by Wieden + Kennedy that portrayed girls in a positive light backfired when women's groups came forward to publicize the exploitation of women and girls in Nike plants in Vietnam, China, Korea, and Indonesia.

Levi Strauss, a company known as being socially responsible, promotes itself as a "people before profits" business. They partnered with the 1998 MTV Video Awards to launch their celebrity Levi's Original Spin program. The jeans were auctioned off and the proceeds went to "Peace 2000," whose primary objective is to establish internal peace in youth communities everywhere. "Meanwhile, they are running some of the worst sweatshops in the developing world."[15]

Benetton

The clothing company Benetton persists in running highly controversial and often offensive ads that portray social and political issues. They have experienced consumer and media boycotts around the world, but continue to run campaigns that earn them sales and free publicity.

Benetton's "journalistic" campaign style, created by advertising director Olivieri Toscani, has caused controversy since its inception in 1984. The company's 1984 campaign began with "The Colors of the World," which consisted of a series of photos of ethnically diverse children playing together. Then came Benetton's International theme, "United Colors of Benetton," which portrayed people from all walks of life joining hands. Since then, some themes for Benetton ads have contained images of poverty, photographs of dying AIDS patients, Albanian boat people, and an African gorilla grasping a human bone. As part of their AIDS campaign, on World AIDS Day they distributed condoms in collaboration with Act Up, the AIDS activist group. *Colors* is a visual magazine published by Benetton presenting an atypical perspective of the world, focusing on topics such as racism, AIDS, multiculturalism, health, and educational issues targeted toward young people aged fourteen to twenty.

In an article about *Colors* magazine, Hugh Aldersey-Williams writes, "There are many contradictions in the position Benetton has taken in its publishing and advertising."[16] He goes on to prove that the company fails at following its own advice or living up to its moral ideals. Williams gives examples of Benetton's hypocrisy, such as using the image of oil-soaked seabirds and then featuring their involvement with motor-racing activities in an issue of *Colors* magazine.

The advertising world has been extremely critical of Benetton campaigns, which have given rise to ongoing debate. According to Jerry Della Femina, "This is desperate advertising." He suspects that the real aim of the Benetton AIDS ad is free publicity, and blasts Benetton ads as "sensationalist garbage."[17] Benetton's ad campaigns have one of the highest international profiles. They spend $80 million— 4 percent of their annual budget—on advertising to promote themselves worldwide, and do no market research for their ad campaigns.

Image Builders

"Image builders" are corporations who use marketing strategies to enhance their reputations, to increase profits, and to possibly defuse negative publicity. Image builders support the arts, sponsor events, or donate money to cause-related organizations. Image advertising seeks to show that the corporation has a human side, persuading the public that they care about people and issues.

Denny's

In some instances, corporations that have been sued try to enhance their images through socially conscious advertising strategies. The restaurant chain Denny's was charged with discriminating against their African-American clientele and in 1997 they paid a $46 million settlement.

The solution to win back their reputation was a diversity campaign. Denny's restaurants, Spartanburg, South Carolina, launched a $5 million TV, radio, direct-mail, and print campaign created by Chisholm-Mingo Group targeting African-Americans. These ads promoted a national dialogue about race: "Diversity. It's About All of us."

Lewis Williams, a vice president of Leo Burnett U.S.A. in Chicago stated in an interview that these ads are public relations disguised as advertising. "Denny's is trying to rebuild their public image to the community." His reply when I asked if he thought it was working was, "I don't think so, they don't go in and stay in," alluding to his belief that there is not a deep community involvement. He offers McDonald's as a good example of a company with a long-term commitment to their community "way before it was a trend to do so."[18]

Denny's diversity efforts received national recognition in March 1998 when the CBS news show *60 Minutes* ran a story on Denny's diversity training. The program cited Denny's as a model for other corporations.

Lewis Williams disagrees: "I think it is a good idea for a company to promote diversity, however, in Denny's case, it was a little too late. The timing of such an effort made them look more than suspect. Texaco was put in the same position. These were basically public relations efforts or old fashioned damage control."[19]

Chevron

Chevron, the oil company situated in San Francisco, has been involved in and has lost numerous court cases—from being sued by workers in their oil refineries due to poor health conditions, to the San Francisco Public Utilities Commission (PUC) filing a lawsuit against them to force them to move a pipeline for fear that it would split in an earthquake and contaminate drinking water for the 2.5 million Bay Area residents. One day, Chevron publicly announced that they would move the pipeline; the next day they were in court trying to block San Francisco's attempt to force the removal.

When asked why Chevron had been refusing to budge on the issue, Marion Otsea, chairwoman of the San Francisco Public Utilities Commission, replied, "because they're Chevron, and People Do"[20]—evident sarcasm directed against the semi-documentary style advertising campaign Chevron adopted to promote its environmental record worldwide.

Many advocacy groups have questioned whether Chevron's "People Do" message misrepresents the facts. According to the UCLA program in environmental geography, "Chevron did the things it is advertising in the campaign because it was compelled by court action, not altruism."[21]

Jonathan Polansky, the creative director for the Public Media Center, San Francisco, commented about the ads in an interview. "Chevron's 'concern' is compelled by federal and state law. Chevron is simply trying to get some PR mileage out of what it must routinely do to ameliorate some of the damage its operations cause in the U.S."[22]

Research conducted has shown that the ads have had a positive impact and have resulted in increased sales of Chevron gasoline.

Komen Race for the Cure

BMW, Buick, Ford, and General Motors have focused on campaigns for breast cancer research and participated in the "Komen Race for the Cure." Ford Motor Company has participated in this effort for seven years and has donated over $10 million to the cause. They have publicized their partnership with "The Race" nationally, which enables consumers to see them in a very personal and human way. Research indicates that there has been an increase in Ford's female consumers since the breast cancer initiative began.

General Motors has seen a positive shift in consumer opinion of its brand since being involved in fundraising for breast cancer. Thirty percent of consumers are now more likely to consider purchasing a GM vehicle since General Motors became involved in the "Concept Cure" campaign. Meanwhile, socially responsible investors have left companies such as Ford and General Motors off the list of social investing because of their involvement in military contracts or ties to South Africa. General Motors has been noted for poor working conditions in its factories, low wages, and each have been noted for contributing to environmental problems.

Both companies launched advertising campaigns to prove they are responsible, caring corporations dedicated to protecting human health, natural resources, and the global environment. They have each partnered with various environmental organizations and donated millions of dollars to fund conservation efforts.

Starbucks

Starbucks, the coffee company that originated in Seattle, has been around for over twenty-five years. CEO Howard Schultz claims that his company does not have political leanings. "Contributing positively to our communities and our environment" has long been part of Starbucks's stated mission.[23] Starbucks has won industry accolades for its partnership with CARE, an international relief organization that sponsors health, education, and other humanitarian aid projects. Jon Entine claims they began the campaign only after an exposé he wrote for the *Chicago Tribune* stating that Starbucks was buying beans from Guatemalan suppliers who paid workers $2.50 a day.[24]

Starbucks launched its partnership with CARE in 1991 and committed to annual donations of $100,000 as well as integrating CARE into every aspect of Starbucks's business. Starbucks liked the idea of giving back to coffee-origin countries through CARE. They have featured CARE in in-store promotions and articles in their magazine and have organized benefit concerts for the charity. There is a Starbucks brochure entitled "A World of Coffee," with a map of countries from around the world where they buy their coffee. This marketing strategy has been instrumental in Starbucks's success.

More recently, Starbucks felt a backlash from nonprofit organizations. A Chicago-based group of Guatemalan labor activists leafleted that coffee workers who were on Starbucks's payroll worked under inhumane conditions and earned only two cents a pound, while Starbucks sells the beans for $9 a pound.

"Starbucks Commitment to Do Our Part," was the company's defense outlining its beliefs and aspirations—setting short-term commitments for helping to improve the quality of life in coffee-origin countries. The Starbucks Foundation was set up in 1997 in addition to an environmental committee—a group that looked for ways to reduce and recycle waste as well as contribute to local community environmental efforts.

Starbucks went mainstream with an advertising campaign developed by Goodby, Silverstein & Partners, San Francisco. Scott Bedbury, Starbucks senior vice president of marketing, says "advertising can help address the issue of Starbucks backlash."[25]

To add more controversy, Starbucks has partnered with Phillip Morris. In 1998, Kraft foods (owned by Phillip Morris) and Starbucks announced a licensing agreement to accelerate growth of the Starbucks brand into supermarkets across the United States. (Many consumers question buying food from a tobacco company.)

Pros and Cons of Cause Marketing

* Cause-related marketing proceeds are mainly directed to large, visible causes that appeal to a private-sector constituency. Less "marketable" but equally worthy causes may not benefit.
* There are risks in pursuing cause-related marketing campaigns. If a company supports a particular cause, it risks alienating market segments that oppose the cause.
* A nonprofit's credibility could be damaged if alliances aren't chosen wisely.
* Charities have become cynical about corporate support that is "hit and run" and 100 percent self-serving.[26]

* "Insincerity may turn to 'causeploitation' just as green marketing for some companies turned into 'green scamming,' says Carol Cone. (Green scamming is exploitation of environmental marketing.)[27]
* Corporations are looking to "own" causes, by setting up 501(c)3 organizations benefiting themselves tax-wise, rather than supporting existing nonprofit organizations.
* Corporations are "insincere" because they donate such a small fraction of what they earn from the campaigns. Companies put a cap on the amount they will donate, but they don't tell consumers when the cap is reached.

Altruism or Exploitation

Is there such a thing as true altruism when it comes to business? From all of the evidence I have gathered, my conclusion is no.

Evidence shows that companies are doing socially responsible advertising to stand out from the crowded market. For example, a company is involved in a breast cancer awareness campaign, which helps to connect it to female consumers. Most marketers admit that by doing so they are creating a brand and that their main interest lies in profit margins. As far as they're concerned, there is everything to gain and nothing to lose.

The consistency of consumer opinions strongly signals that cause programs are not a passing fad but rather have become must-do for brands seeking to strengthen relationships with their customers, employees, communities, and business partners.

Some critics feel that cause marketing is opportunistic, a chance for companies to get cheap publicity and the appearance of social responsibility with relatively little investment. Companies are trying to persuade consumers to buy their products by portraying themselves as having progressive value systems similar to their own.

As Larry Keeley, president of Doblin Group, a Chicago-based design-planning firm, puts it, "Companies are using brief philosophical statements which have nothing to do with their products as a means of marketing the company and brand."[28] Larry Keeley has coined the term "Philofrags," a term which means fragments that suggest the "company is full of caring, concerned, and thoughtful people who have their hearts in the right places."[29] However, companies are taking partnerships to a new level. In many instances the philosophy of the corporation is becoming the brand image rather than just a slogan or "philofrag."

For years, museums have partnered with corporations. Still, examine corporate partners like General Motors, Exxon, or Phillip Morris and the damage they have done to our environment, the dangers of tobacco, the lawsuits against these companies for their business practices, and the controversy surrounding them. Phillip Morris has sponsored art exhibitions, museum publications, and literacy campaigns. It donates money to "good causes," but does the public really feel any better about it? Instead, people are acutely aware that Philip Morris is a huge capitalist conglomerate, dominating the tobacco industry.

On the other hand, companies like Chevron and General Motors, who are doing this type of marketing to enhance their image, and not for altruistic reasons, actually "do good." Society does benefit. The groups they support do benefit. However, it is ultimately about the bottom line, not trying to raise consciousness or benefit society. In business, no matter how emotionally involved in a particular cause a company might appear to be or how loudly it preaches about values, in the end the bottom line is profit and self-interest.

Notes

1. Dave Plank, "States Looking Closely At 'Cause' Marketing," *Natural Foods Merchandiser News*, September 1999.

2. Cone/Roper poll, data from International Events Group (IEG), which tracks sponsorships, verified by telephone.

3. Lisa Belkin, "How Breast Cancer Became This Year's Cause," *The New York Times Magazine*, 22 December 1996 (cover story).

4. Carol L. Cone, "Doing Well by Doing Good," *Association Management*, April 1996, 103.

5. William M. Bulkeley, "Ben & Jerry's Is Looking for Ben's Successor," *The Wall Street Journal*, 14 June 1994, B1.

6. Jeff Glasser, "Not Exactly a Shell Game: Ben & Jerry's Shelves Inaccurate Rainforest Pitch," *Boston Globe*, 27 July 1995, 3. Online, Internet.

7. Joanna Coles, "The Joanna Coles Interview: Tubs Who Is Cream of the Crop—Some Claim this Man and His Chubby Schoolfriend Have Revolutionized Capitalism. Oh Really?" *The Guardian*, 28 December 1996, 7. Online, Internet.

8. Regina Eisman, "Sweet Charity," *Incentive*, December 1992, 24.

9. Astrid Van Den Broek, "Benevolent Dictators: the Tricky Task Facing Companies Engaged in Cause Marketing Is How to Target Their Philanthropy Without Crossing into Crass Commercialism," *Marketing*, 7 September 1998, 14.

10. Jon Entine, "The Messy Reality of Socially Responsible Business," Proactivist.com, 11. Online, Internet. (Editor's note: This article originally appeared in both *At Work* and *The Utne Reader* a few years ago.)

11. Daniel, Kadlec, "The New World of Giving," *Time*, 5 May 1997, 62–4.

12. Belkin.

13. Nancy Arnott, "Marketing with a Passion." *Sales and Marketing Management*, January 1994, 7. Online, Internet, 31 March 1999.

14. Betsy Reed, "The Business of Social Responsibility," *Dollars and Sense*, May/June 1998, 7.

15. Jon Entine, "The Messy Reality of Socially Responsible Business," Proactivist.com, 3. Online, Internet.

16. Hugh Aldersey-Williams, "Voice of Colors: Tibor Kalman's *Graphis*," May/June 1994, 50–1.

17. Bruce Horovitz, "'Shock Ads: New Rage That Spawns Rage," *The Los Angeles Times*, 22 March 1992, D1.

18. Lewis Williams, personal telephone interview, 18 June 1999.

19. Ibid.

20. Susan Sward, "Chevron Talks Nice, Sues S.F./Two Responses to Pipeline Concerns," *San Francisco Chronicle*, 14 March 1996, A1.

21. Ibid.

22. Jonathan Polansky, personal interview via e-mail, 14 June 1999.

23. Howard Schultz and Dori Jones Yang, *Pour Your Heart Into It* (New York: Hyperion, 1997), 292–305.

24. Romesh Ratnesar, "Doing Well by Doing Good," *The New Republic*, 6–13 January 1997, 18–20.

25. Alice Z. Cuneo and Jeff Jensen, "Starbucks Breaks Largest Ad Blitz," *Advertising Age*, 19 May 1997, 3.

26. John R. Graham, "Corporate Giving: Is It Good for Business?" *USA Today*, January 1995, 60–1.

27. Susan McChesney, "Champions of a Cause," *Electronic Perspectives*, March/April 1995, 5. Online, Internet.

28. Larry Keeley, "Homespun Marketing Philosophy: Do As I Do, and Not As I Say," *Brandweek*, 21 March 1994, 20.

29. Ibid.

Ethical Design Education

Confessions of a Sixties Idealist

Susan S. Szenasy

"Sustainability is not my issue," protests one senior, a student in Parsons's product design department. She's presenting her term paper on a designer and maker of lamps. Two others in the class, also product majors, are appalled by this statement; so am I. We've just spent a semester returning, again and again, to discussions of our degrading natural environment and the need for everyone to figure out how to use this knowledge to design more sensitively.

We're a group of twenty-eight fledgling professionals, pursuing courses of study in architecture; interior, product, and graphic design; fashion; and photography; I'm number twenty-nine, their teacher and a design magazine editor. Having observed every kind of designer at work for several decades, I know that the creative professions make a huge difference in the ways we live. I see designers as active participants in the decisions businesses make about the land they occupy and the resources they use, the technologies they rely on, and the ideas they communicate.

Every Tuesday afternoon we gather in a windowless room in a hulking New School building on Fifth Avenue (New York)—the kind of soulless, mechanically aired space we've all grown to tolerate—and discuss the Ethics of Design. I have been teaching this senior seminar, part of Parsons's liberal arts offering, since 1997, when the school first asked me to develop it. The course is all about responsibility:

to the planet, to the regions we live in, to the community, to the profession, to the client, and to the self. I interpret ethics to mean that we have a moral duty, an obligation to our fellow humans and to other living creatures. And that obligation calls on us to be prudent stewards of the natural environment that supports and sustains our lives. Sustaining the environment, in turn, is our highest priority as thinking, verbal, tool-using creatures blessed with free will; yes, we have a choice. In my view, it's ethical to choose fresh water, clean air, nutritious food—the bounties our home planet provides for us—and safeguard these for future generations.

We begin each September by watching *MindWalk*, a 1991 film that argues for abandoning the Cartesian, mechanistic, linear thinking that lit up the road to industrialization and made the modern world possible. Now, if we are to survive, we need to switch to an ecological-systems thinking which considers interconnectedness and relationships. This is the crux of the 110-minute conversation between a politician, a poet, and a physicist—a brilliant script based on the thinking of physicist Fritjof Capra. There's no sex, no drugs, no rock and roll, nothing but talk about life, all kinds of life, and glorious views of Mont-Saint-Michel, a tiny island built up during the Middle Ages in France's Gulf of St. Malo, photographed to the music of Philip Glass.

As they watch the video monitor, the students see a gigantic metal mechanism in an ancient tower and hear the physicist say that the microchip has taken the place of the clockwork. This is a dramatic visual and verbal reminder of how invisible technology is replacing much of the bulkily visible. What's called for, says the scientist, is a drastic change in the way we see the world: no longer as a machine with replaceable parts, but as a system of relationships modeled on nature's own systems.

And so we build on this thought throughout our four months together, probing how designers can become active participants in the great system of living organisms that dwell on our fragile, blue-green planet. We try, as the physicist urges us to, to figure out how we might live and work inside a "web of relationships" and connect to the "web of life."

The first to resist ecological thinking this semester are the fashion students. They're skeptical, even cynical. Their lament: The big companies are in control. There's nothing any one designer can do. We're all slaves of seasonal trends and fickle consumers; we're creatures of a throw-away culture. Why should we care about being sensitive to the environment when nobody wants us to be? The world is a polluted, mean, ugly place ruled by greed and ego. To be part of the fashion industry, to make a living in it, we need to figure out how to make money, how to become stars.

I, the sixties idealist who wholeheartedly believes we can turn that ugly world into something more beautiful, try to keep my cool, though I hear my voice turn shrill. I bring up examples from Paul Hawken's 1993 book, *The Ecology of Commerce*. (I've stopped assigning it this year. Experience tells me that only a few students would actually read any part of it, so why waste all that paper?) I call their attention to large, multinational businesses like Ikea that are making changes in the way they procure and use materials and distribute their furniture, all to reflect their own, and presumably their customers', growing interest in the environment. I mention post-consumer materials now on the market, like the luxurious fleece we wear as parkas and use as blankets, made from recycled soda bottles. Yes, but look at us, we're slaves to mindless acquisition. You're dreaming a naive dream, Susan, argue the students.

We press on and read William Morris on the "morality of materials," on the importance of craft and the human touch in an industrialized world, on the social responsibility of designers. We learn about his interest in and advocacy of such varied but related areas of aesthetic expression as historic restoration, furniture and furnishings, wallpapers and textiles, polemical writings, and book publishing. Through this eccentric nineteenth-century genius we are introduced to the designer as an advocate, a revolutionary who looks back to medieval times to reclaim human creativity. His life and work teach us that a strong and brave designer can take on the powerful socio-economic forces, like Morris took on the Industrial Revolution, and have influence far beyond his own times.

We read Walter Gropius on his struggles to establish the Bauhaus, a breakthrough art school in a provincial town in war-ravaged Germany. We learn about the dire economic conditions that plagued the early years of his school and how Gropius overcame these limitations by sheer will and conviction while collaborating with like-minded people. Though his ideas helped bring our world into modern times, we also learn that initially the Bauhaus was shaped by Morris's thinking: a deep understanding of craft materials and methods. We discuss how a great hardship, like the post-World War I collapse of social and economic values, can propel creative thinking and awaken social responsibility among form-givers. We talk about the need for material invention in such times. And we realize that design, as Gropius saw it (as Morris did before him), has a significant contribution to make in the reshaping of institutions as well as our lives. The word "responsibility" runs through our discussions.

We watch *A Story of Healing*, a short film that follows American surgeons and nurses in Vietnam doing reconstructive facial surgery on children. Working under primitive conditions, these highly skilled professionals bring all their technical knowledge and love of humanity to the task. It's a heartbreaking and an exhilarating thirty-three minutes that leads to two hours of spirited conversation on professional behavior: It's important, at times, to step out of our comfort zone. For the medical team, that meant leaving behind the fancy, well-run, high-tech hospitals they worked in every day. What does it mean for designers? We wonder.

The nurses and surgeons set up shop in a small, provincial hospital, some spending their vacations working there. They talk, between the many procedures they perform, about finding satisfaction in the work. No one mentions money or wealth or prestige. Their faces beam as they come to realize, one after another, "this is why I went into medicine in the first place." They all talk about the joys and surprises of helping those in need, being part of a dynamic team, testing their skills and imaginations at every turn, and learning that even though people's circumstances and cultures are different, they value the same things. They teach us that acting on our obligation to our human family can result in rewards far beyond our expectations.

Then, sometime around midterm, a fashion student mentions that an instructor gleefully showed off a forbidden cache of monkey fur in class. The room blows up. The kids are outraged. The architects, interior designers, and the product and graphic designers face the fashion designers, arguing the immorality and illegality of hunting monkeys for their fur. The thought of killing primates purely for their coats so some fashionista can parade around in them offends all of us, including the fashion designers.

One architecture student starts talking about hearts of palm. Apparently, she says, whole groves of a kind of palm tree are cut down and wasted so that some gourmand can buy a precious little snack in a can. Monkey fur and hearts of palm. Everyone agrees, eventually, that we can do without these ill-gotten luxuries. What else can we do without, I ask.

But the bigger question now, for everyone in the room, is how to think about the materials we use and what designers must teach themselves about these materials. One industrial design student explains that we have to look at the full life-cycle costs of materials, from resource harvesting to processing to manufacturing to distribution to use and recycling or, better yet, working to engineer materials for nontoxic degradation. It took monkey fur and hearts of palm to grasp the complex system lurking behind every material choice designers make, from the paper we print on, to the clothing we wear, to the furniture we sit on, to the buildings we live and work in, to the appliances we use.

Last year, our second class of the fall season happened to have been scheduled for 9/11, and so, of course, did not happen. The semester was foreshortened by the attacks on the World Trade Center. For a while the New School buildings served as staging areas for some emergency services. Several students came closer to the carnage than anyone should. Our academic world became more real as we talked about America's arrogant and profligate energy use, which was dramatically embedded in the twin towers, now turned to one big toxic pile of dust. The rubble was burning not far from where we sat. Those who will give forms to our physical environment—my twenty-eight hopes for the future of a new design ethic—had a hard time ignoring this fact of their lives. The collapse shows, among other things, that our current American lifestyle is unsustainable.

But what can we do? Ask the students. Henry Dreyfuss provides a helping hand from beyond the grave. He got involved. We discuss Dreyfuss's dogged concerns about how people use things, what we need to lead useful and happy lives, how we see the world around us, how our unique body measurements and movements determine our relationship to tools and rooms and other things. He reminds us that there is considerate, sympathetic thought behind every great object.

Dreyfuss learned to type before he designed a typewriter, he drove a tractor before he designed one, he hung around department stores before he would design a shop. It's inspiring to talk about this "man in the brown suit," as the conservatively suited, Depression-era industrial designer came to be known. He connected with humanity. That's what a responsible designer does. This gift for making connections becomes the glue that holds us together after our world is torn apart on that sunny September day.

Also providing inspiration are Charles and Ray Eames. We read about their irrepressible, all-American, mid-century-vintage enthusiasm for both the designed and natural environment. What would they do with the information we now have about the life cycles of materials, we wonder. They would use it to great effect, we surmise. This was, after all, the couple who explored interconnectivity in a most memorable way. In their now classic film, *Powers of Ten*, the Eameses showed the many scales that make up our knowledge and experience of the world, zooming from the molecular to the cosmic and points in between. How about re-examining these scales of existence to help us think about our resources and ourselves, I ask, and prod the students to imagine how they would see the world with the Eameses adventurous, educated, and playful eyes.

Standing on the shoulders of these design giants, who have laid the foundations for responsible behavior, we get ready to explore the ethics of today's designers. To that end, each student has chosen a practitioner they'll interview, preferably in person. This exchange becomes the subject of their presentations and final papers. Incidentally, the fashion designers end up choosing small shop owners, independent shoemakers, up-and-coming dress makers—more in line with William Morris's thinking than Ralph Lauren's—creative and principled people struggling to find their own way.

What of the student who professed to be untouched by sustainability? Though her presentation shows a shocking insensitivity to the subject, her paper does not. As I read it, I'm gratified to learn that the lamp maker she interviewed uses recycled materials and searches out nontoxic processes. Perhaps her disclaimer was a moment of youthful rebellion or an honest confusion about the meaning of a difficult word; sustainability, after all, is hard to wrap your brain around. Perhaps when we understand that good design is responsible design, we will no longer need to rely on clumsy, descriptive words. We'll just call it design—a noble and necessary human activity.

Beyond Pro Bono
Graphic Design's Social Work
Anne Bush

Manifestos are meant to get under our skin. Committed to their biases, brevity, and zeal, they do not rehash established positions but underscore the questionable ones. They invite and expect response. Not surprisingly, it is rarely the manifesto itself, but rather the ensuing dialogue, that is of the most interest—a dialogue in which ideas are tested and ideologies revealed. The "First Things First Manifesto 2000"[1] is a case in point. Circulated last year on the Web and in the professional design press, this manifesto professed the importance of design that attends to social needs rather than pandering to the prescriptions of capitalist consumption. The response to this was varied. Predictably, some took issue with the over-simplification of issues and with the unspoken agendas that were attached (fair enough, but it is a manifesto after all). Unpredictably, some toyed with the very structure of the manifesto itself by cagily inserting abbreviated commentary into the list of signatures. Akin to graffiti or tagging, these interventions combined banal sarcasm with pointed critique. In so doing, they occupied a conventional space in an unconventional manner and served to underline an incredibly simple, yet often overlooked, point about communication—that it is fundamentally about exchange. It is an engagement with a real audience, one that doesn't always fit neatly into original assumptions about interpretation and, in some cases, can reconfigure a message entirely. Moreover, nowhere is such an understanding more important than in discussions about social responsibility itself.

I have always felt a certain unease with the general ways in which the design profession has framed notions of social responsibility. Frequently defined by acts of generosity (i.e., pro bono designs for not-for-profit agencies) or environmentalism (i.e., the use of recycled paper and soy-based inks), the design profession, in many cases, limits social responsibility to acts of benevolence or good will. Recently, this situation has been complicated further by the increasing celebration of design authorship. Although the inclusion of varied voices should be a welcome initiative, too frequently the overriding voice is still that of the designer. As a result, both civic benevolence and authorship tend to maintain (in many instances perhaps inadvertently) the historical notion of the designer as master communicator, the problem-solver. Yet, communication is dialogic. It depends on exchange. Thus, a more accurate understanding of visual communication invokes not only the voices of designers, but the voices of designers in concert with the voices of the audience. It is here, in the virtual space of dialogue, that social "response-ability" takes on the full complexity of its meaning and that the challenge for graphic design unfolds.

Most designers, I believe, would agree that design has an important social role, and that design practice should be anchored in the very reality of its social consequences. To understand these consequences, however, is to understand how messages function—that they are completed by readers who bring their own expectations and interpretive practices to the exchange. This is a scary proposition for many designers. As long as the design profession continues to celebrate the designer-as-author, it continues to hold onto the means of production. It maintains a sense of control, and in a discipline whose professional identity is increasingly threatened by the democratizing effects of new technology, control is security. Yet such security is an illusion. Instances of miscommunication continually remind us that visual communication is a collaborative process. More important, it is this dialogic process that defines visual communication as a social activity. To teach social responsibility, then, is in part to foster an understanding of visual communication as exchange and to understand that such exchanges are never entirely predictable or neat.

In a graduate seminar that I facilitate at the Universidad de las Américas (UDLA) in Cholula, Mexico, students study the relationship between designing and reading practices as different, yet connected, forms of making meaning. In the course students are asked to select an example of visual communication and then to examine the similarities and differences between the intended meaning and the eventual response to the message. Questions they are asked to consider include: what meanings are shared and by what groups; what intended meanings are contested and what counter-meanings constructed and circulated; how is the visual and verbal language that is employed constitutive or reflective of certain groups and positions; and how does the struggle for meaning reflect or resist institutional power structures. The ultimate goal for students is to recognize that meaning is always the result of a range of cultural and social negotiations and the designer is not the sole determinant, but rather a participant, in these dialogues.

In her analysis of a poster campaign developed by the Mexican government, Erica Wong examined the discrepancy between an institutionally designed message and its community reception.[2] The goal of the governmental campaign was to provide information about health and nutrition to rural indigenous communities. The posters, which featured a single image of a smiling boy in traditional dress, were produced in black and white and were posted in the local health clinics as well as on trees and lampposts in the rural towns (see Figure 1). Unfortunately, despite the best of intentions, both the government and the designer underestimated the ways in which the posters would ultimately be read by the local population.

Wong points out that the design of the poster, which uses a grainy black-and-white image, fails in very fundamental ways to communicate to its audience. First, by referencing the documentary fine-art traditions,

Figure 1

epitomized in the images of Mexico by Alvarez Bravo and Tina Modotti, the photography attempts to capture indigenous culture as a kind of romantic and static essence. It becomes a kind of visual anthropology that says more about the conceptions of its makers than the reality of its intended audience. More disturbingly, Wong discovered through interviews with the local communities that many people misunderstood the intention entirely. For citizens bound by a strong sense of community and family, the boy in the image appeared abandoned. The people of the villages couldn't understand why he had been left alone. They also couldn't reconcile this sense of isolation with the posed quality of the photograph. If he was alone, why was he smiling for the camera? The synthetic, portrait-like framing combined with the celebratory dress (normally saved for special occasions) further confused the reading. Many said that they initially overlooked the poster, because they thought it was an advertisement for tourism, since similar portrait images of traditional culture (usually in black and white) were a common visual theme in the marketing of Mexican heritage. Wong reminds us, however, that although depicting indigenous culture in black and white is a common representational practice, it reinforces nostalgic ways of seeing and continues to locate indigenous culture in a perpetual past. Moreover, it differs greatly from the sense of color and activity that is a part of everyday reality in rural Mexican communities. For the local population, then, the poster not only mirrored the imagery of travel and promotion, but,

Figure 2

unfortunately, also served to reinforce regional fears of governmental encroachment and the dissolution of traditional ways of life.

In another example from the same course, Manuel Parga analyzes a poster campaign for the New Liberal Party in Colombia and points out how a message of economic opportunity, extended to the working classes in the 1989 presidential campaign, actually raises more questions than it answers (see Figure 2). For the New Liberal Party, progress translated as technological development, economic diversification and growth, and the elimination of premodern bad habits (i.e., political and economic corruption, informal business alliances, etc.). Thus, modernization, as Parga explains, was understood by the New Liberals as advancement, as an important step toward being a participant in the global economy. Yet Parga goes on to explain that because modernization in Colombia, as in other parts of Latin America, was aligned initially with colonization, it tended to support the privileged rather than the working classes. Instead of working to secure more opportunity for the average citizen, modernization, in many ways, has solidified social and cultural distinctions. As a result, Parga explains, many of the lower and middle classes are suspicious of modernization rhetoric, as, all to frequently, they see governmental invocations of progress and working-class solidarity as a facade sanctioned by the upper classes to keep social divisions in place.

Parga explains the intentions of the Liberal Party by analyzing the reading of the visual symbols (i.e., the Colombian flag, the juxtaposed images of candidates past and present, the arms of the candidate raised in a V shape, and the typography). What is more interesting in the campaign, however, is the manner in which classic images of working-class empowerment (rolled shirt sleeves, the raised arms of victorious defiance against an image of a flag, for example) are problematic because of the specific social and cultural context in which they are circulated. Industrialization in Latin America, while creating jobs and energizing economies, has had both positive and negative consequences. Imported primarily by European colonizers, the celebration of industrialization meant that the tenets of European modernism were mapped onto a reality that was far from homogeneous. Yet, according to Parga, Latin America is better understood "as a more complex articulation of traditions, as well as diverse and unequal modernities, a heterogeneous continent formed by countries where, in each one, multiple logics of development coexist."[3] Such a diverse landscape necessarily contains multiple audiences as well. Thus, ultimately, by packaging the notion of progress as an overall call to the fictional working masses (exemplified in this poster by the image of the triumphant worker), the New Liberal Party, in many ways, reinforced the rhetoric of existing power structures rather than interacting with a more conflicted social reality. It attempted to represent rather than engage potential readers. Parga concludes his analysis by calling for more inclusive communication agendas—ones that respect and address the diversity and traditions of their readers.

What these examples underline is the fact that messages never occupy an objective position in relationship to meaning. They are always completed by readers/viewers anchored in very specific contexts. Moreover, these interpretations often differ from a message's (or action's) intended meanings, since every response is a contingent one (personally and collectively). Not only do readers approach texts from differing degrees of literacy, but readers who do share a common reading ability do not always read messages in the same manner.[4] Consider, for example, the ways in which different audiences respond to different typographic or image choices and their combination. Media only complicates this further. Computers and the myriad of complimentary hand-held electronic devices have changed forever conventional ideas about reading practices. They also demonstrate how individual communities, in turn, possess their own modes of legitimizing particular communication media and methods of interpretation. Ultimately communication is a dynamic process that inserts certain preferred meanings into sites where they are accepted, rejected, or reinterpreted. To understand the dynamic of this exchange is to have what C.W. Mills refers to as the sociological imagination, to understand one's position and how it is conditioned by the world in which it is developed and voiced (professionally, intellectually, and socially).

Such understanding is also, in the end, linked to culture since social actions cannot be understood outside cultural contexts. Understandings actually construct our social worlds: Culture creates a world that makes sense. "In order to conduct a social practice we need to give it a certain meaning, have a conception of it, be able to think meaningfully about it. The production of social meanings is, therefore, a necessary precondition for the functioning of all social practices and an account of the cultural conditions of social practices must form part of the sociological explanation of how they work. Cultural description and analysis is, therefore, increasingly crucial to the production of sociological knowledge."[5]

We accept that part of the way in which we know the world is through representations, the contexts in which they circulate, and how such languages are read, used, and subverted. It is here, in my opinion, that the academy performs its most significant role, since fostering the ability to analyze and question encourages debate and action.

A potential theoretical model for such analysis lies in Michel de Certeau's discussion of the distinction between strategies and tactics.[6] According to de Certeau, strategies constitute the official languages of a discipline. Promoted through education and disciplinary assimilation, they circumscribe the accepted views of a group. In graphic design these views translate into the preferred visual languages of the profession (the result of the marriage of American advertising and European modernist aesthetics). In the discipline of graphic design, our strategies frequently conceal the power relations that sustain them, and separate us from the potentially productive, resistant, and contestatory interpretations of actual users. They reinforce existing notions of graphic design from the safe distance of conference rooms and classrooms rather than investigate the full dimensions (including successes and failures) of a communicative act. For designers to understand the social dimensions of professionally sanctioned languages, they have to study the tactics of actual users. Like reading itself, a tactic is a seized opportunity. It does not rest in a consistent and comfortable place, but acts in real time. It turns ways of reading into ways of speaking—passive readers into active readers who have a definite say in the interpretation of any message. Reading, then, embodies its own rhetorical constructions and these underline the need to study the total communicative act as one that empowers speakers on both sides of a message. For design education, such a reception theory of design means studying the actions and interpretations of audiences as well as those of designers, and potentially finding ways in which both sites of making become more consciously integrated. This study would inform (and probably alter) many conceptions of socially responsible design, as it would reveal how the profession of graphic design, as a discipline occupied with its own official strategies, works in many cases to suppress rather than enable the interpretations of individual users. Although, one could argue that such interpretations cannot be anticipated, it would be interesting to explore ways in which an active dialogue between the client, designer, and audience could result in more collaborative (and ultimately productive) communications that are interactive in their actual intent and that function through joint design rather than prescribed condition. In the best sense, such visual messages would work to encourage self-cultivating publics[7] rather than mass conformity. In the design classroom, this begins with encouraging critical and self-aware citizens.

It has been said that the role of professional education is to make the framework of a discipline explicit. Yet such defining should be done not to curtail discussion but to encourage it. As C. Wright Mills points out, definitions invite others to see the world in a particular way. And, in so doing, they change the discussion from an argument over terms into a disagreement about fact, and thus open arguments to further inquiry.[8]

This expanded inquiry finds fertile ground in the classroom, since this is the place where debate is unbounded by commercial and economic restrictions. It is the place where one practices the art of thinking out loud but intelligibly—where all viewpoints can be explored, and assumptions, methods, and judgments can be laid bare.[9] This is not to say that classroom discussions should dissolve into subjective relativity, but that they should maintain a sense of free exchange, even when positions champion less-popular views. If graphic design education is, in large part, a study of the preferred definitions of the profession, it is also, in its best sense, a site for contests and reinterpretations—a site for students and teachers to pose critical and thoughtful questions about professional ideologies and ultimately their own.

In the most fundamental sense, then, responsibility is the ability to respond. It is not just the willingness to act, but also the ability to understand one's actions, the context in which they are applied, and the widest range of implications for their reception and potential reinterpretation. To teach this ability is to teach a critical awareness of the entire communicative act, not just an awareness of one's personal contribution. When we teach critical understanding, when we investigate our own positions (what we take as fact, the methods that we invoke, and the judgments that we make) as well as the contexts of specific social situations, we encourage accountability. In my opinion, this is the role of the academy. What design education can contribute to participatory society is the engaged and aware citizen who understands the ramifications of action and inaction, yet (ultimately) is given the option to choose.

Author's Note

I would like to thank Erica Wong and Manuel Parga for allowing me to discuss their work in this essay. I am indebted to them and other graduate students and faculty in the department of design at the Universidad de las Américas in Mexico for the opportunity to share ideas and, in the process, learn a great deal about communication and myself.

Notes

1. The "First Things First Manifesto 2000" is a new version of the original "First Things First Manifesto" written thirty-seven years ago by Ken Garland. It was published with thirty-three signatories' names in *Adbusters, Emigre,* the *AIGA Journal, Eye, Blueprint, Items,* and *Form.* A copy of the "First Things First Manifesto 2000" is currently posted (along with the original version and readers' responses) on the *Adbusters* Web site: *www.adbusters.org.*
2. Erica Wong, "Designing the Marginal: Mexican Assumptions in Representation" (unpublished essay).
3. Manuel Parga, "Beyond Instrumental Power: A Critical Analysis of Cesar Gaviria Trujillos Political Campaign" (unpublished essay), 6.
4. Roger Chartier, *The Order of Books* (Stanford: Stanford University Press, 1994), 4. Chartier makes an important correction here when he points out that the essential but oversimplified separation of the literate from the illiterate does not exhaust the full range of differences in readers' relationships to writing.
5. Paul du Gay, Stuart Hall, Linda Janes, Hugh Mackay, and Keith Negus, *Doing Cultural Studies: The Story of the Sony Walkman* (London: Sage Publications, 1997), 2.
6. Michel de Certeau, *The Practice of Everyday Life* (Berkeley: University of California Press, 1988), xix.
7. C. Wright Mills, *The Sociological Imagination* (Oxford: Oxford University Press, 2000), 186–187.
8. Ibid., 34.
9. Ibid., 79.

Timing Is Everything
Lessons from Sphere Magazine
Peter Hall

In 1994, New York–based artist Alfredo Jaar visited Rwanda three weeks after the end of the genocide in which an estimated one million people were murdered. His first project was to send out to friends 200 picture postcards he had purchased of the Rwandan landscape. On the front of each card was a scenic view of Rwanda, and on the back Jaar wrote the name of a person he had met while traveling who had survived the massacres, such as, "Caritas Namazuru is alive!" A prepackaged souvenir thus became a political art piece, with a subtle reference to the existential work of conceptual artist On Kawara. In the 1970s, Kawara mailed daily picture postcards stating the time he got up, as well as telegrams with the message, "I am still alive."

When in January 2001 I met with my fellow editors of *Sphere* magazine to decide on a theme for that year's issue, the postcard idea seemed to offer a great deal of potential. In its five years of sporadic existence, *Sphere* had always positioned itself at a point where design meets pressing social, political, environmental, and educational issues. We'd previously devoted the annual publication to themes like gun control, domestic violence, and boundaries and racism.

Though it's hard to remember with everything that has happened since, in January 2001 we were in the wake of a particularly disempowering election fiasco.

To appropriate writer Joan Didion's phrase, public awareness of the disconnect between the political class and the nation that sustains it had reached a critical level. After the Supreme Court's historic ruling granting the presidency to George W. Bush, we felt the need to affirm the existence of a world—with its urgent needs—outside of the cynical machinations of the Florida election battle.

When reports surfaced that our unusually inexperienced new president had only made one official foreign visit in his political career, I suggested to the *Sphere* editorial team that we turn the issue into a collection of postcards created by artists and designers from around the world. Their subjects could be issues they thought were worthy of the president's attention, and the tagline could be the old picture-postcard cliché, "Wish You Were Here."

The idea went over well with *Sphere*'s founders, David Sterling and Mark Randall, who have an impressive track record in setting up collaborative projects. Their not-for-profit Worldstudio Foundation was founded to redress the dearth of diversity in the creative community through scholarships for minority and economically disadvantaged students and mentor programs pairing these kids with artists. To help raise funds for these activities, the foundation stages an annual event inviting celebrity artists, architects, and designers to redesign an everyday object—one year a chair, the next a clock, and in 2001, a lamp. The results are auctioned off at a gala. The "Wish You Were Here" magazine would operate in the same spirit, with the postcard as our everyday object.

The designs, as they came in, were varied and, in many cases, compelling. Some touched on local politics: The architecture firm Lot/Ek illustrated New York's homelessness problem, for instance, with photos of shanties rigged out of discarded cardboard, doors, bricks, and urban deritus. Others drew attention to problems overseas. Bombay artist Deborani Duttagupta depicted Indian children sitting in the dirt of a rural "outdoor" classroom, deprived of walls, chairs, and writing materials, in a country that spends less than 3 percent of its state budget on education. Milton Glaser illustrated an African man dying of AIDS, the postcard text noting that with a pledge of $3 billion a year, the United States could finance a credible assault on an epidemic that has killed 15 million people.

Many of the designs were sharply ironic. Art director Chris Dixon drew a paper-doll outfit showing the protective dress worn by residents of Punta Arenas, Chile, which is situated beneath the ozone hole. Musician and artist David Byrne came up with a witty response to the Republican election victory, using a photo of a stuffed animal donkey and elephant caught in a compromising position in front of the American flag.

The two most controversial designs, however, were by Seattle artist Shawn Wolfe and the Dutch design firm Wild Plakking. Wild Plakking's showed an aerial image of a military building under the crosshairs of telescopic sights, with the caption "Cleared by U.S. Military" and text questioning the wisdom of the $305 billion-a-year U.S. military budget. Wolfe's satirical design railed against the "rigging and sabotage," as he called it, of the 2000 presidential election, in which the will of the people was subverted (the national majority did not, after all, vote for Bush). His card showed a grotesque cartoon version of Dubya with bleeding eyes, and a tagline neatly reversing our theme: "Wish You Weren't Here." On the reverse side of the postcard were two dotted circles marked "Poke here," implying that the reader could create, with a pointed instrument, two hanging chads (the terminology for half-poked ballots in the contested election) exactly where the cartoon president's eyes were aligned on the front side.

At a subsequent editorial meeting, we decided to use Wolfe's design for the magazine cover, where, with some hand-daubed red stripes, it was incorporated into a variation on the American flag. Little did we know how emotionally charged the flag would become later that year. The issue emerged from the printer in August and we began distributing free copies to our usual list of recipients (mostly designers) by mail later that month. People began to receive their copies in the first few weeks of September, and inevitably, in some cases, our politically charged issue bearing the "Wish You Weren't Here" Bush flag plopped on doormats during the week of the worst terrorist attack on American soil in history. Our timing was unfortunate, to say the least. Bilious e-mails and faxes began to pour in, and the Worldstudio telephone began ringing off the hook. In some cases the calls were fantastically stupid. One faxed message likened the issue to a "rabid KKK or Aryan Nation publication," while a caller described the magazine as "shit produced by faggot-loving Nazis"—a phrase that seemed to raise the novel prospect of progressive fascism. But many e-mails reflected a recurring theme, suggesting that the magazine was "un-American" in its criticism of the government. These ranged from the hysterical, calling the magazine "vile, hateful, and partisan," to more reasonably worded criticisms: "While I too believe that the most wonderful aspect of the U.S.A. is our right to disagree, I am saddened by your lack of respect for the flag and general tone of the piece." It became clear to us that our mis-timed issue had become the object of misplaced anger at the terrorist attacks. Patriotism was at a feverish pitch, flags lined the streets, and *Sphere* had become a flag flying in the wrong direction. Even one angry posting in the "soapbox" section of the Graphic Artists Guild Web site admitted as much: "This is where I'm not sure if I am over-reacting. Had I received this publication a month earlier, I would have just thrown it away without such strange feelings."

Our first response was to draft a message to post on the Graphic Artists Guild site. We explained that the issue was planned and developed months before the events of September 11 and was intended to encourage "positive interaction" with our newly elected government and among our readers. We argued that publishing *Sphere* was to us an "intensely patriotic act" because it was based on the very American right to free speech, and on the belief that people can still participate in political change. Shawn Wolfe's response, which touched on similar territory, took a more sorrowful twist: "Perhaps intolerance, rage, and self-righteousness are indicative of an emerging tenor of our times," he wrote. "If so, if we no longer have the freedom and latitude to express an unpopular idea, then the enemies of democracy are winning already." In my mind, Wolfe nailed the most disturbing characteristic of the "Wish You Were Here" flak, which is the way it reflected a lack of tolerance for dissent. This became more prolonged as war was declared and bombs were rained on Afghanistan. Dissent had become taboo in America. The author Edward Said described the atmosphere in his December 2001 PEN lecture: "Unless you are vying to provide descriptions of outrage and anger that say 'On with the war,' then you are un-American." A few weeks earlier, the actor and Buddhist Richard Gere was booed at a benefit concert in New York for preaching compassion rather than vengeance. It was a stark contrast to the situation in Europe, where the logic of bombing the Middle East drew heated debates. Jonathan Freeland, a Washington correspondent for the *Guardian* newspaper in England, argued that Democrats were unanimous in their support of the war front for tactical reasons: to prevent Bush gaining political advantage from it and to leave themselves free to attack him on other fronts. "The result is total, bipartisan consensus," wrote Freedland. "There is no debate about the rights and wrongs of the war in Afghanistan—none at all. A single congresswoman spoke out against it, and she has been all but ostracized by her Democratic colleagues."

As I write this, we continue to bomb villages in Afghanistan, and self-censorship is in full evidence on the streets. New York City hoardings are not spattered with anti-war posters in the vein of the Vietnam War era, or even a level of graphic dissent akin to the previous Bush era, when artists as diverse as Robert Crumb and the Guerilla Grrrls were producing posters protesting the war in the Persian Gulf. The shock of the attacks on September 11 seems to have silenced us all into submission.

America is still nursing its wounds, and it takes considerable strength to voice an opinion against a tide of hurt and anger. The philosopher and critic Christopher Hitchens writes in "Letters to a Young Contrarian" that "one of the hardest things for anyone to face is the conclusion that his or her 'own' side is in the wrong when engaged in a war. The pressure to keep silent and be a 'team player' is reinforceable by the accusations of cowardice or treachery that will swiftly be made against dissenters." Hitchens eulogizes the courage of his friend, an American serviceman, Ron Ridenhour, in exposing the evidence of the 1968 massacre of Vietnamese villagers in My Lai. The resulting "And Babies?" poster by the Art Workers' Coalition featuring R.L. Haeberle's photograph of the massacre is one of the most important design works of the era. I would hazard a guess that at the time it provoked a flurry of bilious complaints by the public.

Our "Wish You Were Here" issue was not so bold. Its theme was not anti-war, but simply to call attention to matters that artists felt were of importance: the unfairness of the electoral college, homelessness, excessive military spending, lack of education funds, and so on. We were, we felt, continuing a strong American tradition of graphic dissent. In response, more than one graphic designer suggested we leave the country and move to Afghanistan.

I learned three lessons from the experience. One is that timing is everything. Political graphics are best produced swiftly, when the events they protest are still fresh in the public memory. Two is that many graphic designers prefer their graphic agitation in historical books, at a safe distance of at least ten years. The third lesson is that, as Socrates argued a few thousand years ago, the unpopularity of an idea does not prove that it is false. It does, however, prove that it is unpopular. Or, as Hitchens puts it in his letter to a young contrarian: "Don't expect to be thanked, by the way. The life of an oppositionist is supposed to be difficult."

Healing with Design

An Educational Approach

Chase A. Rogers

The ideas presented in this essay cross many boundaries. But why should I write this paper now when we are at the very early and controversial stages of a quest to understand how we behave, think, reason, and respond using physics, brain theory, and vibrational therapies? The reason is that I believe this essay brings together diverse experimental data and theory that support a new educational model for designers—a model that successfully combines design and communication art with innovative healing therapies.

Steve Heller, in response to this essay, offered this wise quip: "Not all communication arts heal, but all healing arts have roots in communication." The idea that graphic design has curative powers may not be the first thing on a designer's mind, but it is a power that, if harnessed, can be among the most responsible things a designer can do.

Introduction to Energy

When communication arts and healing arts merge, the potential for vast systems of healing and learning can occur. In the recent past, vibrational studies and therapies have focused solely on the individual. Believably, vibrational medicine combined with communication and design techniques opens the door for systematic healing and learning far beyond individual therapies. Through the appropriate uses of sound, light, color, pattern, and symbol, it is possible to change vibrations and currents in the mind and body. To understand this theory, we must explore the nature of medical science in its current and evolutionary state and its relationship to both Newtonian and quantum physics. If designers, like the medical profession, begin to incorporate the multidimensional systems of life—molecular biology, biochemistry, quantum physics, as well as ancient modes of healing—into design strategies, the potential exists for extending the framework of communications into a vast system of creativity, learning, and healing.

In the recent past, medicine has viewed the human body as a biomachine, a mere clockwork of biological gears and parts that can be tweaked and replaced. A new worldview emerges, however, that regards the body as a complex energy system. Both quantum physics and Eastern medical practices view reality as a continuous flow of change. There are observable, definitive connections between emotions, sensations, nerve impulses, chemical reactions, images, sound, and light. The human body is composed of dynamic chemical, electrical, light-based, biomagnetic, spiritual, subtle, and magnetic energy systems that work together to create harmony in our bodies in relation to our environments. Therefore, *energy* is the common link between mind, body, and soul.

Accordingly, the body has a unique energetic relationship to the world, taking in, processing, and emitting various forms of energy on a constant basis. Vibrating protons and electrons that make up every cell in the body form everything in life. Matter itself is simply congealed energy, slow-moving molecules frozen in form. Thus, biochemical molecules that make up the human body are forms of vibrating energy and emit wave patterns of varying frequencies. If everything has its own unique frequency system, then it stands to reason that the human body is a vast system of energy that resonates, expands, and contracts to other frequencies emitted from other substances around it. These patterns or scientifically measurable energy fields that make up the body include properties of light, color, sound, heat magnetism, and electromagnetism. Since energy moves in the form of wave patterns or frequencies, movement, thoughts, and emotions must elicit specific brainwave patterns. As such, our energy fields are already reacting to any external energy with which they come into contact even before we are consciously aware of it, if ever. William Collinge states, "Einstein showed through physics what sages have known for thousands of years: everything in our material world—animate and inanimate—is made up of energy, and everything radiates energy . . . energy is the bridge between spirit and matter."

From ancient practices to contemporary scientific thought, the body is viewed as a system of energy to which new vibrational approaches are being introduced regularly for increased emotional and physical health. Vibrational medicine simply provides a scientific model that suggests possible ways that health or illness might be affected via the body's energetic relationship to the world around it. The mental body, where and how the mind receives, processes, and distributes information, has a correlating effect on the physical body. Psychic distress often manifests itself physically when left untreated. The fundamental rule in treating the body energetically is in treating the whole individual, taking into account experiences and environment. Therefore, every identifiable system in the body must be kept in relative balance, internally and externally, in order to promote proper health and functionality. The use of vibration—light, color, sound, and biofeedback—on the body reveals the importance of restoring normal vibratory frequencies to help achieve that balance.

Biofeedback

The study of brain wave biofeedback can be used as the foundation for frequency theory. Defined as the science of quantifying subtle electrical information from the brain and activating a corrective frequency to normalize or stabilize brain frequencies, it is proven to enhance function and well-being. What biofeedback demonstrates is that the brain emits waves and responds to different frequencies and that in altering frequencies in the brain you can alter emotion, function, and behavior in very subtle ways. Research shows that the brain's electrical signals are subject to change and that people can be taught how to change them. Therefore, designers, through a concept known as *bioentrainment,* can utilize these vibrations to effectively regulate normal patterning on an energetic level for designing products and environments.

According to bioentrainment, the brain responds to oscillating light, sound, or magnetic field energies by becoming entrained, or in sync, with the frequency at which the energy is pulsating. Entrainment is a phenomenon of resonance in physics. It is more easily defined as the synchronization of two or more rhythmic cycles. This principle exists universally in chemistry, biology, medicine, psychology, sociology, astronomy, and architecture. The classic example shows that when individual heart muscle cells are brought close together they begin pulsating in synchrony. Mozart's music has a similar effect on the cells in the body, producing a harmonious, elevated vibration that opens the mind for learning (this is regarded as the Mozart Effect). The process of reproducing the entrainment effect using audio technology was developed in the early 1970s, and with that came the process of creating audio-entraining binaural beat frequencies.

Brainwave entrainment and binaural beats occur naturally in our environment. Via sonic entrainment, brainwaves are synchronized to achieve states of relaxation, productivity, and learning. In essence, normal vibratory frequency is restored to the mind. Sonic entrainment can affect the body on an emotional level, which can then correspond to a change on the cellular level. Sound can transform negative repressed emotions into a state of equilibrium that has direct and immediate effects on our physiology. Entrainment music has the potential to (1) resonate with the listener's feelings energetically, (2) transform negative into positive, and (3) promote states of liveliness or serenity. Therefore, designers, as sound coordinators, can match appropriate brain wave frequencies to transform the moods of individuals or large groups of people.

Light

Light therapy works in a similar way. Syntonics reveals that varying frequencies of light will affect different energies in the body. The most basic form of light, sunlight, is critical to our health on both a cellular and material level. Sunlight, containing all wavelengths of light, consists of the entire electromagnetic spectrum on which we depend to exist. Numerous studies have shown that only natural light and full-spectrum artificial light have an altering effect on the body. As light changes in the natural environment, so do the body's daily rhythmic patterns involving mood, fertility, and enzymatic and hormonal stems. Studies in syntonics demonstrate the use of different portions of the light spectrum to treat an array of mind and body conditions, specifically through the eyes.

Harnessing full-spectrum lighting and implementing it in all aspects of environmental and product design can only improve the way people function in the world. Artificial lighting that does not utilize full-spectrum patterns can cause *malillumination*, thereby depriving the body of the most basic nutrient essential for continued growth and development. Studies show that when fluorescent lights are replaced with full-spectrum lights in classrooms, attention deficit disorders (ADD) and hyperactivity decrease while learning, memory retention, and optimism increase. Such studies demonstrate how a tiny adjustment of environmental design, such as lighting, could incur profound changes in both attitude and health.

Color

Another design adjustment includes color. Color comes from light as a distinguishable frequency in the electromagnetic field. Light visible to the naked eye is known as the visible spectrum, which consists of the colors red, orange, green, blue, indigo, and violet. Each color found in the visible spectrum has its own wavelength. Each color frequency produces its own energy and has a specific effect on the body. The body absorbs color through the vibration it emits. Through color, we receive most of the energies we need to maintain the health of mind, body, and soul. The National Institute of Mental Health has done studies showing that our mental health, behavior, and general efficiency depend largely on color balance.

Accordingly, one often uses color to describe physical, mental, emotional, or spiritual states of being, but can color actually alter these states? Yes. Color can excite, sedate, balance, and motivate. Color preferences can reveal information about psychological states. Color/light therapists use these principles to restore cells to a level of balance and to stimulate healing processes. By learning how each color influences the mind and body, designers can effectively use color to alter energetic and physical states.

The effective use of color in design is not a new concept. Marketing and package designers associate color with sense response. For instance, the color red is often used in fast-food restaurants because it stimulates the nervous system and increases appetite. The objective is knowing *how* to use the vibrational frequencies of colors to promote health and healing on a large scale. Studies have revealed that when disruptive students were placed in blue classrooms, their aggression subsided dramatically. Even more interesting reports show that when England changed the color of its bridges from black to blue, suicide rates decreased by 50 percent. These studies prove that small changes in our education as designers can be instrumental in saving lives.

Imagery

Even the imagery a designer chooses can have a powerful effect on wellness. Medical use of imagery has existed in many cultures for many centuries from ancient Egypt to Biblical times, Freud, Jung, and present-day therapies. Connections have been made between emotions, sensations, and images, determining that chemistry follows thought. Imagery representing optimism, enthusiasm, and humor strengthens our healing systems. Adversely, imagery evoking pessimism and helplessness weakens them. The effects of this formula were demonstrated in an experiment using two test groups. One group was shown a film about Mother Teresa and her life's work; the other group, World War II power struggles. The first group had lower stress levels and a heightened immune responsiveness. The second group showed a weakened immune response and depression. Thus, when you influence the mind you influence the body.

Conclusion

The new worldview teaches us that illness is not only attributed to toxins, germs, and bacteria but also to chronic dysfunctional emotional energy patterns and unhealthy ways of relating to ourselves and the environment. If we can find ways to design better environments and systems of communications, we have the opportunity to improve the quality of people's lives and the life systems of the planet. We can achieve this by better understanding integral relationships between body, mind spirit, health, and illness and how energetic influences, such as color, sound, motion, light, and imagery, effect them. The exploration of vibrational therapy reveals the power that the elements we use in design have in altering energy frequencies and therefore states of learning and being. We live in an environment of increasing technology and geophysical forms of energy. The more compounded these levels of energy become, the more difficult it is for the body, mind, and spirit to achieve an energetic equilibrium. Knowing the impact of the external environment on energy fields requires that we make more conscious efforts as to how we, as designers, are contributing *vibrationally* to natural environments. It further demands a greater sense of responsibility and attention to each individual as a highly sensitive and resonant antenna in relation to other individuals.

The power to create long-lasting, positive, and meaningful change as designers is in our hands if we can only harness the energies of light, magnetism, electromagnetic fields, and other environmental energies that correspond with our bodies. If, as designers, we can begin to appropriately and positively work with the energy systems we have a greater chance of restoring balance both within the body and in the environment. "When we, as a Global culture, truly begin to use the knowledge of vibrational medicine to appreciate our place in the greater scheme of things, and to understand and respect the spiritual evolutions of all living beings on this fragile planet earth, we will start to heal on many different physical, social, emotional and spiritual levels."[1]

Notes

1. Richard Gerber, MD. *Vibrational Medicine for the 21st Century*, HarperCollins, 2000, p. 406.

Expelling School Violence
Visual Communications as a Catalyst for Change
Carolyn McCarron

Bullets are becoming as common as letters in American high schools: as many as twenty students in a high school of 800 are likely to enact a school shooting.[1] Kids believe violence is a justifiable means to an end when they feel reduced by another classmate, as new studies prove that retaliation against bullying is *the* key factor behind school violence.[2] Parents and teachers are often out of the loop when it comes to grievances among kids, so in most cases they are unable to help resolve conflict before it's too late.

The media, on the other hand, seems to reach kids faster. Today kids are exposed to more sources of information and visual imagery—from the Internet, to hundreds of TV channels, to the proliferation of magazines and newspapers— and they listen to these sources, making them vulnerable to countless conflicting messages.

Because of our media expertise as designers and visual communicators, it is possible that the antidote to school violence rests with us. A change in perception among kids could be more effective than additional metal detectors and school suspensions, and design could therefore be the catalyst for change and help bring about an end to violence in schools.

Same Vehicle, New Direction

Children and teens are the largest, most profitable target audience among advertisers and marketers, as they represent three markets: present, future, and an influence on their parents' purchases. Channel One, a ten-minute daily newscast complete with advertising that is aired in junior high and high schools, is so popular that it is now watched by eight million students—more than any other television program except the Super Bowl.[3] And kids *are* affected by what they see in the media: extensive coverage of the rampages at Columbine and Santana high schools motivated other students across the country to enact copycat shootings.

But even without this proof, it takes little more than common sense to know that visual communications and media influence kids. As Seymour Chwast, founder and director of the Pushpin Group, acknowledges, "I can't quantify it, but we know they respond to things that are visual. Good design and illustration can benefit them socially and culturally, as well as contribute to their knowledge and spiritual well being. It is up to the experts in child psychology to tell us what children understand and should know, and it is the designers who must implement that information." In communicating that information, we can use the same vehicles of media that may have helped to escalate violence among children and teens to *reverse* violence.

Exemplary Efforts

Some creative professionals have already begun to address these issues. The Worldstudio Foundation directed a campaign against gun violence. The campaign of blunt ads resulted from a mentoring program called "Help Kids Create," in which high school students who were directly affected by incidents involving gunfire were paired with creative professionals to create works of art about their experiences and feelings. David Sterling, founder and president of Worldstudio, says, "Because of the spate of gun violence perpetrated at American high schools, we became very concerned and wanted to do something. The name of our program came about when we envisioned taking away children's guns and giving them paintbrushes. We believe that creativity empowers; that if people are given opportunities to explore creatively, they may be more likely to imagine their way out of desperate situations—such as poverty or troubled families—rather than be limited or oppressed by them." In one project, sponsored by Polaroid and Neiman Marcus, mentors and students created stories with large-format Polaroid cameras. The images appeared in Worldstudio's magazine, *Sphere*, as well as in an exhibition in San Francisco for students and parents. Another collaboration with artist and photographer Janiel Engelstad resulted in six billboards in Los Angeles and bus shelters in Washington, D.C. Many of these images were aimed at grabbing the attention of adults and legislators. It worked, because one of the student artists was invited to testify before the California legislature about her experiences with gun violence.

The Advertising Council in Washington, D.C., aired a television commercial on the one-year anniversary of the Columbine tragedy on all major networks during prime time. The public service announcement, targeted toward parents, featured President Bill Clinton as the spokesperson, and encouraged parents to be attentive and to communicate with their sons and daughters.

A large number of Web sites address school violence, but for the most part these sites remain invisible because students have to first be aware that they exist in order to log on and seek support.

Other types of creative professionals are stepping up and offering their services, such as architects who are redesigning schools to make them safer. Gary Prager is designing such a school in Colorado in response to the Columbine tragedy. He is eliminating blind corners in hallways, putting windows in the classroom that overlook the hallway, and replacing bathroom doors with walk-around partitions.

Musician James Brown wrote a hit song, "Killing is Out, School is In," to motivate kids to do away with guns and be more proactive in keeping their friends, classmates, and teachers safe in school.

Addressing the issues of gun control, parental participation, online forums for students to anonymously seek support, and the safety of school building layouts are critical, and these exemplary efforts are all effective ways in which to do this. But more work needs to be done in reaching kids on a peer-to-peer level about bullying and seeking vengeance. The "I Will" pledge, penned by high school students in Nashville, Tennessee, proves that peer-to-peer communications may work best. The intent of the oath is to dissuade students from making fun of those who dress, act, or look different, demonstrating that students just may have a better understanding of the root of the problem than their parents, teachers, school administrators, and community leaders. The campaign has been so successful that one has to wonder why it has not been expanded nationally.

It is possible that more has not been done in this area because there are always the issues of finances, resources, and time when doing not-for-profit work. It can be difficult to find a sponsor willing to finance such public service campaigns, and when sponsors are secured, they often have their own agenda. In doing work for an individual school, one often has to get past the politics of that particular school board. But these are obstacles that can be overcome.[4]

A Message of Hope

At the time this essay went to press, it remained to be seen what long-term effects the terrorist attacks of September 11—which profoundly affected children and teens all over America—would have on the rate of school violence. Would it make violence seem more justifiable? Or would it show teens how devastating violence really is, and how it can destroy a family, a community, and a country? Only time will tell. Even so, many of the issues that needed to be addressed with teens before September 11 have been brought out into the open by the terrorist attacks, a key one being *tolerance*. The concept of tolerance, taken for granted or dismissed as political correctness prior to September 11, has become *the* catchword among adults around the world, as demonstrated in numerous ad campaigns targeted toward adults both in America and overseas. But this is not enough. Tolerance needs to be communicated and taught to children of all ages and backgrounds, especially given the diversity of American schools today.

To prevent the terrorist attacks from escalating violence among teens, the National Association of School Psychologists recommends addressing the following issues with children and teens:

- ✱ Violence and hate are never solutions to anger.
- ✱ America is strong because of our diversity. Our democracy is founded on respect for individual differences.
- ✱ All people deserve to be treated with fairness, respect, and dignity.
- ✱ Vengeance and justice are not the same.
- ✱ History shows us that intolerance only causes harm. Some of our country's darkest moments resulted from prejudice and intolerance for our own people because Americans acted out of fear.
- ✱ We need to work for peace in our communities and around the world.
- ✱ Tolerance is a lifelong endeavor. It does not stop with high school.[5]

Both Worldstudio and the Ad Council are attempting to address this specific topic of tolerance. After September 11, Worldstudio changed the title of its "Help Kids Create" campaign to "Create/Not Hate" to shift the focus from guns and violence to a more positive focus of humanity. David Sterling confirms, "In this revised program, we are trying to give kids alternate views of looking—with open minds—at the people in their schools, neighborhoods, and communities. It became important for us at this point in history to shift the focus in this way."

The Ad Council's campaign, "E Pluribus Unum," which means "Out of Many, One," is a message of tolerance and unity. (This motto originally signified the union of the thirteen colonies into one nation.) The "I am an American" television commercial is one of the first installments on this international campaign that is directed to a very broad audience. Susan Jacobsen of the Ad Council confirms, "We can't predict how much of an influence this campaign will have on our nation's youth, but we certainly hope that it will encourage all Americans, young and old, to embrace the ideals of tolerance and unity." Nevertheless, the flood of thank-you letters the Ad Council received after the campaign was launched is proof of the strong response it has generated among adults, offering hope that children and teens will be influenced as well. In broadcasting this moving campaign, the Ad Council generated higher visibility for the creative professionals who collaborated to produce this campaign, and the need for visual communications in times of crisis and tragedy—proving we can persuade, inspire, and motivate.

We Can

Some will argue that design and advertising cannot solve this problem. We need greater parental and community involvement and collaboration, counseling, gun control, and tougher school policies on bullying. But design and visual communications *can* be part of the solution. Given the new research, this is not a problem of guns but largely an issue of perception due to various influences, and we can help to promote a new philosophy among kids when it comes to violence and using guns. We can reach kids when teachers and parents sometimes cannot, because as communication professionals we are trained to listen to an audience and form a communications objective in response. Seymour Chwast adds, "If designers can 'speak' the same language as young people, they *can* have an impact."

History proves we can. During World War II, visual communications convinced people to buy bonds and travel America and motivated women to take jobs outside of the home. A single photograph of Jeffrey Miller lying on the concrete pavement at Kent State helped Americans to realize the divisive effect the Vietnam War was having on American society. Seymour Chwast's "End Bad Breath" poster became an icon of the anti-war movement and helped us to see the futility of bombing Vietnam. Likewise, the images of two planes crashing into the World Trade Center towers in New York City are forever seared into our psyche. That's how powerful visual imagery and communications are, whether a communications objective is intended or not.

In this case, a communications objective is badly needed, and at such a critical time in history. These teens are the next generation of leaders, workers, teachers, and parents. How do we want them to relate to world neighbors with views different from ours and resolve world conflict?

Notes

1. Sue Fleming, "Bullying Seen as Key Factor in School Shootings," Reuters/ABCNews.com, August 28, 2001.
2. Michael Josephson, "The Ethics of American Youth: Violence and Substance Abuse, Data and Commentary," released April 2, 2001, by the Josephson Institute.
3. Ellen Goodman, "Turn on Channel One, Turn off Values," *Los Angeles Times*, March 8, 1999.
4. The following are three organizations that can be considered by visual communicators looking for a forum or resources to pursue work on social or cultural topics, including school violence: (1) The Artist's Call to Justice, a new organization established for design students and professionals to submit art and design work on various social topics. The Artist's Call to Justice will annually recognize and award effective communications efforts and help with resources to publicize winning work (*www.liberation.org*); (2) To Make the World a Better Place, similar to Worldstudio, this youth organization, founded by artists Elana Gutmann and Daniele Robbiani, pairs creative professionals with kids to help them find avenues of constructive self-expression. An annual exhibition showcases photos and literature by students who share their vision of the world and how to make it better. This type of creative mentorship is critical because it helps kids to see that their voices and visions are valued in the world around them (*www.makeabetterplace.org*); (3) Ideas That Matter, a program in which Sappi Papers annually awards grants of $5,000 to $50,000 to winning applicants around the world to help them realize their creative concepts and campaigns in print (*www.sappi.com/itm/global.htm*).
5. "A National Tragedy: Promoting Tolerance and Peace in Children," handouts and press release by the National Organization of School Psychologists, September 15, 2001.

Brand Name Dropper
Steven Heller Interviews Shawn Wolfe

Shawn Wolfe does not preach anti-branding on weekends while designing corporate annual reports on weekdays. Rather, he devotes a sizeable share of his graphic design business (he also creates flyers and logos for alternative music groups) to perpetuating a "brand" of his own called Beatkit™ used to promote the radical idea that branding, which many of us designers have come to practice, is morally dubious and downright unsavory when exported from the haves to the have-nots. So, if one accepts that consumer culture is based on devious manipulation designed to stimulate excessive material desire, and one objects to the growth of crass materialism throughout society, then one will certainly appreciate Wolfe's foray into mythical branding. However, if one has no such axe to grind against corporations or capitalism or materialism, one can still appreciate the wit and humor of Wolfe's Beatkit™ (its motto: "Since 1984 Until 2000") because it is hard not to be amused by this self-obsolescent (indeed as promised it met its planned demise in 2000), anti-brand, corporationless-corporation. Wolfe's message is imparted through such universally wry sarcasm and sly subversion of consumption habits that it touches the funny bone of even the most rabid materialist.

Wolfe invented an ersatz product called the "RemoverInstaller™"—a mechanism that is void of any utilitarian purpose other than to titillate desire and increase expectation. Yet, like the Pet Rock, it has such a beguiling folklore that it could possibly enter the marketplace where it might sell by virtue of its fake allure, even though it does absolutely nothing. Through clever graphic persuasion Wolfe imbued the RemoverInstaller™ with the kind of authority that makes it as indispensable as ball bearings and iconic as widgets. In a weird way, one is almost convinced that it is an essential mechanism with incalculable attributes, even though in reality it merely perpetuates its own existence, adding nothing to the world, yet taking up space and begetting waste. RemoverInstaller™ is a concrete metaphor for planned obsolescence and conspicuous consumption. And by framing the entire enterprise in a pseudo-seventies rainbow and glitz graphic style, Beatkit™, RemoverInstaller™ and the faux worldwide advertising campaign devised to promote it, (which Wolfe calls "Panic Now"), mimic one of the most superficial periods of American cultural history.

SH: What does the word, indeed the notion, *responsible* mean to you?

SW: I suppose at root it simply means being accountable. Basic *personal* accountability. All people, ideally, are accountable for the burden they place on their environment, their impact on their surroundings, their influence on those closest to them as well as those they affect indirectly. Not to suggest that anyone's morally bound or obligated to live in any particular way, only that they should be accountable for whatever effect their life choices have on others. And maybe both words mean roughly the same thing. They certainly go hand in hand. But I think from accountability comes responsibility. I'm accountable for everything I say and do. In *principle* anyhow. *Ideally.* So I try to speak, act, work, and live responsibly, motivated to be aware of the facts of my existence. It's true for a designer just as it's true of anyone from any walk of life.

As I see it—in this world at this time—the activity in which all people are engaged, the activity that is having the most profound effect on everything from the human condition to the condition of the planet itself, is the activity of production and consumption. Whether at any given moment you are a have or a have-not

Brownout Blowout (2001)

or something in between . . . whether you're the faithful consumer of cultural products or you're the instrument or mastermind of some faithless cultural production . . . *you are involved* and you're accountable for the part you play. That involvement, for better or worse, could take many forms and have many effects and countereffects. And it's going to be impossible to have foreknowledge of them all. But if I'm being responsible I'm taking steps, making reasonable efforts to know the facts, gaining some sense of likely outcomes . . . for the offshore sweatshop worker filling quotas at gunpoint . . . for Johnny Have-Not who will live with that gnawing sense of festering inadequacy that advertising exists to breed . . . and for the landfill that will choke on those sneakers and handbags and portable minidisc players by the time we all buy enough of them to keep the economy on the upswing, forever and ever.

Whether you're designing products or packaging products or both—I think a designer has extra responsibilities that the average consumer doesn't. Anyone on the production end of the cycle has to recognize that his or her actions will be multiplied and whatever effects resulting from those actions are going to be manifold. Whatever value or ill effect designers' works have is magnified through repetition and mass distribution to every corner of people's lives, whether those people like it or not. And whether one labors behind the corporate armor-plating of Monsanto or Martha Stewart Living Incorporated, each is accountable, personally, to the extent that he is an accessory to the vitality of their employer. Consumers have special responsibilities too, and they have a role in deciding who and what is going to survive on an open market. They are at a disadvantage though—always on the receiving end of imposed and intrusive things—and it's nearly impossible to stage an effective resistance to powers that are entrenched or have the momentum or the kind of bandwidth that the consumer can't hope to compete with.

Having said all that I also realize that there are limits to how responsible or accountable any of us can be at any time. We can't all afford to *not* shop at Wal-Mart. We have obligations. We can't all afford to turn down work we find objectionable or change jobs as soon as we start to feel lousy about our situation. We're all leading compromised lives, and whatever we do, no matter how carefully we step, our actions are going to compromise the quality of some other life, somewhere in the world. I'm probably helping to make extinct some species of beetle in the Amazon basin somewhere as I speak, without even lifting a finger. The best we can hope for is to stay mindful of it and own up to our contribution, for better or worse.

SH: How do you gear your work as a designer/artist toward, shall we say, the public good?

SW: Hard to say. I guess I don't proselytize. Or I try to avoid that if I can. As a designer, and even as an artist, I don't necessarily have an agenda or an informed idea about what "the public good" is or should be, only opinions on the subject. I suppose I do enjoy exploring the possibility of a "public good." With the Panic Now and RemoverInstaller™ campaigns, for instance, as well as pieces that have spun off from these, my aim primarily has been to provoke, give a person pause, anyhow, and put them into a questioning state of mind that maybe

Just Add Life (2001)

they weren't in until this incoherent, irrational thing crossed their path. Not that people have no defense for the irrational or that they are unprepared for it. People are accustomed to processing thousands of incoherent and irrational messages and ideas every day. We're all really good at it, whether we realize it or not, and even if we'd prefer to *not* be good at it . . . we are. We've developed this shiny callous hull called "ironic distance" to keep us well and help us deflect all the nonsense. By way of an alternative, Panic Now is not necessarily the voice of reason, nor is it saying anything that the beauty industry is not telling us constantly. It's irrational. Panic Now is a last-ditch solution to an unspecified, maybe nonexistent problem. Panic Now is also the impulse to buy. "What if I don't? How can I not?" But whether it provokes a laugh or an annoyed grunt, if it makes someone stop long enough to look to see if something's there . . . even if it's only an exercise in futility, maybe it throws other selling messages into question, as they should be. Or maybe a habit of mind is broken, long enough to actually chew on what would have previously just been swallowed whole.

SH: Can art and design make changes in our collective lives, and if so, how do you see your work having such an effect?

SW: I guess they are two different things, right? Art is essential as a proving ground for ideas, especially ideas that do not necessarily have any exchange value, yet maybe never will, or ideas that are just not popular or are outrageous or completely offensive. The proving ground is a necessary thing for a people whether

Panic Now Poster (2001)

they realize it or not, to see ahead, to imagine a way out of the bag the present has them in, or just see the present more clearly for what it is, or the past. Artists supply the beer goggles we need to get a good look at ourselves as we are. Or as we hope to be. Or not be. Whichever.

There is room for some of this in design, in advertising, fashion, even in architecture, but only to an extent. Mostly these things—the good, the bad, and the ugly—are a cluster-fuck manifestation of the marketplace, all competing with each other, jockeying for space and consideration, making trashy, incomprehensible, and oftentimes wonderful noise together. The sinews of the marketplace reach everywhere now. New occasions for design are proliferating and synergizing themselves all over the place. And that means surfaces to cover. I'm thinking of the Internet, for example, and the segmentation and branding of the television screen we've seen with the recent overhaul of CNN *Headline News*. But also there are things like the billboard advertisements that are now on the floor of the supermarket aisle, and bus wraps. And I still hear rumblings about that low-orbiting Golden Arches. The heavens redefined as previously underutilized design surface. How long before we're walking on streets paved with ads, under a sky dotted with low-orbiting burger beacons and a fifteen-mile-tall Carrot Top telling us to use AT&T when calling collect? Certainly the personal computer and the mass-market conquest of cool that's taken place over the last thirty years have produced a couple of generations that are far more aware of design than their predecessors. There's already a heightened design literacy, heightened expectations for more and more people. Hopefully the powers of bullshit detection are heightened as well.

As far as how do I see my work having an effect one way or the other, I only know I am fortunate to be working now, as opposed to ten or twenty years ago. I don't think that design was something the average person had an awareness of, at least not nearly to the degree that people do today. I think that only in the kind of blizzard of advertising and design like the one we now live in could something as absurd and fatalistic as Panic Now have any currency. And if the RemoverInstaller™ provokes a stray thought or two about obsolescence, or our appetite for extinction, or the futility of trying to fill that emotional void with cute products, or if it functions simply as a tangible expression of some kind of vague disgust or resignation that the consumer is feeling anyway, if it does any of that—and I know it has, for me anyhow—then I see my work having a therapeutic effect. Just as Wacky Packages and *Mad*'s parody ads had a therapeutic effect on me when I was a boy.

But I'm not kidding myself either. This stuff often mostly amounts to pissing in the wind or preaching to the choir. Pissing and preaching.

SH: It is one thing to have a social conscience, it is another to make serious contributions—and by this I mean actions that are not just pissing in the wind. What areas do you believe are vulnerable or susceptible to meaningful action, and what action might this be?

SW: Meaningful action? I don't know. As [the band] Negativland said, ours is a "slow and indiscriminate culture, sauntering through the last phases of the American Dream Era." Certainly designers should have an idea of what that word "responsibility" means to them and what they're prepared to do about it. But it's important that everyone else recognize that they are accountable too. Let's help them see if and where they have a hand in determining *how things are.* Convince them that it *actually matters* how things are. This may fly in the face of thirty years of detachment, cynicism, vanity, first-world privilege, and glut. But now that they are attacking our cities maybe we can all at least agree that it matters. It matters what we did, what we didn't do, who we elected, what they did and didn't do. We need to enlarge that kind of awareness I guess. Popularize it. Get parents interested in teach-

Bush League cap patch (2003)

ing it to their children. As far as meaningful action, ultimately that's going to mean action in the marketplace. Our culture *is* a marketplace. Our homes are lifestyle showrooms. Our bodies are surfaces where advertising goes. And the marketplace is a tepid Ganges contaminated with all of our worst leeching tendencies, false appetites, treachery, and raging psychoses. Wherever we're headed, the market is taking us there. Downstream.

The culture jammers are all working in—or in relation to—the marketplace. It defines them. Even those who lash out against it are spawned from it. It preceded them and it's bigger than them and, like it or not, it sustains them. Their way of life. As individuals, as packs of street artists, even as organized consumer advocacy groups, often our efforts amount to little more than posting bills along the base of a vast cultural edifice that is not about to move or dismantle itself. As amazing and inspiring as the WTO protests were here in Seattle back in '99, I think we all have to hope that there is a better means to an end than open revolt. I think we have means at our disposal, particularly as designers, to communicate with our fellow man using the same voice and the same platform as the big boys. We lack the billions needed to be heard during prime time, but we still have the Internet, for now. And there are those among us who are willing to risk incarceration for the defacement of those billboards. And the rest of us work within the system, playing by the rules but also making the world we all have to live in. *We are us* in that respect, and *we* can change if we want to. A corporation or an industry may not be vulnerable or susceptible to meaningful action, but people are always vulnerable and susceptible. We have to work on *them*. And that is what culture jammers are doing. We groan when we see advertisers co-opt our semiotics, but this is only an indication that these ideas have mass appeal.

SH: Who do you aim to influence—is there an age, profile, demographic that you can honestly say is within your grasp?

SW: I don't know. I suppose I'll take all comers. Although I have to say, I'm not always hoping to influence or grasp someone. Often I'm working to suit myself, for my own satisfaction, or to satisfy my sense of how something ought to look, or what it ought to say.

SH: After 9/11, did your strategies change, were they put on hold, or did they stay the same?

SW: I tried hard for a few weeks to just watch and listen as closely as I could to what was happening. The first thing I remember thinking, or feeling, regarding "my strategies"—or "the stuff I do for a living," as I would think of

Vending Machineries (2001)

it—was that it all suddenly seemed completely trivial. It pissed me off that I was made to feel that way. I definitely felt stifled by sudden history. Creatively and in general. The gravity of what happened, the scale of the loss, not to mention the high drama, the staging of the event by the terrorists . . . "out of the clear blue sky" as it were . . . it captured our imaginations, to say the least. We were at a loss for anything to compare it to, therefore it was deemed "unreal," despite the grim and gritty realism. I can't tell you how many times I heard people say "it was like a movie," reaching for irony's crutch out of habit. Since then, though, the New Normalcy has started to take shape, I guess. Still waiting for some other shoe to drop, but getting on with life too, picking up where I left off wherever it's appropriate to do so.

SH: How would you categorize your main weapon: parody, sincerity, or something other?

SW: My main weapon has to be sincerity. That sincerity is slathered in winks, nods, and air quotes at times, but underneath all the cloying is a sincerity. Ha. I tell myself that I should only make images that are worth making, or only do something that is worth doing . . . that *that* should be my guide in how I divide up my energies. It's childish and unreasonable, but it makes a good enough rule of thumb. I think to myself . . . while you're going to the *bother*, make sure whatever you're doing is worth doing and not just some wasted effort or added clutter.

SH: How would you teach responsibility?

SW: By example I guess. Or intimidation? Heck, I don't know.

Not for Profit
Steven Heller Interviews David Sterling and Mark Randall

David Sterling and Mark Randall are principals of Worldstudio, Inc., a for-profit graphic design studio (*www.worldstudioinc.com*). David is president and founder of Worldstudio Foundation, and Mark serves as vice-president.

David Sterling conceived of the idea of Worldstudio in the fall of 1992. He had been working with Jane Kosstrin for the past twelve years in their company, Doublespace, which he cofounded. As he tells it, he felt like he had taken it just about as far as it could go. There was a disconnect in his life between the graphic design work he was doing and his desire to contribute to the larger community. Always interested and active in social causes, Sterling spent many evenings and weekends volunteering. But the split between the world of commerce and the world of community service became too much for him, and he began to seek out ways in which work and life could be more seamless.

After working for Vignelli Associates for several years, Mark Randall struck out on his own, running a small design studio, and had begun to have many of the same feelings that Sterling had. Randall wanted to work on projects that felt more meaningful to him personally. Randall and Sterling shared similar concerns and both wanted to work on projects that reached beyond the bottom-line needs of clients. They also wanted to work on projects in which they could feel a true sense of ownership. Worldstudio was a way to integrate both the need to make money and the need to fulfill a more basic human desire to give back to society in some way.

The foundation was truly a grassroots initiative. Neither Sterling nor Randall had had any experience in starting, let alone managing, a nonprofit foundation. Through a continuing dialogue, the goals and the vision of Worldstudio Foundation evolved and became more concrete.

SH: What is the foundation on which Worldstudio operates?

DS and MR: We did not want to follow in the footsteps of many graphic activists creating provocative posters about a range of social issues. Instead, we sought to create programs that would directly impact people's lives. Our collective interest in culture and diversity—and David's experiences teaching design at the School of Visual Arts—led us to create the scholarship program for disadvantaged and minority students. At that time, there were many industry discussions about the lack of diversity within the creative community and major corporations were looking to diversify their workforces. But while the topic was discussed at industry conferences, no one seemed to be tackling the problem. We felt like this was something that we could do that would directly give back to the creative community in a tangible way. To date, we have awarded over $500,000 to students across the country in art, architecture, and design. In keeping with our initial concerns of a more socially aware creative community, we focus our awards only on seniors and graduate students who demonstrate their desire to give back in some way.

SH: When speaking about a designer's responsibility to society and culture, I suspect there are many responses, but Worldstudio seems to focus on issues that most designers would not incorporate into the professional realm. How do you manage to balance profession and good works?

DS and MR: We draw our salaries from Inc. and donate our time to the foundation—often after hours. The workload at Inc. determines how much time each of us is able to spend on the foundation. Besides us, Worldstudio, Inc. has a staff of four designers, a couple of marketing types, and basic support staff. The foundation has two full-time employees who primarily run the scholarship and mentoring programs. In addition, a percentage of the profits of Inc. are directed toward the foundation.

Initially we were trying to develop a studio where the work of the for-profit business and the work of the foundation could go hand in hand. We quickly discovered the difficulties in this. Design exists to serve commerce and there was not much we could do beyond specifying recycled paper. We separated the two organizations and they work independently of one another. Occasionally a project comes along—managed by the foundation—that needs a graphic design component, so we are able to hire ourselves, in a sense. In the future we hope to bridge the gap more by working on cause-related marketing programs for various industries.

The nature of graphic design often leads a designer to fulfill the role of social commentator rather than a true activist. The operative word is *act.* You can design a poster about literacy or you can teach a kid to read. While the poster may be a valid and important part of the equation, we wanted to act more and comment less.

While attitudes can sometimes be affected by commentary, we decided to follow our core belief that true change comes through action and *not* commentary. It's been our experience that the graphic design community often responds more to commentary than to action. Commentary is visual; it is sexy and can grace the pages of industry publications. Action is not: what would you show your peers in *Graphis?* Because of this, it is often hard for us to engage the design community.

The issues we chose to tackle were ones that we hoped could effect measurable change. We wanted to fulfill a recognized need within the creative community. The scholarship and mentorship programs go hand in hand. We introduce high school students to the creative professions through our mentorship program. At the same time, we sow the seeds of social responsibility. The students are paired with mentors to work on community-based projects. These projects range from a Los Angeles billboard campaign against gun violence to a newspaper art journal tackling issues of homophobia that is distributed to school and youth groups. Then, by the time these students are ready to attend college, if they have decided to enter careers in the arts, we step in and offer a helping hand through our scholarship program.

SH: Design is about making and packaging things and ideas. Historically, design has been seen as a force for changing the world. Realistically speaking, how much can design actually change the world?

DS and MR: We believe design can change the world. It may not be huge, all-at-once, sweeping change, but over time we can chip away with one idea at a time. (Unless you consider Guttenberg a graphic designer and Henry Ford an industrial designer, then the changes can be pretty sweeping and pretty fast!) We never underestimate the power of human beings—much less designers. Think of it this way: if every graphic designer absolutely stopped specifying any paper other than recycled paper tomorrow, imagine the change that would transpire! Still, design must go hand in hand with individuals willing to do the work; design can't do it alone. The designers in Gran Fury were not just commentators from the sidelines. They were directly involved with the fight against AIDS. Their work gave vision and voice to the fight and had an impact. To use another example, currently the architect William McDonough is working with Ford Motor Company to re-envision its River Rouge plant, cleaning up a contaminated site while creating an environmentally friendly manufacturing plant on a huge scale. McDonough, who inspired Ford to go in a more "green" direction, can't do it alone: He needs a client with the vision and foresight to tackle such a project.

Often design that effects true change goes unnoticed because it is not sexy or glamorous. It is often more about function than form. While trekking through Nepal professor David Irvine-Halliday from the University of Calgary paid a visit to a local school only to discover darkened rooms with little light for the students to study by. Artificial lighting was infrequent and costly. His reaction was to initiate the Nepal Light Project. Halliday developed safe, reliable, affordable, and healthy lighting using small white-light-emitting diodes, which run off 12-volt pedal-, solar-, wind-, or water-rechargeable batteries. This simple solution has had a direct and measurable impact on the students of Nepal, but will probably never grace the pages of *ID* magazine because it was not "beautifully designed." In an ideal world the light would be "designed"—but that is not the point. It's more important that it work and solve a problem than be beautiful. Too often in the design community the interest lies in the form, not the function.

SH: What is the purpose of your magazine?

DS and MR: In order to establish ourselves within the creative community—and to define what our organization was about—the first thing we did was develop *Sphere* magazine. Our goal in creating *Sphere* was to highlight the social and environmental work of artists, architects, and designers from around the world that we admired, and, in effect, to inspire other creative professionals by example.

Paper companies collectively spend millions of dollars promoting their paper with elaborate promotions designed by "design superstars." Many of these promotions travel from the mailbox right into the garbage can. We proposed to Gilbert Paper the idea of a "paper promotion with a purpose." They agreed and generously gave us money and paper for our first issue, which mailed in the summer of 1994 to 15,000 creative professionals across the country.

We like to think of our annual publication, *Sphere*, as the inspiration and our quarterly newsletter, *1/4 Sphere*, (previously called *Atlas*) as the impetus. *1/4 Sphere* is meant to provide factual information on how you as an individual can become involved in the issues that concern you most. We give practical advice and sources of information, from where to recycle old computer equipment to which congressman to write to in order to share your thoughts on a particular social issue. We developed the idea of producing *1/4 Sphere* as a series of postcards. Each card would introduce the reader to a particular subject in a condensed form, and if he or she were interested in learning more there was a link to our Web site with the full story. This was a way to make the newsletter a bit more interactive—give it a pass-along quality—as well as make it colorful yet cost effective.

We think of these publications as the voice of the foundation. And, in pure marketing terms, they help to put us on the map. But in the overall scheme of the organization, the publications do not receive as much of our attention (read: time commitment) as do our scholarship and mentorship programs.

SH: How do you fare in this role of humanitarian design firm? How do you measure success?

DS and MR: While the road we have chosen is sometimes rocky and difficult, we continue to grow and garner the support we need from the industry. We can't do this alone—nor do we want to. The purpose of the Foundation is to engage the creative community and every year we manage to get a new individual, corporation, or foundation on board.

We measure success in the stories and letters we receive from students we have given awards to; in the continued support that we receive from the creative community; in the ever-increasing grants we receive from foundations that fund our programs. Since we have a small staff, and must balance our own time between our for-profit design business and the foundation, it is a constant struggle for money, support, and recognition.

The fact that we are able to earn a decent living running our design studio, and maintain a thoroughly functioning and active nonprofit, is success enough. It proves that with a bit of ingenuity and commitment you can accomplish a lot in a short period of time.

An excerpt from one of our mentors: "Working with [my mentor] gave me an idea of the direction I want to pursue in school, and even motivated me to skip my well-dreamed year off of volunteering and go straight to school." Knowing that we've had an impact on someone's life is our true measure of success.

SH: What are your now and future goals, given the fact that society, indeed the world, has changed since 9/11?

DS and MR: I think our perception of our place in the world certainly has changed, but I think it is a bit self-centered to say that the "world has changed." A more interesting question might be, "Will *we* change?" Granted terrorism has achieved an unprecedented level of horror, but the root causes of that action were always there. Devastating events happen all too often. Hatred of one group toward another has existed from the inception of humanity. In 1994, when the West largely ignored the genocide of over 800,000 Rawandans, did we ask if society or the world had changed? Did we change when the Union Carbide gas leak killed 15,000 Indians, displacing millions from their homes?

The issues that affected us before 9/11 still affect us now. We will continue to build our scholarship and mentorship programs. But it is now more clear than ever that the mentorship initiative that we began over a year ago is more important than ever.

As for the future, we want to provide even more impetus for professionals to get involved. So we are slowly developing a grant program for creative professionals which will assist them in their work on vital social or environmental issues.

SH: Indeed, do you see a changing role for design in general since the events of 9/11?

DS and MR: After the events of September 11, we've noticed a lot of talk in the graphic design community about what we as designers personally can do in response to such a devastating event (aside from the designers who dealt with the event in their daily work as editorial, broadcast designers, etc.) "When Something Terrible Happens People Wake Up," a Jenny Holzer truism we put on the cover of *Sphere* several years ago, has never had as much resonance as it does now. The arts have played a role in the response to the events of 9/11. Photographers created images that not only defined the event but were a true expression of the feelings we all had, and helped bring us together. The advertising community banded together to donate their time to create television spots which were meant to help shore up New York's weakening economy. Architects and urban planners rushed to their drawing-boards to begin the task of rebuilding. Everyday citizens—many of whom were not artists—covered the city with handmade posters and signs. I think this underscores the lack of awareness in the graphic design community. Instead of rolling up sleeves, diving in, and tackling a problem head on, we all approach it from the side and just discuss it. There's something sterile and rather safe about that, isn't there?

We think that it is our responsibility, not only as designers but as individuals living together on this planet, to be more socially aware, to understand that the decisions that we make in our daily lives may have a negative impact on another life. If the tennis shoes you love were reportedly made by child labor, maybe you should not buy them. If you know that a potential client uses child labor to make those shoes, maybe you should not work for them. We were recently offered a small project to design an elegant invitation to an event at the Waldorf Hotel here in New York. The glamorous affair was to raise money to support the war against the Palestinians in Israel. The idea of taking on such a project ran counter to the work we are trying to do in our "Create! Not Hate" mentorship program. It was an easy project to turn down. In the future, when the stakes are much higher and if it required either laying off an employee or working for the war in Israel, it might not be as easy. That would be the true test.

SH: Of all your achievements, what is Worldstudio's crowning one to date?

DS and MR: That's easy: awarding over $500,000 in scholarships to disadvantaged and minority students across the country.

Reporters Without Borders
Véronique Vienne Interviews Robert Menard

Information frontlines are as dangerous as military ones. The barbaric execution of *Wall Street Journal* reporter Daniel Pearl in February 2002 was a shocking reminder that journalistic freedom comes at a price. According to *Reporters sans Frontières* (RSF) (a.k.a. Reporters Without Borders, a Paris-based freedom of press organization) in the last fifteen years, more than 775 journalists have been killed worldwide—nine of them in Afghanistan in 2001. That year alone, at least twenty-seven journalists were murdered worldwide, compared to sixty-six during World War II. And in ninety-five percent of the cases, the killings of journalists are never prosecuted.

And every year, an even greater number of reporters are kidnapped, wounded, beaten, and thrown in jail without trial. As this book goes to press, as many as eleven journalists covering the Iraqi conflict have been killed in the last month. Today, RSF is assisting more than one hundred journalists languishing in prisons—a third of them abducted in the last twelve months. Kept behind bars, unable to communicate with the world at large, the silenced journalists can no longer generate the very pictures that could make their story—and their plight—newsworthy. "That's why we are communicators—not journalists," explains Robert Menard, who founded RSF in 1985. "Our job is to create news—even when there is no news."

Human rights transgressions are only meaningful when translated into photographs. In today's media, a story without a picture is not a story. So the challenge for RSF—often called the Amnesty International of the press—is to put a human face on faceless crimes. "In most cases, we can only take credit for accelerating the process that leads to the liberation of jailed journalists," says Menard. "The nature of our mission is at times bleak and unremitting: all we do is criticize, criticize, criticize."

A case in point is Menard's criticism of the way the United States is handling the war against terrorism. Since September 11, Menard has denounced the wave of restrictions imposed by the U.S. government on all journalists. Access to information regarding military operations is now strictly controlled. The Pentagon has bought the rights to all high-resolution commercial satellite images of Afghanistan, and the *Washington Post* has been publicly reprimanded by Defense Secretary Donald Rumsfeld for endangering American soldiers' lives with its reports of U.S. troop movements in Afghanistan.

Freedom of press was further curtailed when White House officials asked TV networks not to broadcast videotapes of Osama bin Laden when an Al-Jazeera correspondent in Washington was taken in custody by the police for questioning. And when, right after the September 11 attack, journalists were barred from the World Trade Center's Ground Zero—a gory scene by all accounts—and directed instead by authorities to take celebratory images of firefighters doing their patriotic duty.

Although the bulk of RSF's caseload is in countries ruled by authoritarian regimes, such as Burma, China, and Rwanda, Western democracies are scrutinized as well. "Our communication style must be direct, without subtleties," laments Menard. "That's our force. That's what we have to do in order to have impact."

Born in Algeria in 1952, Robert Menard grew up in the French city of Montpellier. Not one to make much of his Marxist youth, he is nonetheless tagged as a leftist. Open to attack from the Right for his left-wing leanings, Menard is vigorously criticized by fellow left-wingers for not being active in the pursuit of a political agenda. But for him, the first priority is to support the freedom of journalists to report—regardless of their political allegiance or personal motivations. Often the jailed journalists are radicals, even fanatics, with a self-serving agenda. "Victims are not always heroes," notes Menard.

Renowned and respected throughout Europe, Menard is so far totally unknown in the U.S. In his book *Les Journalistes que l'on veut faire taire* (the journalists they wanted to silence), he outlines the growth and challenges of Reporters Without Borders. Financial survival is always an issue: Few governments or companies will risk damaging future trade relations with repressive regimes by being publicly associated with RSF. Small grants, donations from private companies, and contributions from individuals are welcomed—but rare. So Menard has to raise most of the money for his organization through sales of monographs of famous French photographers, such as Robert Doisneau and Willy Ronis. Sold at newsstands, not in bookstores, the paperback monographs cost less than six dollars and are popular with the French public.

Thanks to networking, lobbying, press releases, media events, and awards ceremonies, Reporters Without Borders keeps the plight of endangered journalists in the mainstream media. But the organization also provides whatever help it can to all those who fear the threat of censorship, jail, or death: grants for legal fines, payment of fines, and financial support for the families of imprisoned journalists. In an interview last summer in Paris, Robert Menard spoke of his main goal in life: to negotiate the release of all journalists worldwide.

VV: Reporters Without Borders is not known in the United States, yet it is very popular here in France. Would you mind explaining to our readers what you do?

RM: Our work is first and foremost to gather information. We have correspondents in more than 103 countries worldwide. With the information they gather, we try to put pressure on whoever holds journalists in custody.

But there is only one way to put pressure on governments, you know. The one thing these people are afraid of is getting bad press on the international scene. They are usually looking for money from the United States, from Brussels, from Paris, from London, or from Tokyo—and a bad image makes it a lot more difficult for them to get the credit they need. "Oh, shit," they think, "it's going to make things much more complicated."

So that's where we come in. Each time freedom of press is in jeopardy, we inform the press, in the West in particular, to warn the folks who help authoritarian governments by lending them money. "Look," the moneylenders tell them, "sure, we can help you—but can you fix this little problem first?"

We focus on two major areas. First, we disseminate information to alert the various media of the seriousness of the situation, exposing the predators who are a threat to the freedom of press. But our second mandate is to help journalists who are stuck in prison, by assisting them as well as their families by providing lawyers, doctors, cash—whatever is most needed.

We can also send money to an association of independent journalists, as we do in Cuba. We can help people flee to safety and survive in exile if that's the case. We buy airplane tickets. We buy paper to print newspapers. We try to provide all the material help that you can imagine.

VV: How do you get your own financial resources?

RM: Seventy percent comes from selling our photography monographs. They are sold in thirty-five countries in five languages: French, English, Spanish, Italian, and German. We are preparing a Japanese edition. We survive on the revenue from these paperback albums, published twice a year. One comes out May 3, the day of the freedom of press [which was created by RSF in 1992], and another on November 28, which is the day we celebrate the "sponsoring" of jailed journalists by various media worldwide.

When a journalist is in jail, we ask a newspaper, a magazine, a television or radio station to become his or her *parrain* (the French word for "godparent"). On November 28, all the media in the world do a global action, and we sell our second album of the year. Last November, we published a monograph on William Klein. What sells better is "art" photography. Controversial topics do not sell and thus do not serve our fund-raising purposes.

VV: And how do you keep the various media informed of the situation of the journalist they sponsor?

RM: We send press releases. But we also update our Web site (*rsf.org*) daily (at 5:00 P.M., punctually) with current news. Here in the office, we have twenty people who gather information from every source, including our foreign correspondents—about a hundred of them worldwide. And all day long, three people call the media to keep them posted. Let's face it, we spend most of our time pestering the press.

VV: What's the most effective way to get stories published?

RM: Concepts, ideas, and numbers do not move journalists to write stories. You are a journalist, so you know. What works are precise case histories. If you tell me that in Burma there are thirteen journalists in jail—it's true—it doesn't galvanize you to action. On the other hand, if I send you a picture of San San Nweh, a Burmese woman journalist, writer, and political activist who is serving a seven-year sentence in a cell measuring only ten square meters in the women's wing of the Insein prison in Rangoon, you'll listen. If I also tell you what she wrote, how she was arrested, what she had to suffer, her family background, why her innocent daughter was jailed . . . and if I add to this report a couple of interviews with people who have been incarcerated in the same prison, then, indeed, you have a story!

That's what we are trying to do. Personalize the victims.

But we also do vivid portraits of the enemies of freedom of press. In our monographs, we list about thirty of the top culprits and we published their pictures and biographies.

The essential difference between Reporters Without Borders and other human rights organizations is that we work with the media. We believe that they can make a difference by putting pressure on public opinion, and by extension, on the various governments that jail journalists. The media can also put pressure on the heads of Western democracies who can help the cause of human rights by speaking up. When Mr. Bush, or Mr. Blair, or Mr. Chirac meet other heads of state and mention to them their violations—with a list of the reporters who are jailed in their countries—they can have a tremendous impact. The only way to communicate with everyone concerned is through the press. So our obsession is to mobilize public opinion.

VV: Do you write stories as well in order to feed them to the various journalists?

RM: Yes, we write detailed reports that we send to the press, but just as important, we create occasions for the various media to talk about it. For example, yesterday I was in Geneva where we launched a campaign against the 2008 Peking Olympic Games. Considering China's human rights policy, it would be madness to sponsor the games on their turf. So, for the occasion, we brought one of the most famous Chinese dissidents, Wei Jingsheng, who lives in the United States, so that he could describe the daily reality of Chinese human rights violations.

VV: So you create media events.

RM: Exactly. We are always coming up with new ideas for events that would generate press coverage. We understand the psychology of journalistic stories. We know that when someone has been kept behind bars for ten years, there is nothing new to report. Whether the story is published today, next month, or next year—makes no difference. There is no sense of pressure. So our greatest challenge is to make a current story out of old news.

People in jail have two things going against them: no news, but also no images. Often, we have no photograph of them. No visual record of their arrest. It's very difficult to do television without images! So we have to imagine what gripping visuals the TV crew should show to illustrate a case history—a case history whose subject is invisible, cooped up behind thick walls.

VV: So how do you tell a story that has no pictures?

RM: The best tactic is to stage press conferences on location. We try to have journalists meet the families, we try to "steal" photographs from prison walls, we try to meet friends of the victims—anything that gives the story a level of reality.

VV: How many prisoners are you following at any given time?

RM: Last year, we took care of about 400 cases during a twelve-month period. Some journalists were liberated, others are still in jail, and still others have been arrested again. The figure I am giving you today will be different tomorrow.

How can we measure our efficiency? Now that's a difficult question. In the last six years, we were able to find media sponsors for about 150 jailed reporters, but sometimes a popular journalist will have up to twenty media sponsors. Half of them were liberated, but we don't take full credit for their release. Other factors have worked in their favor.

It's not a great record, but it's not bad either. Not a week goes by without some good news. Take San San Whet in Burma, for instance. She is not liberated. But for the first time, she has been able to see her family. You know, if you have been in jail for seven years, and at long last you can see members of your family . . . that's quite something! Of course, if you compare our modest success rate with the staggering number of dramatic human rights violations worldwide, it's not encouraging. But if a prisoner were your sister or your mother, then you would begin to appreciate our efforts.

For instance, I remember visiting a Turkish prison—I did that many times—to help journalists kept behind bars. Once, the director of the prison took me aside to tell me he should not be held responsible for the treatment imposed on convicts. We had a nice chat during which he offered to help us—giving us permission to send medication and food to jailed reporters in his prison. Again, that's not a release, but it's a form of progress. I don't consider this sort of action negligible. I was able to reach an understanding with a man who did his job—but who wasn't a blind instrument of an authoritarian regime.

To be totally forgotten is a second prison. Being allowed contacts with the outside world is already a form of freedom. We are aware that it is a formidable moral booster for the prisoners to know that 5,000 miles away people are working for their release.

VV: How do you effectively communicate with the prisoners?

RM: It depends. Often through the families. But sometimes we can't reach anyone. There is a man, Abdullah Ali al-Sanussi al-Darrat. He has been incarcerated for twenty-seven years in Libya—the longest period a journalist has been in prison in the world. We know his family, yet we don't even know if he is still alive. No one has been able to see him for all this time. But as long as we don't have proof of his death, we are not going to forget him. Every month we plead with the authorities in Libya to get some information regarding his fate, with no result so far.

VV: How do you get in touch with local governments?

RM: We write letters. We go to embassies. We try to put pressure on international organizations they belong to. But with Libya, it's almost hopeless. It's one of the worst regimes.

We get best results, unfortunately, with the poorest countries, who need money from Western democracies in order to survive. We have more ways to put pressure on the Central African Republic or on the Ivory Coast than on Libya or on China. It's terrible. In Libya, they have oil, so they don't need foreign help. They don't give a damn when the Western media give them bad press. Same with China. We cannot put pressure on them—no matter what. Except for Mr. Bush who recently took a much tougher stance toward China, the majority of European countries are cowardly noncommittal toward China.

VV: How do you keep informed of the violations?

RM: First, we have a twenty-four-hour SOS line, and we receive calls on it all the time from family or colleagues of journalists in trouble. Our policy is to do something at once. We know that torture is most dangerous in the first twenty-four hours. It's often in the police stations, during the first few hours of detention, that people are tortured. It's before they are officially arraigned. Before any official action takes place.

We have 103 foreign correspondents who I can call to go to police stations at once—in the middle of the night if need be—to see what's happening. We call diplomats, embassies, the Red Cross, you name it. We do everything that's in our power. The faster we are, the more successful we become. That's why we have such a large network of correspondents worldwide. They are paid by us. Unfortunately, their task is not easy—they too are vulnerable.

When I, a white man, go to Africa, I am relatively safe. People are going to think twice before killing me. But someone who is local doesn't benefit from the same international protection. A year ago, as many as six of our correspondents were either thrown in jail or put under arrest, pending some judiciary action. In some cases, our correspondents are well known by the local authorities; in others, they are undercover. Whatever gives them greater protection.

VV: Men and women work for RSF?

RM: Yes, though more men than women—that's the nature of the profession. And in many countries, women are not allowed to hold jobs. And if they did, they would be more vulnerable, because of their children.

VV: Are you also following people after their release?

RM: We try. Let's take Peru, just to mention another continent. President Alberto Fujimori had arrested a lot of journalists under the pretext that they were terrorists. Once they were released, we helped them find jobs—menial jobs if need be—so that they could make some money. Often, unfortunately, there is little we can do, because we lack the financial backing.

In Cuba, for instance. If we want to help alternative journalists, we have to give them money on an everyday basis. Otherwise they get in trouble dealing on the black market and are arrested again. Today we pay the salaries of twenty Cuban journalists. If we didn't, they would not be able to work as reporters—they would have to flee or be arrested again because they cannot obtain regular jobs.

VV: Do you care to comment on the Brice Fleutiaux suicide? [a French photographer who was prisoner in Chechnya, released thanks in great part to RSF, made into a national hero in France—but who took his life at the end of April 2001. His funeral was May 2, 2001—ironically the day before the May 3 RSF freedom of press yearly celebration.]

RM: It was our fault. Brice was behind bars for eight months. Because he was French, we were able to galvanize the public opinion and eventually force his release. He was the twentieth journalist held as hostage by the Chechen. When he was freed, we wrongly assumed that we had done our job. In hindsight, we realized that we didn't pay enough attention. We feel terrible about it.

Now, we have learned that our role doesn't stop with the liberation of a journalist. We have to provide a follow-up as well. We were lulled into thinking that he was fine—he himself assured us that he felt great. But he had personal problems, of a sentimental nature, and instead of getting over it, as you and I would have, he became despondent.

The lesson is that post-traumatic stress disorder is a real thing. Our work doesn't stop the day people are freed. Now we know: we call lawyers, experts, judges, but also therapists and mental health professionals.

VV: How can you hope to increase your financial resources? Can you find rich sponsors?

RM: Very few people, organizations, companies, or governments are willing to help us openly. To give RSF money today means jeopardizing one's commercial ties with the Chinese market tomorrow.

You have to realize that our job is to say terrible things about people and governments. I am not going to celebrate the good deeds of others. Things are swell in Denmark? I am not going to talk about it. It's quite understandable that commercial entities are reluctant to be associated with a muckraking organization like us. I can't blame them. And since in Europe there is not a tradition of grand charitable foundations, we are left with no other choice but to raise money ourselves—thus the photography monographs, which are designed to have a wide appeal.

We only get some funding from the European Union (EU). Why? Because it is a union of fifteen states. They don't have a common foreign policy, they help human rights organizations. But if we were to ask for the support of, let's say, the French government, or England, or Germany, they would all individually make excuses for not helping. I have a very bad relationship with French diplomats, for instance. Even though France is supposed to be the birthplace of human rights! I ask for help with prisoners in Cameroon? Oh, no! It's a former French colony. We have to maintain good relations with the region! The Ivory Coast? Nope. Algeria? Are you out of your mind? Tunisia? Get out of here! Do you want me to go down the list of the forty countries that do not deserve French support when it comes to human rights?

Now, if I ask for money to defend the freedom of press, let's say, in Burma, maybe I will get an audience. It's far enough, and Burma is not a financial or commercial partner of France or Germany.

VV: What's your relationship with Medecins sans Frontières (Doctors Without Borders)?

RM: None. They are just good friends. They helped us at the beginning set up our organization, but that's all. And their role is very different from ours. Their task is essentially humanitarian. Ours is to sensitize the media to safeguard the freedom of press.

Our one solid partner is American. It's the Committee to Protect Journalists, based in New York. But in the United States we are not known. We have almost no presence.

VV: Yet your monographs, translated in English, are available in the States.

RM: But the distribution is lousy. We go through LMPI, a Canadian subdivision of Hachette. We only distribute 2,500 albums in North America—that's pathetic. But we have to find people who are going to volunteer to help us. We function on a friendship basis—our network is based on personal affinities. That's how we have been able to grow so far.

One of our next projects—in collaboration with the Committee to Protect Journalists—is to find American newspapers that would be willing to sponsor jailed reporters. It's inconceivable that the top newspapers in the U.S. would not jump at the opportunity to take under their wing a jailed journalist and do what's necessary to get them out of prison. But so far we haven't had time to approach them. Help us get known over there!

Originally published in Aperture *magazine, Summer 2002.*

Professional

Part II
Professional Responsibility

The Cultural Influence of Brands
In Defense of Advertising
Chris Riley

I'm an advertising guy.

I wanted to make that clear as you and I engage in this conversation about "sustainability." Advertising is intrinsic to consumerism and, as you know, consumerism is about creating desire. I am very happy in this environment. I like advertising, I enjoy helping create it, and I enjoy being associated with strong businesses that are growing. Strong businesses are important. I grew up in Manchester, England, in the seventies. Let me tell you, you learn a lot about the importance of strong businesses when they are in short supply. So I come at this question of sustainability from that place. I am not an environmentalist in the classic sense. I have not dedicated my life to protecting our environment, though I have huge respect for those who have.

One of the big inventions of consumerism is the brand. We all intuitively know what I mean when I talk about brand. Yet there are as many different perspectives on what brands are as there are brand owners. It may help if I share with you the way I think about brands. I think of brands as business ideas that have achieved cultural influence. Big brands influence culture in a big way, small brands in a small way.

What interests me about this perspective is that it hinges on two huge ideas. The first is that a brand is a "business idea," and the second is the notion of cultural influence.

Let's talk first about a business idea. There has been a lot of work done on this subject. On the one hand, you can focus on the business model. The business model is all about the way a business creates wealth. For the last few years many young technology entrepreneurs have been presenting their business models to venture capitalists for investment. The VC looks at their presentation and asks two questions: "Is this a good business model that will generate a return on my investment?" and "Is this person likely to do it for me?" The business model is about *capitalism*. It is about *return on investment*. It is about the *commodity*. In one of its most refined forms, the business model's effectiveness hinges on the financial value ascribed to relationships. This is the way capitalism renders everything as a commodity to be bought and sold. For example, the value of AOL exists within the relationships created by the service. These relationships are then exploited to create wealth.

The problem with this way of thinking about business is that it underrepresented the social and cultural role of business. When Time Warner merged with AOL, what kind of business would be created as a consequence? Is AOL's commodity its relationships with people, like my daughter at her iMac in her bedroom, to be traded as, well, just any other stuff? I understand that the contents of, for example, an oil field are an easy commodity to understand, or the value of owning land, or the ability to make a fine automobile or . . . but wait. Things are looking harder as I go through that list.

In the film *Wall Street* we are introduced to Gordon Gecko (remember "lunch is for wimps"?) The film reveals the way business commoditizes everything within a capitalist system. The futures of the workers' lives are in the hands of traders who care little and understand less about them. The young adventurer ends up in a limo with a beautiful women who informs him that he has earned a reward from Gecko—her. The film uncovers the ugly truth about pure capitalism: the human experience is simply another commodity to be traded for financial gain.

It need not be so. In fact, some experts in the field of business analysis suggest that a pure focus on the capital aspects of business is a deeply flawed way of thinking about how business works and how businesses can succeed in the long run. Some early pioneers of consumer businesses seemed to understand this: Ford, Kohler, Cadbury, and Lever, to name a few. In their world, business was an integral part of society. The role of the business was not only to generate wealth for the business owner but to create opportunity for all who engaged in the business transaction, from the entry-level employee to the most distant customer.

Business is a process, not an entity. It is entirely the product of relationships. Technology has helped business operate at a global scale. Consequently, as business became more complex, embracing a multitude of human relationships and organizing them into systems driven by economic models, the perceived value of human relationships was eroded. In essence, humanity has begun to serve capital rather than the other way around. Capitalism has been a great system, unleashing the innovative powers of the human mind, the creativity of the human spirit; but capital is not the ends, it is the means. Today we find ourselves in a difficult situation: The success of capitalism has concealed the erosion of the basic underpinnings of business—human relationships. Capitalism has bred corporatism, which has enabled good organization but has also removed personal responsibility from business planning.

The emergence of corporatism as the dominant ethic of business analysis is recent and will be transient. Kees van der Heijden made the following observation in his book *Scenarios: The Art of Strategic Conversation:* "We define structural profit potential as an attribute of a system capable of creating value for customers in a unique way that others find difficult to emulate."

To repeat: "Profit is an attribute of a system." Obviously, every business wants to make money, but it also has many other attributes, and if this attribute becomes the sole purpose of the business and drives every business decision it has the effect of commoditizing everything—including people. Business exists to serve human needs and desires, not capital requirements. The levels of growth preceding the dot-com crash in the United States were obscene. Growing capital became the sole reason to invent business ideas. And how many of those ideas still exist today? A business designed only to grow capital is far more likely to create distress and cause destruction than one within which the total value of the business, its role in the lives of the people involved with it, is the purpose.

Many who have started small businesses or are part of family enterprises understand this deeply. Those who have lived through harsh times in Flint, Michigan, or Liverpool, England, are also aware of this simple, human truth.

In America there is the extraordinary situation that the food industry now produces far more calories on a daily basis than is needed (or really wanted) by each and every American. Do we really need access to donuts when we buy gas? Is it really a good idea to commoditize food so absolutely that America is the only country in the world where the relatively poor are relatively fatter? Where the rich pay more to consume less? This is a corruption of the role of business. Corporate capitalism is founded on the idea of growth, not growth in the holistic, developmental sense, but growth as in "Get bigger!" This seems to me to be at odds with what I hear coming from the hearts and minds of people I talk to around the world. They are interested in sustaining and developing their lives, their cultures, their families, their cities, their minds, and so on. It is not about getting bigger, it is about getting better. A worker in a factory in Vietnam dreams of improving the lives of his or her family, that the kids will be educated and enjoy a risk-free, healthy life. This is a dream of development, it is human, and to be nourished by business, not exploited and dashed. It is central to the concept of the "business idea" as opposed to the "business model."

What seems to be happening as we enter the next phase of our economic evolution is that many of these chickens are coming home to roost. Businesses that focused solely on maximizing financial ROI seem to have become disconnected from their customers, their employees and their shareholders. This powerful alliance—with many individuals participating in all three experiences—can be credited with driving a fundamental change in the environment for business in the twenty-first century.

Information technology has stimulated the creation of a culture of knowledge and it is sweeping the world. In the culture of knowledge, everything seems knowable and everyone wants to know. From the vicarious experience of survival to a basic understanding of the capitalist system and its attendant marketing habits, people feel smart and informed. And guess what? They are.

The world of marketing and the world of brands have been rocked by these changes. Nothing seems to work quite as it used to, which brings me on to that idea of "cultural influence." It turns out that the degree to which businesses engaged with their public, creating relationships that either sustained, evolved, or eroded value, was linked less to their ability to create powerful business models and more to their ability to create valuable relationships. Now, this is news to many in the MBA world of U.S. consumer marketing, but it is an unquestioned fact of life in Asia and Europe. Here's what happened: As marketing mechanized the process of relationship management, the consumer got less emotional value out of the relationship.

The spreadsheet was invented in the early eighties. The power of the spreadsheet is that it renders very complex mathematics into simple actions. Spreadsheets revolutionized the stock market. The measurement of things became simple. Anything and everything can be measured. The complexity of society, the complexity of war, the complexity of the mind, all seems measurable. Marketing was a craft, a creative act (the Jolly Green Giant predated spreadsheets, as did Snap, Crackle, and Pop), it was about individuals imagining the relationship they could create between a business and a customer, then going about the business of creating that relationship. The advent of the "anything can be measured" philosophy meant that business became mediated by measurement technology rather than human experience. Numbers on a research chart were supposed to reveal the reality of customer behavior. This approach is so pervasive that many of the most corporate businesses have lost all real connection to the customer. They simply do not know the people they rely on to sustain their business. The customer has tired of this; it feels abusive. I constantly hear the word "corporate" used to explain loss of human contact. The relationship between consumers and business has been deeply eroded.

Customers simply reduced the amount of money they were willing to pay for the relationship they had with what they perceive to be amoral marketing companies. These companies are not bad, but they are sort of culturally autistic. By remaining unable to engage with consumers as human beings with rich cultural lives and complex social environments they are unable to communicate. Thus, they tended to scream and become abusive the more they craved and needed consumer attention. We see the results of cultural autism on our screens every day: persistently aggravating advertising that sends manifestly corrupt messages into our homes.

But in the culture of knowledge, the consumer knows and is rebelling. Recent research we have been involved in at Wieden + Kennedy (W+K) has begun to highlight what is going on. We were interested in the evolving relationship between the consumer and big business. We had already come to the view that the brand was a surrogate for the business idea, and that if we were to evolve and grow the brands we worked on, we needed to understand more deeply what they symbolized and how people were relating to them.

As part of one study, I was in Tokyo talking to a producer of Japanese hip-hop records about the idea of being "modern." I mention this because in some ways the transcendent themes of the modern experience were there to be witnessed within that conversation. He was twenty-six. I was forty-two. He was from Tokyo. I was from Manchester. Yet we were both intimately aware of and engaged with the work of Ian Anderson and the Designers Republic. When I asked him, through our excellent translator (who herself had lived in Kensington, London, only three blocks away from my old home), how he perceived the idea of modern and where he saw culture evolving, he said, "To a more mental place." He went on to discuss in depth the fact that products have narratives as well as benefits. We know about the ways of these products, the whole story. From the vantage point of someone born in 1975, business had to engage with the whole truth of consumerism. That involved two important and related realities: Firstly, that unsustainable consumption would destroy everything we have and could have, and secondly, that the consumer experience was deeper and richer than is ever acknowledged by mainstream marketing.

As we travel the world and talk to people for all types of reasons these themes emerge. Big business is not perceived to be a de facto problem: it is the lack of imagination, creativity, and responsibility within the idea of corporate business that sucks. Brands are seen as manifestations of, and as surrogates for, the business people that create them. The consumer wants—no, *demands*—a relationship with those people. A young media entrepreneur from Brazil said, "I just have one question: Who are you?"

And who can answer that simple question? The emergence of a culture of knowledge that is global in scale due to the attendant networking that now defines communication and social interaction has brought the real issues facing our postindustrial-age culture to the fore. Brands can no longer survive on a diet of artificial benefit creation or the assumption that somehow we are dysfunctional and need to be "fixed." We, the individuals who consume, whose money oils the wheels of corporate capitalism, are not broken. We don't need to be fixed. We, to paraphrase an old Subaru ad I was involved in, don't need to use what we consume to increase our standing with our neighbors. We can relate to the size and shape of our bodies in a way that helps us enjoy the life, liberty, and pursuit of happiness promised in our Constitution. We do not need products to be symbols of empowerment: We have power. We do not aspire to manufactured dreams that reduce our capacity to feel individual. In short, nearly every branding tactic of the past will fail in the future.

This is because the nature of the transaction between consumers and businesses has moved on.

The cultural role of brands is to respond to the spirit of the times. In the early 1930s, when Coke employed Norman Rockwell, the company transcended its role as a purveyor of refreshment and became deeply embedded in the emerging identity of American consumerism. These values were to sweep the world: optimism, faith in the possibility of harmonious diversity, and egalitarianism. In an era when students were being shot at Kent State and carpet bombing was destroying the lives of hundreds of thousands of people on the Southeast Asian peninsula, Coke tried to "teach the world to sing . . . in perfect harmony." Like it or hate it, it was an attempt to project more than the benefit of refreshment. Its power lay in the confidence with which it voiced its perspective.

If we were to respond today we would respond to the culture of corporate repulsion. By which I mean this: The transcendent themes of new consumers emerge from their experience as the progeny of the consumer age. They have known little else. They have engaged with and then experienced the emotional hollowness of the consumer promise: that what you buy dictates how well you feel. They still felt bad when things didn't go right. They have learned through experience that promises are shallow and that there must be an ulterior motive for everything. Some would say that they are cynical. But I don't believe that they are. I believe that they are aware.

As today's consumers view the world they are aware of how everything is all linked together. They did media studies in elementary school. They watched *Sesame Street* and learned about ecology from the movie *Ferngully*. What seems to be the case is that they have a different narrative than previous generations of consumers. Their narrative embraces their position within a complex and interlinked world. As millions of kids swap banalities yet create networks of relationships on AOL Instant Messenger, they understand only too well the power of causality: that what you do has an effect, somewhere.

They are translating that experience into their lives as consumers. In fact, they are rethinking the ways they consume. Rather than be trapped within the manufactured aspirations of the mass market, they are seeking to create experiences that connect them in a meaningful way to ideas and ideals that are worth something. They take control over their futures by taking control over their expectations. And, talking about futures, they are very concerned about the legacy of wanton, excessive consumerism practiced by the previous generation. In their view, they have inherited the consequences of consumption for consumption's sake with scant regard for the long-term future of either themselves or their children. Or, to put it another way, scant regard for meaningful human relationships and responsibilities.

Surveys such as those by Yankelovich have for years directed our attention to the evolution of a fresh perspective on consumption among the young. Well, it seems to be here, and if you are in any doubt you only need to look at the fortunes of the Fortune 500—the near total collapse of the great marketing brands as they surrendered to the ultimate comodititizing business: WalMart. What happened to Kellogg, McDonald's, P&G, Coke, Oldsmobile, and a host of others is that they ceased to maintain and develop a dynamic business idea that intersected with the values of their customers. The brand is the manifestation of that relationship; as I have said, it is surrogate. Van der Heijden would refer to this as a squandering of two things: distinctive competencies and a dynamic relationship with customers. Over time the values of our consumers evolve and competitors emulate our core competencies, delivering them for less cost and reducing distinctiveness.

There are two distinct developments, one in the realm of competencies and one in the realm of consumer evolution, that threaten established brand owners who fail to create a dynamic model for brand and business development.

First, we need to acknowledge that the singular pursuit of capital growth has thwarted attempts at creating a sustainable model of consumerism. Technology has been evolving at a hair-raising rate but business models have not. Detroit and the oil industry remain locked in a death grip grounded in the idea of exploitation for enrichment. The consequence: a pathetic response to increasing anxiety regarding all forms of pollution and near indifference to the issue of gradually disappearing resources. The automobile industry has been the bellwether of all consumerism but seems intent on donating that leadership to other categories that more effectively respond to the spirit of this age.

At a time when technology is delivering the means to reduce the impact of the car on our environment, Detroit is marketing machines that speak to the command-and-control exploitation culture of the past: the Lincoln Navigator, the Chevrolet Suburban. This is seventies technology, but more importantly this is seventies culture. It is about dominance, power, exploitation, and it is deeply masculine, or rather, a kind of warped version of masculinity that finds an echo in the corruption of sports at the hands of capitalism: the NFL, the NBA. This is how the new consumer sees the old brands.

Second, we need to accept that things are different now. The world in which our children have developed has taught them much. We have taught them much. They are individuals existing in complex cultural systems. They have transcended vague notions of monocultural national values and the politics of supremacy. They do not trust the previous generation. Their version of leadership is not command and control, it is not J.F.K., L.B.J., Churchill, Thatcher, or Reagan. If the Clinton presidency taught this generation anything it was surely this: Leadership is about acknowledging uncertainty rather than manufacturing certainty. We are all flawed and it is how we respond to that fact that defines our future. This sensibility is endemic among new consumers. The Cluetrain Manifesto reflected this as its authors indicated a way forward: Markets are conversations. Absolutely, and so are brands. The question is, what do we want to discuss?

The answer is: kind of everything.

At the top of the list is the identity question and the values consumers wish to be associated with as they engage in transactions with companies. Deeply embedded in this question lies the consumers' relationship with a world they feel increasingly connected to and in a small way responsible for. Consumers no longer accept the cultural autism of corporate brands. They want a conversation about where we, as designers, stand, what we are doing, and how we can do it better. They want to enjoy the benefits of a healthy economy (don't we all?) without the guilt of screwing it for everyone else. How could they enjoy their smart new shoes if they knew there are unhappy people living in dangerous conditions so that they could have them? This was never part of the promise but it was always part of the reality. Now, that reality is visible and the new consumer is aware and engaged. This means we, as designers, have to be also.

The sustainability question is intrinsic to the identity question. In a culture that has rejected exploitation, has confronted inequity, and is striving for a utopian ideal of life, liberty, and happiness, sustainability has huge cultural value. Within the semantics of the word is the resolution of a paradox: It is about keeping what we love, not losing it. This means everything.

When you talk to new consumers, the idea of impact, or the idea of sustainability, is right at the front of their minds. It is in lockstep with a variety of other humanitarian issues. It may be part of a mystical or spiritual value system. It may be part of a reality check and related to their immediate urban environment. It may simply be a part of their general awareness of the world in which they live. Whatever the reason, it is there. It is part of their response to the disappointment of mass consumerism, particularly the mass consumerism created and fueled by the growth of television:

> While our cars may be shiny, and our stocks may be booming, there is another story to be told. There is an emptiness inside, a void in the soul of America.
> The TV functions as a conduit for the lowest common denominator of public dialogue. Whether it be Regis Philbin or Beverly Hills 90210, the world learns about America by the cotton candy that we call Must See TV. And it works. Only 25% of teenagers between the ages of 13–17 can name the city where the U.S. Constitution was written, but a full 75% know that you can find the zip code 90210 in Beverly Hills, California.
> —Adam Werbach, The Thin Green Line

I quote Adam Werbach because he is a particularly eloquent representative of the new consumer generation. Passionately committed to the environmental movement, he was the youngest-ever president of the Sierra Club (at age twenty-six) and now propels his agenda through a video production company and Web site called The Thin Green Line. As a media sophisticate he understands the relationship between the issue of environmentalism and what he would consider to be the insidious actions of mass marketers in concealing the truth of consumption from the consumer. Of equal importance is the connection he draws between the feeling of loss that exists within our mass consumer culture and the explosion of environmental concerns. This connection is the critical link between the history and future of brands.

Consumerism's great contribution to Maslow's hierarchy is desire. In many cases branded goods are promoted as a means of (help me) self-actualization. The notion is that, fully empowered by access to the right stuff, an individual can get a grip on his or her own reality and project a kind of instant individuation, a personality that is both unique and yet belongs to a larger group. The trick is always, as we know, for the brand to influence the idea of the group to which people aspire. And people seem to like this.

It turns out that buying stuff because it satisfies a desire is O.K. In fact, it is rather pleasing. There are many people in the world today who would love the opportunity to get stuff because they want it rather than be restricted to satisfying only their needs. And before we run off in an apoplectic rage about the sinfulness of desire I am afraid to tell you that it is a basic human truth. We *want* as well as *need*. The experience of desire is nice! We love it! In my view the crisis of consumerism is not that it creates desire but that it fails to satiate. Most critiques of consumerism and the advertising industry it created seem to focus on how bad creating desire is rather than asking if we can create desire for, well, something else.

This turns out to be on the mind of the new consumer: I want to want but I want to want what will actually satisfy me.

So imagine if we, as designers, and as the creative fuel of an evolving consumerism, were to shift the focus of desire from something we can never satiate to something we can. To me that is the essence of the new consumerism. It has all the thrill of the old but this time it actually delivers.

This is where we can begin a serious conversation about sustainable consumerism. This is when we can look brand owners in the eye and talk honestly and openly about the challenges they face. The ability to create great stuff is not necessarily correlated to the ability to create great relationships. Within relationships that thrive, all parties are able to enjoy the experience. The brand owner who ignores the consumer values part of the equation fails to acknowledge the human dimension of the relationship. As we proceed into a consumer world within which many different versions of the same stuff offer marginal differentiation for the consumer, we will become ever more reliant on the quality of the relationships we create. While the Internet utopians of rationality argue that information technology will reduce everything to price-value-based comparisons, the consumer is mourning the loss of human contact, the loss of valuable relationships. Just look at the mourning ritual of the recently bereaved Oldsmobile franchise.

In a recent speech to a conference hosted by *Metropolis* magazine, I put up the following slide:

The modern consumer adds environmental impact to the perceived cost of consumption and is attracted to companies who acknowledge their responsibility by embracing incremental improvements in environmental impact.

This observation was grounded in conversations we had with consumers in the research we do here at W+K. Here is what seems to be going on: The sustainability question has become a flash point for the anxiety that permeates the relationships people feel they have with business. The continuing lack of interest expressed through brands by business in this question is seen as symptomatic of the corporatization of the consumer experience. The profit motive is seen to have trumped basic human decency. Carl Pope of the Sierra Club once told me that the environment was the issue that almost guaranteed a young voter turnout. It has become a focus of young voters' fears that they will lead meaningless lives in servitude to massive businesses whose sole concern is shareholder value. It signals the threat they feel: that they have little control over their lives and that business cannot be trusted.

The upshot of this is that sustainability has become their issue. The new consumer owns the new consumption and his or her values will dictate which brands succeed and how. There is no barrier being put up by the consumer to the idea of sustainable consumption.

I was discussing these issues with designer Alex Gajowskyj. Alex had designed the "world shoe" for Nike. The idea was to create a product with minimal waste, designed for manufacture, and useable by the people who made it. In a deep way, the project reflects the response a good company like Nike has when confronted by this issue. Nike has started to move toward sustainable consumption as it acknowledges the feelings of both its consumers and its employees. Alex's experiment was a central part of this evolution. In his words, this is what they learned:

> Tradition; natural opposition to change and a reliance upon "tried and trusted" business practice represent the biggest obstacles for any business seeking global growth.
>
> —Alex Gajowskyj, shoe designer

In other words, if the consumer is not the barrier, then the business is. Part of the dynamic evolution of distinctive competencies, to use Kees van der Haijden's idea, is to evolve away from the traditions and practices that hinder the ability of the business to engage fully with the consumer.

Evolving consumer values demand that modern brands rethink the transactions they rely on for consumer attention. This is why brand owners need to care about the sustainability question. It is a cultural phenomenon as well as a real issue. If brands are to respond to the spirit of the times, then they need to respond to this most crucial element of contemporary culture. Furthermore, they need to acknowledge that, as a symbol, it is also a symptom of a deeper dysfunctionality between brands in general and the consumer. The relationship between consumer and mass brands has decayed to such a point that the days of premium-priced, high-margin branded products seems to exist only in our fantasy world. We need to change that: People want more! But now they want more from us as people rather than more of our stuff.

Here is a comment by Clive Whitcher who oversees Strategic Planning for Saatchi & Saatchi on their Toyota business:

> Prius buyers are ecstatic about the car and what it says about Toyota. Toyota's their hero for finally doing something tangible about the environment—one guy came to a group with a collage featuring evergreen sprigs and a rose stuck to (re-cycled) paper! The love is akin to what people felt in the 1970s when Toyota was their savior—saving them from bad gas mileage when prices went up and there were lines at the gas station and of course from bad domestic quality and ridiculous domestic "downsized" compacts.
>
> —Clive Whitcher, Saatchi & Saatchi

The movement has started. There are companies, like Nike and Toyota, who are responding to their consumers' deeply felt issues. But on a broader scale my question is: Where are the designers? Where are the ad guys? How can we develop skills and practices that respond to this evolution? How will we determine the effectiveness of what we do when the entire industry is trapped in an unevolved capitalist paradigm? How can clients trust that the advice they are being given responds to the reality of consumer culture when that advice remains locked in process-based thinking from the 1970s? It is time to challenge these traditions, as Gajowskyj has stated. We have in our midst the most well-informed talent in the history of our young industry, coupled with mind-expanding technology that helps us learn and execute ideas better and faster than ever before. We have no excuse to fail the people we create our work for, both clients and consumers.

Sustainability is just that: It is about sustaining, providing nourishment, keeping going. Brand owners who nourish their consumers with meaningful ideas and representation, and designers and advertising people who take a similar approach and help their clients keep going, will recognize that consumerism is, like everything else in our world, about evolution. In this case, it is the evolution away from the self-destructive impulse of mass commoditization and toward a sustainable consumerism that satiates our desires for strong relationships grounded in our common humanity.

The fact of our connection to the extended network of humanity has been tragically brought to our attention by the horrible events of September 11, 2001. That markets are dynamic and conversation-based has been clearly revealed. Many Americans felt attacked but none more so than those at ground zero of the capitalist movement: corporate Americans. This did not seem like an attack on American teachers, American nurses, American software designers, teenagers, hip-hop artists, production-line workers, bakers, and so on; it seemed like an attack on corporate America, and those deeply protected and nourished by corporations suddenly felt particularly vulnerable. For the first time the connection between their world and the seething experiences of the rest of humanity was brought into terrible relief.

I was fortunate enough to be invited to participate in some deep conversations about the near-term future of business in the light of the global economic downturn that had begun before the so-called War on Terror. These were conversations between business people who are many degrees removed from the world of marketing, advertising, or design. They were economists, bankers, engineers, HR directors, corporate strategists, and the like. Eamon Kelly and his team from the Global Business Network in Emeryville, California, skillfully led a group of 150 of us through these conversations to imagine scenarios for the business environment in 2010. For me, one of the most striking elements of the conversations that I participated in was the emergence of a more urgent awareness of the relationship between the cultural and economic value system of business itself. For some, there was a reappraisal of the value of their brand. They saw their brand as their company's reputation, symbolizing not only the performance of their organization, the innovation and service values they excelled at, but also the cultural values it symbolized. They sensed a big change in their future: an unbundling of the economic model of business from its intrinsic cultural values such that the cultural impact of business behavior could be evaluated and reintegrated into business planning. A very smart and articulate participant claimed that the cultural impact as well as the economic impact of business planning would, in the future, be central to the way he thought about his work. To me, this could herald real change in the way business relates to society and culture. Moving from exploitation to sustainability as a strategy for development could be part of that change.

Rethinking the conversations that brands as surrogates for businesses have with people the world over is a necessity if we are to continue to use the incredible power of creativity in a free world to generate development on a global scale. Business can bring development and growth to every corner of the world, but not at the expense of destroying the environment, both physically and culturally. Individuals want to sustain themselves and grow. They want to develop their own skills, enjoy a good life, and create opportunity for their children. This is true for every single human being ever created. Businesses that fail to relate to these twin desires—to sustain a life, a culture, a society, a family, an ideal, and to develop it—will loose traction at home and abroad.

The simplistic attitudes that have characterized an increasingly dysfunctional corporate world cannot continue if business itself is to be sustainable. After being given free reign for a generation, capitalism will be constrained by culture. This will radically transform the way we think about brands. The days when the goal was to manipulate the cultural context of business to ensure success (to present smoking as glamorous, personal transport as a surrogate for power, consumer products as empowering) are over. Finito, gone, gone, gone. Assuming that competition takes place within a stable environment and is about differentiation alone is also obsolete as a philosophy. The future is about adaptation to the cultural context of the business transaction, both at the micro and the macro level—at the level of a toothpaste sale in Sri Lanka and at the level of a Maglev urban transport program in Germany. Oh sure, there will be a transition period during which conservative money will be poured into maintaining a semblance of a status quo. But also there will be and are businesses that are fully engaged with the transition out of this period of history dominated by economic capital and into a period balanced by the values of cultural capital.

Listen to the young and you hear a clear voice. The fundamental change they bring is from hierarchies based on power to networks based on influence. Influence relies on the art of listening, not the deployment of power. Listening is a human skill, not an organizational attribute. A new semiotics of communication is being created in the crucible of Internet-enabled networks of youth. Ethics are being evolved into business assets. Global strategies by multinational corporations are evolving from imposition to participation. America has been the model; only the monocultural theists ever dreamed of America as a melting pot. The rest of us wanted something more chunky and less palatable and we got it. Managing diversity is a different challenge than creating uniformity. Managing a sustainable business is a different challenge than driving fourth-quarter profit growth. Listening is a different challenge than broadcasting.

So we return to the idea of sustainable consumerism. It is about sustainable businesses also. Sustainable brands listen, respond, and create value within relationships for all participants. A consumerism that satiates desire by creating value rather than extracting it. Our challenge will be to wrench branding and communications from the cultural autism of corporate marketing and hand it back to the creative community: the thinkers, writers, inquirers, and designers who are intimates with the emerging culture of business and can interrogate their clients as effectively as the customer.

Mental Whiplash
The Subjects of Our Affection
Leslie Becker

Because "whiplash" implies a wrenching change in direction, it is a good metaphor for contemporary graphic design practice and education. Our discipline continues to address unlimited variations in and unpredictable genres of content. The antithesis of rote activities like working in a canning factory, we are afforded the luxury of learning about the world as we work. One morning we might be developing an instructional poster to explain the Heimlich maneuver. Later that day we might be designing the interior surfaces of a trendy store. We engage topics ranging from serious information to commercial seduction, from science to pop culture. Graphic design practice finally requires more than skilled eyes, honed craft, and wit. Because contemporary design presupposes strong involvement in content development, our students need to learn what qualifies as research in service of developing a responsible voice. How do students learn to conduct research appropriate to their projects? What types of research serve design activities? How do our students learn more about how to research effectively, understand the limits and usefulness of their findings, and then translate those findings into informative, poignant, or provocative communications?

Popular culture's preoccupation with surface and ephemera has diminished empiricism. We collect our "impressions" and confuse their authority. Students may research without considering less obvious research options like interviewing, consulting mentors, and testing hypotheses. When using academic research forms, often they get mired in unwieldy branching, hoping to develop a personalized "truth" so that ultimately they can make something. They tend not to know when to stop reading and start making, when to stop making and start reading. They tend not to see the nonlinearity in creating a communication. Making something directs research as much as research directs making. We need to examine design choreography so that students can learn methodologies that work for design. Responsible representation emerges from solid research that is project-appropriate and wisely used.

Variables Affecting Learning

Following is an abbreviated design education matrix that hints at the confluence of classroom complexities.

Project Content/Project Form

Content may be specific or implied, imposed on or selected by the student.

Research may be personally intuited, empirically gathered, mentor-driven, and/or scholarly. How do we teach graphic design students responsible representation of subject, particularly when accuracy of information is critical? What happens when communication must be abbreviated but content is complex? What happens when mimetic style dominates design activity? Do we really want a postmodern air traffic control screen? Caught between science and intuition, typically we request that our students research content when making something and hope that they will translate their research into responsible and compelling visual/verbal representation of content.

The form a project takes is often specified in order to achieve a skill-based learning objective. If the student selects the form, he or she must question why that form and not another, considering content and audience. Preselecting form for the student when a specific skill acquisition is not the focus of a project diminishes understanding of the relationship between subject matter and how to best represent it. In order to make learning possible, we need to respect individual interests and abilities of students and make certain that what can be learned, such as the options for inspired research, is learned.

The Teacher

What is your professional background? When and where were you educated? Do you acknowledge your own biases in the classroom? What must the teacher learn?

If we acknowledge our design biases (for example, a die-hard modernist educated in the seventies who is trying to teach a group of MTV fans to simplify, eliminate, and make hierarchies), then we create a forum for students to learn about differences, impermanence, and historical influence.

The Students

What is your student's age, maturity level, life experience, educational back-ground, culture, and type of intelligence? It has been clearly demonstrated that people have different kinds of innate intelligence.[1] This translates to different abilities and learning styles. Part of education should concern itself with what one innately does well and what and how one might learn to do better.

Educated students learn re-invention rather than mastery of a single skill or a single style. Ease of invention and reinvention varies from student to student. One may have a previous degree in comparative literature and be an avid reader and meticulous writer and researcher. Another may be an eighteen-year-old non-reader who knows everything there is to know about contemporary music. Another student may have a passion to explore a specific topic. One of my classmates at Cooper Union was a pre-Colombian fanatic. Everything he made at school looked like it surfaced from an archeological dig, patinaed and distressed. The last information I heard about him was that he runs a pre-Colombian gallery in New York. Another student may be interested in a specific form design takes, such as film, video, or sound design. In addition to our own formal contributions to our students, others will need to be involved in a student's process so that the student internalizes a professional ethic of responsible representation.

Case Studies

Following are a few examples of how different students in our thesis class at CCAC learned to combine research and representation.

Holly Holmquist

A sophisticated student with a previous degree from U.C. Berkeley in the social sciences, Holly's starting point was a literary inspiration, an essay on oranges. Here is how she describes her own process:

"My approach included a combination of observation, intuition, and academic research. The book leading to my final project documents this research, and in the process locates complexity in the mundane object. In the end, it informed a piece describing the essential parts of orange: word, color, and object.

"I will elaborate on the various components of my investigation.

"Observation: drawings, photography over time, everyday encounters

"Intuition: collections—that is, anything that feels relevant regardless of its title or appearance(and personal intersections, for regardless of how "neutral" a topic might be, it is inevitably loaded with more meaningful associations; the visceral experience is also included here.

"Academic: libraries, books, words

"A combination of observation, intuition, and reading lead to the development of the subcategories or 'branches.' The academic route is most directly responsible for the development of the 'tree.' Each branch representing a different aspect, including color, etymology, byproducts, botany, nutrition, ornamentation, sensory experience, migration, and representation. The goal here is to not only show how diverse the topic becomes but also how connections are found within that diversity. What they hold in common is the center seed—the orange."

Holly learned to create something manageable as she discovered the enormity of a presumably simple topic.

Jerome Maureze

Emerging from his graphic design education and its preoccupation with typographic impact, Jerome questioned the limitations of braille when compared with the typographic richness of the sighted world. His project included formal research on both braille parameters and typographic history with a focus on what is experienced in typographic style. His goal was to create a richer reading experience for the blind. He used empirical learning, diligent experimentation, and usability testing. His subject mentor was Lighthouse for the Blind, essential because there was no way for Jerome, a sighted person, to evaluate the success of his proposed braille fonts.

Stephanie Mueller

In her effort to picture a nonvirtual Web, this student researched by making something weekly during the course. Every object Stephanie made was an exquisitely explicit representation of a metaphor under investigation. Each idea showed an understanding of scale, limits, delimits, and connectivity. She had a particularly good understanding of metaphor and a very sophisticated ability, which she strengthened through the intensive process of making things, to evaluate her own work. Self-evaluation is a particularly important learning objective of design education.

Jacqueline Tanudjaja

Chinglish was the result of experiential learning across two cultures and research of the recorded history of language development. Jacqueline tested her new language separately on Chinese-speaking-only and English-speaking-only groups. Her proposition was that both groups should have been equally able to "read" Chinglish. In fact, Jacqueline discovered that because of the heavy reliance on images in her hybrid language, it worked with some reliability for one part of language: common nouns. This, of course, helps to explain why symbol sets are first tested and then implemented across cultures. We considered her project a success because, although Chinglish failed as a language, it was a thorough study of a complex subject and it gave everyone who viewed it an understanding of limitations particular to words or images.

Identifying the various options for conducting and translating research enhances a student's learning experience. Exposure to the different ways in which research can be conducted—i.e., reading, making, interviewing, usability testing, and consulting with a mentor to both offer guidance during research and then respond to the communication—is vital. Everyone has an opinion. Validating beyond a student's comment, "I have a sense that . . ." and perhaps, through an unpredictable sequence of readings, musings, makings, musings, interviews, makings, etc., we can help our students figure out the complex relationship between form and representation of content.

Notes

1. Howard Gardner, *Frames of Mind* (New York: Basic Books, 1983).

Reality Branding
Addressing Real Concerns and Real Needs
Nancy Bernard

Right off the bat, I've turned you off. Reality is good—that's what we're discussing, isn't it? The reality of our impact on the profession, the larger society, and culture? But branding? Yecchh. We're supposed to be talking about design.

We are. The point of using the word "branding" is to put design in perspective. Instead of pretending that design is the be-all and end-all of existence, let's look at it from the outside, be honest about its place in the world, its power, and its potential, and see what we can do with it.

One benefit about looking at design from the perspective of branding is that a brand is a system over which a designer might hope to exert some control. Unlike, say, the world. Who ever said that graphic design could change the world, anyway? Have you seen the world lately? It's huge! The whole premise is out of proportion. For one thing, it doesn't make sense to expect one's practice to fulfill all of one's social, political, spiritual, and cultural ambitions. Presuming that one has a life outside of work—which one sincerely hopes one has—one might dedicate some part of it to good works. At the same time, we need to find meaning in our work—or at least to feel as though we're doing no harm.

So let's get down to it, and run a quick "outside" analysis of graphic design. What do we actually do? How important are the things we make? How much influence can we hope to exert? And what are our real responsibilities?

The problems are obvious.

First, what do we do? For the most part, we make communications materials for businesses that make business products for businesses, or for Hypoallergenic Thigh Wax in your choice of Spring Rain, Scottish Rose, or Asian Bazaar. For balance, the firms that can afford it might take on one or two projects a year for Rainforest Relief and PowrrrrGrrrrls Educational Software (though the truth is they're more likely to put those pro bono hours into things like exhibition posters that'll win awards and get exposure).

What influence do we really have? The media we work in—logos, brochures, annual reports, packaging, labels, signs, and so on—may be ubiquitous, but their very ubiquity, not to mention their obvious self-interest, makes them easy to shut out. The messages we deliver aren't all that powerful, either—whether they're commercial or informational, people only care about them when they're actively looking for an LCD monitor or the way to San Jose. The rest of the time they're a kind of chattering background tappity-tap.

When the design itself is visually cool, conceptually witty, or emotionally vivid, it can of course give pleasure, which isn't half bad. Certainly beautiful or intriguing graphics are better for the environment than ugly, boring graphics, but still, in the context of social and cultural responsibility, so what?

As for influence within the brand system (you really don't want to hear this, I know), design is at the bottom of the capitalist food chain. Audiences neither know nor care who we are. And the people who hire us think that what we do is basically stupid, even though they have fun doing it with us.

As if you didn't know.

Still, without claiming to change the world, we can raise the level of integrity in our piece of it—"think globally, act locally." If bad communications design—manipulative, seductive, intrusive, disproportionate, or just plain dishonest—is undermining the core values of America, don't engage in it. Here comes my great, do-what-you-can-with-what-you-have manifesto. Let's start a new movement in design and call it "reality branding."

In reality branding, our responsibility is to make the communication 200 percent real. Don't make it generic—don't turn your client into a commodity or anything—just build your message on real value. Make it honest. Make it relevant. Avoid hyperbole. Be respectful. Don't be afraid to project a vivid personality. And don't be afraid to let design inform the other disciplines in the brand system.

In reality branding, your client's responsibility—this is really important—is to make sure the organization delivers on its promises.

Every designed object arises out of a brand—a system of ideas, motivations, objects, actions, events, and goals. The thing that gives design its particular power is the fact that it's the last link in the chain, the final initiative. Motive, mission, research, strategy, market position, product design, distribution, and corporate culture all precede it. From one point of view, that makes design an afterthought—but only if you're on the inside, looking out.

From the outside, design is the sole point of contact. Until a person decides to engage with the organization, design is all he sees, all he knows, and all he has to relate to. Design is where the rubber meets the road. And that makes it very, very important. Critical, in fact.

The problem is to convince the powers that be. Sure, all the famous CEOs are saying "the brand is the thing," but when do we get to work with the CEO? And when does the CEO listen to us? Well, right. Never. Okay, hardly ever. And that's what reality branding aims to change.

If we lie down, accept the last-link position, and put all our energy into the look and feel of the design object itself, we're abrogating our gifts, cheating our clients, and cheating the public. If we don't contribute to decisions about strategic positioning, promotional strategy, message, environment of use, product design, and distribution, all we're doing is dressing windows. Strategy may or may not be more important than design, but it does have the strongest material effect on people. It's also the thing that clients understand, respect, and listen to.

Machiavelli, arise! People who hold power, whether over a brand or anything else, seldom hand it over to anyone else. You have to take it from below. Considering our status in corporate America, what do we have to work with? Two things: our attitude and our process.

The attitude part is easy to state, but harder to live up to in the crush of compromise. You have to commit yourself to seek the truth, illuminate it with decent ethical standards, and advocate it.

Reality branding is honest. It reflects the real value of the goods. If the product is frivolous, don't pretend that it's serious; if the organizational culture is obsessed with technology, don't pretend it's about people; if someone else's stuff is pretty much the same as yours, don't pretend that it's unique. Find something else about the organization that no one else can claim. Maybe it's a lifestyle statement, as with Virgin Airlines. Maybe it's a political stance, as with Working Assets' progressive telephone and credit services. Just be sure it's something the client can truly live up to.

Reality branding is relevant. It doesn't decide what it wants to sell, what it wants to do, and what it wants to say, then force people to swallow it. It finds out what is really needed, what is really at stake, and answers that need (even if the need is kind of dumb).

Reality branding avoids hyperbole. That handheld isn't going to "revolutionize business," okay? Meanwhile, we sort of wish it really would so we could have an excuse to buy it because it's so cool. Reality branding says it'll revolutionize business, but uses voice and visuals in a way that acknowledges that we know that you know that we know it's a fantasy.

Reality branding is respectful. It doesn't propound from on high or aggravate people's insecurities, but identifies with real concerns, and talks about them in a down-to-earth way. Sister to sister, guy to guy—it can be heavy, it can be factual, as long as it's straightforward.

Reality branding has personality. It isn't faceless, but full-faced; it isn't institutional, but tribal. It has a story, a mission, a character, a set of ethics and values; it has tastes and preferences. It's actually different from all the other brands on its block. (Red Bull "energy" soda is a good example. Who else flatly acknowledges that they can't get through the day without a huge dose of caffeine using shaky little black-and-white animated cartoons about Rapunzel and Zeus?)

Don't be afraid to let design push back—let design give new perspectives on all that "inside" strategic work. If design tests show that people don't respond to a position, advocate a new position; if pre-research shows that people don't actually like or need the product, advocate a product re-design; if the brand discovery interviews show that the company has an attitude problem ("their service sucks"), get the word out, and challenge management to find out what's eating their employees.

Process-wise, reality branding is wide open. It seeks criticism. It seeks all kinds of input, at every step. It observes real people using your client's stuff. It interviews everyone affected by the brand—customers, employees, the competition, distributors—and asks what it means to them. It makes prototypes of every design, shows them to real users, and compares their reactions to its intentions.

All told, reality branding promises to create more honest, and far more relevant, communications. More powerfully, it can provide strategic checks and balances that the client is unlikely to get elsewhere (what sane corporate courtier is going to stand up and shout "Hey, look! The Emperor is naked"?). It can show the powers that be what the firm's responsibilities are toward everyone who is touched by the brand. It might even persuade them that living up to those responsibilities could have a beneficial effect on both their status and their pocketbooks. And that, my dears, could change a few lives for the better. A very nice thing to be responsible for. And well within our grasp.

Think Globally, Upload Locally
Responsible Web Design

J. D. Biersdorfer

You can find just about anything on the World Wide Web, from dissertations on particle physics to tender photographs of a rabbit in Japan balancing a pancake on its head. Elaborate genealogies of people you don't know, the latest software driver for your printer, handcrafted lesbian fiction starring the main characters of *Xena: Warrior Princess*—it's all out there. The hypertext Web has become a hyperactive populist press that can afford anyone with a vague bit of technical expertise and something to say a public place to put it up there for the world.

In the ten years or so since the Web has been around, people who figured out how to make pages did so—and this was both good and incredibly awful. It made for some very inventive, unfettered creations that found new tools and new ways to use the mass media, but it also paved the way for hundreds of id-driven brain dumps that have clogged up servers and search engines for years.

While there has always been an underground press and various malcontents fixing the world over pints in bars, the information industry used to be the province of large, well-funded organizations with the distribution muscle to get their product out to the public by truck, airplane, or airwaves. Professional-quality publications or broadcasts required money, equipment, and an infrastructure that most amateurs couldn't ante up, and most of these companies accepted the responsibility to provide data to the public in an accurate manner.

In a way, what desktop-publishing software did for 'zine creators and conspiracy theorists in the late 1980s, the World Wide Web has done on a global scale in the late 1990s: It has given a voice to anyone who desires to make a message available to millions of people. But do Web-page creators feel the same sense of responsibility to the public that media professionals profess to feel or are held to by that very, often opinionated, public? As online gossip Matt Drudge has proven, the Web can make everyone a publishing house/TV station with varying degrees of accountability.

Quis custodiet ipsos custodes, y'all, when every Tom, Dick, and Harry Knowles is a watchman? The issue of responsible Web pages is as complex and intertwining as the Web itself, and involves not only functionality, but form as well.

To start off, a Web page should be conscientiously designed so that readers can find what they are looking for with the least amounts of time, effort, aggravation, and snarling homicidal thoughts involving edged weaponry. Part of the problem with the Web is that it is a new medium and many designers do things just a little bit differently.

For example, over the centuries, most people have basically figured out how to operate a book like the one you are holding in your hands. You take the book, anything from *The Book of Kells* to the latest Harry Potter novel, open it up, and turn the pages sequentially to navigate through the material. The only major variance in navigating through the typical book was in which direction you turned the pages—and that usually depended on which language you were reading in or possibly your frame of mind at the time.

Although they both contain text, Web pages are very different from books. Most books cannot instantly link you to a vast resource of collected human experience and knowledge, plus electronic pictures of strawberry Pop-Tarts exploding into flame inside a toaster. Then again, a book is not going to make you wait for a bloated animated toolbar to squeeze through a tenuous dial-up modem connection onto your computer before you can read it, either. Given the vast capacity of Web pages to present anything, from live video clips of Britney Spears to a long text scroll of someone's senior-year paper on the Voynich manuscript, the Webcrafter has a huge collection of potential tools that can be used in creating a page.

Web designers could see that creating pages for online viewing was much different than creating them for the printed world. For one thing, Web pages had to load quickly in order to snare the impatient surfer. Large-image files had to be reduced in size and quality, fonts had to be streamlined and the page had to have a layout that was easy enough to navigate and comprehend at a fleeting glance; because as many quickly found out, unless the surfer was waiting for an extremely detailed picture of a naked woman to download on the screen, he wasn't likely to wait around for a slow-moving document to unfurl in his browser.

Then there is the issue of navigation. Once on a Web page, where do you go from there? With the nonlinear virtues of hypertext, Interactive Alices often have dozens of potential rabbit holes to fall into, and the Web designer must put up obvious road signs for the reader. Responsible Web pages get the user where he or she wants to go, and always gives them a way backward, forward, and out of the site through obvious links and icons.

When the Web emerged from the computer-science department and was dubbed the Next Big Thing by a feisty, inquisitive public in the mid-1990s, more than one Archimedean revelation was had. These revelations led to a stampede of business people hoping to sell things, gleeful online diarists hoping that someone would read their musings about Fig Newtons and give them a screenplay deal, and designers hoping to make the whole thing look just a little bit better.

Software like Macromedia Dreamweaver and Microsoft FrontPage that was designed to help print-based designers, spreadsheet jockeys, and those who knew not a lick of HTML code create slick Web pages easily is both a blessing and a curse. While it did make the creation and design process less fraught with dental gnashing, it allowed just anybody to put just anything up there. The matter of content is another area in which the Web has run willy-nilly with irresponsibility, and we are not just talking about bestiality sites freely finding their way into little Bobby's browser when he is clicking around after school.

The responsibility to the public to present accurate or necessary information can often fall by the wayside for those on the quest for the Holy Grail of Hipster Cred. Take, for instance, the doctored photograph of a scowling Bert the Muppet sitting next to Osama bin Laden that was plucked from a joke Web site and turned up printed on pro-bin Laden posters in Bangladesh in the fall of 2001. Although the creator of the fudged photo apologized and took the picture down from his site (a snarky set of pages called "Bert Is Evil" that showed Ernie's pal craftily Photoshopped alongside the likes of Hitler, Michael Jackson, and other bad influences), it was picked up by anti-American protestors halfway around the world who obviously did NOT get the joke.

This is not, by any means, a call for censorship of the Web. The Bert Incident was pretty darn funny. The right to free speech is celebrated wonderfully and exuberantly all across the Internet, from the most uplifting tales of surviving oppression to the vilest hate site. But when one is practicing the art of free speech, one should make absolutely clear that everyone reading or looking at a site understands exactly what it is the creator is trying to communicate. Although sites like the clever creation for "The Blair Witch Project," which provided back-story about the movie's fictional spook, proved to be an excellent marketing tool, doing this sort of thing sparingly can cut down on the amount of misinformation in the world. The Net has established itself as a fertile breeding ground for all kinds of rumors, hoaxes, and flat-out untruths to run wild, and purposely adding more junk data is irresponsible. It's almost like falsely yelling "Fire!" in a crowded theater.

Deception is another irresponsible practice. JavaScript programmers should not redirect surfers to unwanted sites. Designers should not try to mimic the look of other sites in an effort to dupe people into thinking they are in a place that they're not.

Keeping the Net neighborhood orderly is important, too. If they are going to put up that page, the creators should take the effort to maintain it—making sure links are always functional, outdated information is corrected, general relevance sustained, and the page removed when it has outlived its usefulness. Stumbling across a stale page in the search for fast, accurate information is a real buzz-stomper for most surfers unless they are in a nostalgic mood.

Seeing how things have progressed over the past few years, Ease of Use is going to be a smoother task to accomplish in the area of Web Responsibility than will be Useful Ease. In the hands of designers and design conventions that will inevitably begin to take hold in the Darwinesqe march to get attention, making Web pages intuitive, accessible, and nice to look at will be a snap compared to screening out or shoveling off the scads of pointless pages, screeching scrolls of hate, and other detritus from the collective consciousness that finds its way online.

True responsibility is shown not necessarily by censoring others, but by censoring one's self and the more churlish impulses we all have. (So the next time you get dumped, keep those revenge notions out of your public HTML files and scribbled in your private Hello Kitty diary where they belong.) Web-site creators should think long and hard about what they are putting up there and who is going to read it. We need to think globally as we upload locally. The Web may have given everyone a voice, but responsible folks know when to shut up.

The Weaving of Design and Community

Julie Baugnet

"Devote yourself to a cause."
—Robert Bellah

This essay is about how artists, specifically graphic designers, are weaving a strong bond between themselves and the communities in which they live. It is about humanity, generosity, and characteristics innate to human beings that encourage us to try to make this a better world.

Graphic design has experienced a drastic change even during my short career of the past fifteen years. When I started using the Macintosh and doing work for nonprofit organizations in 1987, the economy was somewhat depressed in the Midwest. Designers took the projects they could get and worked on budgets that were controlled by reasonable profit margins. The world of design was very tame and practical and it seemed to do the job that it had done in the past—to carefully plan and implement a project such as a brochure, a poster, a logo, a symbol, a newsletter, etc. This work seemed very distant from the advertising world. Many designers discouraged work that looked too blatant and showy or full of hype. We looked at advertising as more material and commercial; design was an artistic approach. Designers liked working alone. The short history of design reveals that designers were very much aligned with artists and very interested in aesthetics and beauty.

If you look back at the nineties, you'll see attitudes have changed. Design has merged more with advertising. The information and computer age has allowed us all to change our modus operandi. Design is no longer about methodically and physically cutting and pasting materials together. It is a fast operation of pressing, clicking, and sending, thus without deep thinking and/or meaning. The surge in this design-advertising mode relates to our rampant consumerism and well-to-do economy. Everything seems to be over-advertised and over-designed, which has led to consumers over-buying. Another change in the design procedure is that many graphic artists now work directly with marketing professionals and are inextricably linked to advertising. And with this link comes many political and ethical questions for the designer. For example, many artists working in larger design studios are faced with decisions such as whether to design new cigarette labels or logos for major corporations they may not agree with. They are involved in many dilemmas. Do they express their opinions or say no to certain projects? Or do they just go along with the status quo and disregard the ethical and political implications?

This new approach to design has brought about many articles. This summer, a manifesto was put out by leading designers and educators, and published in seven of the most influential design magazines. The title was "First Things First Manifesto 2000."[1] It blatantly accused designers of using their best energies and skills to "sell dog biscuits, designer coffee, diamonds, detergents, hair gel, cigarettes, credit cards, sneakers, butt toners, light beer, and heavy-duty recreational vehicles." The manifesto goes on to say "Many of us have grown increasingly uncomfortable with this view of design. Designers who devote their efforts primarily to advertising, marketing, and brand development are supporting, and implicitly endorsing, a mental environment so saturated with commercial messages that it is changing the very way citizen-consumers speak, think, feel, respond, and interact." The manifesto calls for "a reversal of priorities in favor of more useful, lasting and democratic forms of communication—a shift away from product marketing and toward the exploration and production of a new kind of meaning."

These are some of the issues in graphic design today. The manifesto calls for meaning in design and asks designers to question themselves. It asks us to look at our culture and our communities not just to see how we can make money, but to see how we can weave a stronger thread into the fabric of our society.

This brings me to the core of this essay. I would like to focus on a few unsung heroes of the design community in Minnesota and show you how they are helping various organizations that cannot afford to hire a designer to give them a look that matches the professional work they do.

First, I'd like to talk about the work from The Spangler Design Team. Mark Spangler has worked in the Twin Cities community for over twenty years. He spent much of his time teaching at the College of Visual Arts while continuing his professional work. His design studio has grown into a team of thirteen. Early on, when Mark thought about doing something for the community he realized it would be very easy to donate some money to a cause. After more thought he realized that he could utilize his own talents by becoming involved in pro bono design work—that is, "work for the public good." For him, this seemed more rewarding than just writing a check. He had a sense of wanting to be more involved with people and realized that what he had to offer—simply good design—could be more effective in raising money for key nonprofit groups of his choice. Mark's view is that today's nonprofits must become more competitive. To do this their image must look professional and they must have a strategy. His design team has helped many nonprofit groups in the Twin Cities area. When he works on large campaigns he sees his work out in the community and immediately feels a sense of pride. Mark likes the civic engagement and he says he feels a fulfillment just knowing he's doing something for someone that is helpful to the community. His philosophy in life is that "The positive energy you expel will always come back to you." Currently, the Spangler Design Team donates 13 percent of their gross sales to community work. A few of their pro bono clients include the Juvenile Diabetes Foundation, the Minnesota Orchestra Volunteer Association, and the Minneapolis Aquatennial.

A similar understanding and involvement in the community comes from Ken Friberg Design in St. Paul. Ken had an early start in his career when he taught himself photography. In his early twenties he did many projects without pay mostly because it benefited both him and his client. The pro bono work helped him build up a portfolio while doing professional photo shoots for organizations such as Mothers Against Drunk Driving and the Minnesota Homeless Project. Ken says it wasn't always a conscious decision to do something for nothing—he just really enjoyed doing the work and added that his monetary concerns were not important in his younger days. Extra work allowed him to practice what he really enjoyed—the creative process. His experiences with working for these organizations were always positive and while doing the work he realized he was also making friends. When he takes on a project Ken says his relationship becomes a close connection to the organization and the people. This changes the environment of the work in a way that becomes more valuable and personal to him.

These are two designers that have small studios and are in charge of what they want to do and have created lives in design that are closely linked to their philosophy of helping others in their communities. There are many other designers in the Twin Cities and around the country that portray these beliefs. Together they are the ones that are balancing the imposing commercial ventures that we see everyday.

For designers who are lesser known and are looking for this type of volunteerism, there is an organization in the Twin Cities that will match a graphic designer to a needy nonprofit group. At the Management Assistance Program for Nonprofits (MAP) it is the job of Annie Lewis to find designers willing to do pro bono work. Annie admits that this is often a hard task, since some designers are less experienced and not quite ready to take on a large project. Most often the projects work well and the nonprofits are happy to get the help of a professional organization that can steer them in the right direction. MAP offers expert help in many areas, such as organizational development, consultation, marketing, and staff development. MAP was set up over twenty years ago when top corporate executives from Honeywell, NSP, St. Paul Companies, Bemis, and 1st Bank saw that the nonprofit organizations needed help in order to achieve their missions and goals. Without the work of MAP and the volunteer designers, many of these organizations would go unnoticed because they lack a visual presence.

Sui Lee, a regular volunteer, admits that she is busy working as a designer forty hours a week, but she volunteers for MAP because she truly wants to give nonprofit organizations a helping hand. Her work for the Midwest Rural Assistance Program demonstrates that the work of an artist can give integrity to an organization. Many graphic designers have worked with MAP on projects for organizations such as the Children's Dental Service.

Finally, I would like to talk about Sue Crolick. As a graphic designer she has a slightly different way of offering her help to the community. After spending over thirty years in design she reconsidered what she was doing in her career while recovering from a health problem. After some thought, she decided to team up with the Aliveness Project, a group working with people living with AIDS. Her first creative endeavor, a Paintbox Party, was a huge success. She developed a project where designers gathered together for a day and painted over 650 flat, corrugated boxes. She recognized some of the strong points of graphic designers—they're good colorists, great painters, and they don't mind getting messy. The Aliveness Project filled the boxes with various gifts to be delivered to people living with AIDS during the December holiday season. Sue became well known for her service through this project. She still continues to work with people and to reach out to the community. In 1994 she founded a nonprofit organization called Creatives for Causes. Its mission is to use the power of creativity and self-expression to help children at risk develop new visions of themselves. This project is more interactive than traditional pro bono work. She pairs a graphic designer with a young child for an intensive self-esteem project. The creatives become "Art Buddies" to the kids. In one event design volunteers worked with three hundred children from eighteen emergency shelters. In the "Animal Mask" workshops kids are asked about their favorite animals. They talk about the positive characteristics of an animal and they create their own masks with the help of their "Art Buddy." The event ends in a parade where the children are cheered on and have their pictures taken in a studio by a professional photographer. Sue believes that children at risk need mentoring and she has seen many positive results, including academic improvement, changes in a child's attitude, and higher self-esteem. This program has been a tremendous success and shows the strength of the art process in shaping a child's world.

In the book *The Good Society*,[2] Robert Bellah and others ask us to "devote ourselves to a cause." They encourage us to contribute to a "common good." These designers have all found their own interests and fulfillment by working with a cause that gives them satisfaction and enjoyment. In a similar book, *Soul of a Citizen Living with Conviction in a Cynical Time*,[3] Paul Loeb asks some very big questions. "Which issues should we take on in this complex and demanding time? When do we act, and how do we do it?" More than ever before, our students are faced with these decisions. And as educators we can help them prepare. At St. Cloud State, we are taking small steps and adding this element into our curriculum. We have set up an Open Design Studio, which is run by my colleague Keith Christensen. Each semester Keith works with between six and eight design students on community-based projects. Most recently the students have designed a set of signs. Keith was approached by some members of the East St. Cloud Community Association who were looking for a way to improve and uplift the image of their community. They wanted something that would give the people a sense of definition and show that East St. Cloud is an important place to live. Keith and the students talked with residents and asked them for words about what they thought was important in their lives. Our design students developed icons and added text to create bold signs that are now displayed prominently in an area that is becoming much more livable.

The students working on this project gained an understanding of community and were given the opportunity to work directly with a client in a professional situation. They now have a unique project to show in their portfolios. This is just one example of how we as educators can help students understand the importance of pro bono work and its benefits.

For this sampling of Twin City designers, design and the work they do is very meaningful and reflects the call of the Manifesto 2000. They determine value not by money, fame, or hype, but by meaningful, useful exchange. They take pride in weaving together a stronger fabric that is helping to strengthen our society.

Notes

1. Jonathan Barnbrook et al., "First Things First Manifesto 2000," *Adbusters,* Autumn 1999.

2. Robert Bellah et al., Eds., *The Good Society* (New York: Alfred A. Knopf, 1991).

3. Paul Loeb, *Soul of a Citizen: Living With Conviction in a Cynical Time* (New York: St. Martin's Press, 1999).

Human Values in Commerce
A Profile of Sara Little Turnbull
Véronique Vienne

Sara Little Turnbull, well into her eighties, is still a practicing designer, a strategic planner, a teacher, a cultural anthropologist, a problem-solver—and a self-described "master of the creative accident." A woman of formidable intellectual stature, she sizes you up from the height of her diminutive four-foot eleven-inch frame. Within minutes of meeting her, your perspective on the world changes to adjust to hers. Feeling like Alice in Wonderland—a little too tall suddenly—you are quite willing to squeeze into rabbit holes to follow her nimble mind wherever it wants to go.

In order for Sara Little Turnbull to explain what she does—and why it's particularly relevant to our culture now—she must first debunk some of the current assumptions about design and its function. In the process, she is likely to tell you how she came up with a new design for the lids of baking dishes after observing the way cheetahs in Kenya use their paws to capture and hold their prey, or how she got the idea for a line of energizing bath towels from watching traditional weavers in Malaysia, or how, to design a burglar-proof lock she first interviewed crooks behind bars—the real security experts.

For more than five decades now, Mrs. Turnbull, née Sara Little, has been corporate America's best-kept secret. Working behind the scenes with top product development people at General Mills, Corning Ware, Procter & Gamble, and 3M, just to name a few of her long-term clients, she operates at the intersection of design and commerce. An independent thinker, she is a role model for many women. One of her fans, Los Angeles interior designer Gere Kananaugh, believes that Sara paved the way for "the next three or four generations of female designers." To Sara, though, this is not a compliment. "I am not a female designer!" she exclaims. "I am just a designer." Married late at age forty-eight to forest-product industry executive James R. Turnbull, she was a modern woman before her time. One of her former students, Jennifer Ayer Sandell, a young woman who juggles family and career, considers Mrs. Turnbull a mentor. "She is an informal adviser to me and to a lot of my girlfriends in the corporate world," she says.

If she is so popular, how come Sara Little Turnbull is not a household name today? The reason is simple. Almost no one can explain what it is she does exactly. When she was a consultant at Revlon—a stint that lasted almost twenty years—someone once asked its then president Charles Revson what Sara Little's contribution was to his company. "After all these years," he answered, "I don't understand a thing she says—but I can't live without her!"

Nowadays, Sara Little Turnbull is on the faculty at Stanford University Graduate School of Business as director of the Process of Change, Innovation, and Design Laboratory. She is also a consulting professor at the School of Engineering as part of the Integrated Design for Marketing and Manufacturing program. In this staid academic context, she explores with both business and engineering students "how a deeper understanding of culture can be a competitive advantage in business." Her approach is interdisciplinary—the teaming of business and engineering students is mandatory for the Integrated Design course, a twenty-one-week program. Forty students, divided into ten teams of two MBAs and two engineering graduate students, compete to design, manufacture, and market the same working consumer product prototype—a citrus juicer one year, a mini bike pump the next.

"There is a remarkable amount of reason that goes into coming up with design solutions," Turnbull says. "I see design as essentially creating order, but I also encourage students to learn from their own experience, at times letting their mind meander to discover the unexpected and the creative accident." What she calls the Process of Change is a dynamic development methodology she shaped during years exploring creative opportunities at the corporate level—a technique that's part logic, part chutzpah.

Born in Manhattan in 1917, raised in Brooklyn, Sara Little grew up in a modest Jewish household. Her mother came from a family of Hebrew scholars and instilled in her daughter an intellectual curiosity for all things big and small. To this day, she credits her mother for teaching her to appreciate design. She fondly remembers her mom showing her the meager yet precious provisions for the day—an eggplant, a bunch of scallions, a cucumber, and an onion—and then describing each in detail, from the rotund fleshiness of the eggplant to the gossamer layers of the onion reluctant to reveal its succulent center.

Sara Little graduated from Parsons School of Design in 1939. By 1941, she was an editorial assistant at *House Beautiful*, where she quickly rose to the position of decorating editor. Already she was showing an uncanny ability for defining the next societal trend. Even before the end of World War II, she was developing a series of articles for the magazine addressing the new realities of what she predicted would soon be the postwar boom. Under a "Girl with a Future" seal-of-approval logo, she introduced readers to modern ideas such as sharing an apartment with a roommate, decorating a home for a returning soldier, doing away with the cleaning lady, or making the best of the G.I. Bill.

At the time, she lived in one room in the Lombardi Hotel in Manhattan, artfully turning a couple hundred square feet of convenient real estate into a model of urbane efficiency, thanks to tucked-in storage spaces, folding screens, and collapsible furniture. An experimenter, she derived great satisfaction from taking advantage of every nook and cranny, her restless mind always questioning the reason for everything.

When her sister was diagnosed with cancer in the late 1940s and staggering medical bills had to be paid, she turned her room at the Lombardi into a tiny design office. On the side, after hours, she began to design packaging for Macy's private brand products. Soon, other clients were clamoring for her services, among them Elizabeth Arden and Lever Brothers. Not knowing what to charge, she one day decided to add all the doctor, hospital, surgery, and nursing expenses she had to foot for her sister and make that her fee. To her surprise, her clients didn't balk.

From then on, her freelance practice flourished, and so did the quality of her clients. "I quickly became one of the highest-paid designers in the business," she now says. "I would never have been as successful—would never have done as much as I did—if I hadn't been forced by circumstances. And, you know what, I got paid, and then I got paid, and then I got paid." By the time her sister died in 1954, Sara had grown into a savvy design professional who was not intimidated by powerful corporate clients. In 1958, she quit her day job at *House Beautiful* and officially became Sara Little, Design Consultant. She was forty-one, single, and well-to-do.

The country was ready for its second postwar boom. Many of the patents for advanced technologies granted during the war were on the verge of running out. In the United States, patents are given for a limited time—seventeen years—and unless they are used commercially within this period they fall into the public domain. By 1958 companies like 3M and Corning Glass were in danger of losing ownership of some potentially valuable wartime inventions, unless they created new products with them. They began to scramble for ideas. Many of the novelties introduced in the 1960s, from Tang to Spandex, came about as a result of this second wave of urgent postwar inventiveness.

As it happened, Sara Little had written an article in a trade publication titled "When Will the Consumer Become Your Customer?" In it, she frankly discussed the fact that most companies at the time created products for retailers, not for the people who were really going to use them. This was the only article she ever wrote (Sara doesn't waste her time on paper trails; she only wrote two memos during her career as a designer), but it had a tremendous impact on her life. The head of Corning consumer products division and the senior vice president of 3M, who both had read her article, called and asked her to come over and talk to them. "I came away with a practice that sustained me for thirty-five years," she says. Indeed, brainstorming with heads of companies is really her thing. As San Francisco design consultant Ellen Newman, daughter of the late Cyril Magnum and a friend of Sara's for fifty years, explains: "CEOs in this country just want to talk to Sara. She is one of the few designers who does not intimidate them." To this day, top decision makers still call on Sara Little Turnbull when they need to stretch their minds and discover new opportunities for their industries, from reinventing the way food is stored in a refrigerator to making lipstick colors less arbitrary.

Corning and 3M have been faithful clients, along with Procter & Gamble, Coca-Cola, Ford Motor, General Mills, Scott Paper, American Can, Neiman Marcus, Revlon, DuPont, Pfizer Co., Nissan, and more. But Mrs. Turnbull will not share with anyone the specifics of her contribution to the numerous projects she was privy to. In fact, she becomes very unhappy if you try to find out what she discusses with clients behind closed doors. "I am scrupulous about not taking credit for any idea," she insists. "An original concept may be mine, but the result is only as good as its final implementation."

For Sara, staying on the edge at age eighty-four is a discipline. "I am a young oldie," she explains. "There are very many young oldies like me out there, and society today is somewhat more receptive to us—as long as we are willing to keep learning new things all the time." Her brilliant insights are not the product of serendipitous flashes of genius, but of sustained efforts to keep up with the culture. She reads—and clips—five newspapers daily. The *Wall Street Journal,* the *New York Times,* the *Japan Times,* the *China Strait Times,* and the *Financial Times,* which she thinks is the best paper of all. She also reads about sixty publications a month, everything from scientific journals to consumer publications, trade press, and news magazines. She has archived all her clippings since the early 1960s and they are now the backbone of her "lab" at Stanford.

"Everything that's in my head is in these drawers," she says, pointing at the file cabinets that surround the Process of Change Laboratory conference room. "I have not allowed this information to be put on an electronic database because that's not what I think this material is." Students and clients come to study her files right here, with her. Neatly classified in bright red folders and constantly updated, the information reflects major trends in design directions. There are more than 375 categories, but no cataloging or fancy cross-referencing. More than a systematic research tool, the data is there to stimulate your thinking by providing an interdisciplinary overview from a global, cultural perspective. "Sure, you can go online and get bits and pieces of information instantly," she explains. "In less than twenty-five minutes on the Internet you can sift through material that takes me five hours to read. But I don't think you know the same thing when it's over. When I read material, I look at all kinds of things."

All kinds of things? To explain how her mind works, she tells the story of how years ago she solved a problem for "an international client in the food industry." One of their most popular cake mix products wasn't selling in England. They dispatched her to London to find out why. She stayed at the Claridge, doing intensive research as she always does, frantically interviewing everyone from psychologists to pastry chefs. After ten days, she had not come up with very much, and had to admit that she had failed her mission. She packed her bags and booked herself on the next flight to New York. With an hour to kill before going to the airport, she decided to have a proper English high tea, something she didn't have time to do while at the Claridge, so anxious was she to solve her culinary mystery. Ordering pastries instead of the traditional cucumber sandwiches (she felt she needed a little sweet treat), she was surprised to be served a plate of tiny cakes, but no fork or spoon to eat them with. Just as she was about to summon the waiter, a red flag went up in her head. "I suddenly realized that I had to take this incident seriously," she recalls. "The moist-looking cakes were of a completely different texture from what I expected. They were finger food. This was the answer to my puzzle. The cake mix was all wrong—it had to be more like a cookie mix."

This same pragmatic anthropological approach has allowed her during her long career to come up with freezer-to-oven dishes made of a Corning Glass material originally developed for missiles; design bedroom furnishings to help patients with cognitive disabilities regain control of their lives; invent rope candies to give kids a dietary supplement of soybean protein; and create anti-pollution masks for 3M made of non-woven fibers. Along the way, she gathered an impressive collection of artifacts from around the world—dishes, baskets, bowls, vases, trays, tools, dolls, designer clothes, fabric samples, and more—which she donated in 1974 to the Tacoma Art Museum, Washington, where she had moved to follow her husband.

Between 1965, when she married James Turnbull, and 1988, when they moved to Palo Alto, California, to seek treatment for his brain cancer at the Stanford Medical Center, Sara Little Turnbull kept as busy as ever with her consulting work. She would routinely fly from nearby Seattle to Europe one week and Japan the next, dispensing her sage advice, lecturing, and earning her share of awards in the design field—a Trailblazer Award and a Fellowship from the National Endowment for the Arts among them. So it's no wonder that, almost as soon as she appeared on the scene in Stanford, she was hired by the Graduate Business School. James died in 1991, and Sara has made Stanford her permanent home, living in a one-bedroom apartment that's not much larger than her Lombardi Hotel pad used to be.

Though her teaching schedule is full, she manages to keep in touch with the real world of business. Academia is not a refuge for her. "I tell my students that the chairman of a company who listens to their ideas and says 'Yes, I think we can do it' is as much part of their design process as anyone involved," she says. "I want them to assume right from the start that the client is automatically as creative as they are."

Students flock to her classes and her lab to learn to create "cool new things," as former student Patrick Sagasi explains. Now a product manager at Adobe, he still uses what he calls her "why-why-why-why-how" investigative methodology. "It's about asking *why* enough times to dig down to the root of the problem," he says. "You don't want to design products that only fix superficial symptoms."

For an assignment to design a wakeup device, for instance, he and his teammates Linda Kuo, Maria Olide, and Hua Ji had to figure out (1) why traditional alarm clocks don't work, (2) why their waking stimulus fails to rouse you every time, (3) why both body and mind have to be activated together in order for one to awaken, and (4) why setting up the clock is as critical as turning it off. The final prototype looks like a whimsical cube with feet. Setting it on and turning it off require some ingenious realignment of body parts. The device gets you up by calling upon your mental alertness and your sense of play.

Stanford MBA Norito Ibata, who met Sara when he was a student and is now a retail operation director with Starbucks in Japan, praises Turnbull's ability to ask all the right questions. "There are so few people with whom you can have conversations about *why*," he says. "Sara always asks me 'Norito, why are we talking about what we are talking about?' She always reminds me of what's important."

Her students are sure to become enlightened CEOs who think creatively about design. In the meantime, Sara Little Turnbull says she can't wait to rush to the office every morning, "because I am getting older, and I cannot die until I set the stage for human values in commerce."

Originally published in Metropolis, *November 2000.*

Who Gets to Say What to Whom?

Maud Lavin

Who gets to say what to whom? Who has the means to communicate, the power and money to get a message across, the passion and humor to speak, the openness and confidence to participate in dialogue rather than monologue? In aiming these questions at graphic design and related areas on advertising, corporate identity programs, Web sites, and political photomontages and posters, I'm particularly interested in examining the cottage-industry images printed, broadcast, projected, or digitally transmitted in mass markets. I want to know what happens to private visions in public forums. I'm encouraged that designers have the entrepreneurial power to express themselves in these forums, but cognizant that this power is all too often restricted to formal issues.

As a populist and believer in radical democracy, I'd like to see designers involve themselves more in the content and impact of their messages, participate more in public debate, and enjoy more personal expression. I believe the current trend toward what I call "multitasking practices" can potentially enable this broadening of roles. My hope for the future of design is that more designers function— when so moved and in different ways—as visual editorialists, a practice unconventionally and powerfully exemplified by the writer and illustrator Art Spiegelman in the *Maus* books. The flexing of visual voice muscles is a key to the concept of radical democracy, which emphasizes citizens' egalitarian involvement in debate, representation, change, and government. That's the dream. For the reality now, though, I recognize that most practitioners are in a service role. And designers, like the rest of us, have to pay bills. A more practical version of the dream, then, is that designers realize their power to communicate and their power to earn by developing multi-tasking practices—those that encompass both visual editorializing (usually not a big money maker) and more sturdily profitable work. This new model is more than adding pro bono work to paid work (although it might include that); it's about designers initiating projects with an ambitious reach and nontraditional forms.

Graphic design is an umbrella field, defined broadly as mass visual communication and more fully as "an art form that depends for its efficacy on the degree to which words and images communicate a coherent message."[1] For the most part, at present, it's a hard-working service field, a field that sees itself more occupied with translating speech into visual language than speaking. It is client- and product-oriented. Many of its corporate-client practitioners are instructed to provide order and to clarify, to give their clients' companies the look, sheen, and promise of a clean new world. It's a fairly neurotic expectation, since designers can't really clean—they just cover, wrap, accent, or put into a clean envelope some messy realities. Typically, there is no in-depth communication in corporate design graphics. For me, graphic design fascinates and frustrates because it is a bizarre example of hamstrung power. In corporate service, design's most common function, design is implicated in both cultural stasis and change, but with only partial control.

A while back in Minneapolis, I was on a panel with Ivan Chermayeff, a principal in the design firm of Chermayeff/Geismar. A star in the field, Chermayeff looked the part of the handsomely aging artist: tall, rangy, with longish hair and expensively understated clothes. Chermayeff was well known for, among other things, having redesigned Mobil's corporate graphics. His waves of clean gasoline sloshing inside the orange "O" were seen by millions of people. But as we started to talk in the panel about how that image and its related identity program did and did not relate to what Mobil actually did as a corporation, Chermayeff grew uneasy. He didn't really know or didn't want to talk about what Mobil did. His task was to concentrate on the details of its look. Here was someone who had tremendous power to communicate visually and no power whatsoever to influence the content. And here was a field, graphic design, bent like most fields around self-justification, forced to only talk formal, visual issues and ignore its own impotency.

Because graphic design is so powerful and so warped (in most commercial practice) in its ability to communicate, it provides an exaggerated model for the same questions that dog other communications fields, like photography, film, the Internet, and my own field, writing. Who really has a voice in our culture? Do we have public forums that are democratic, alive, open, fun, make a difference? Or are too many of our public spaces bought and closed off: the town square where speeches are protected by the First Amendment now deserted in favor of the shopping mall where private owners determine what is said in advertising spaces; the cacophony of public access cable ceding to HBO; anything resembling porn on the Net potentially censored by schools and libraries; reporters, TV anchors, graphic designers, and others hired to condense and deliver messages but to keep their own mouths shut?

Nevertheless, it's a time when women have at last come to the fore of the graphic design field—yet they still earn less than their male counterparts. Perhaps because of the continuing economic inequity within design firms, women designers who do self-generated as well as corporate work have turned increasingly to a mix of teaching and self-employment structures that combine to create semi-independent, multitasking practices. Such multitasking in turn has provided a persuasive model for the field as a whole. For instance, well-known female designers who work for institutional and corporate clients and in addition have a strong record of self-expressive work and/or public service include Lorraine Wild, Ann Tyler, Sheila Levrant de Bretteville, Rebecca Mendez, Sylvia Harris, and Marlene McCarty. Their influence spreads in part through institutions where they teach, like Cal Arts, the School of the Art Institute of Chicago, and Yale. Of course there are men with exemplary political and self-expressive multitasking design practices as well, the varied practices of B. J. Krivanek,[2] J. Abbott Miller, and Art Chantry come immediately to mind.

What these women and men do goes way beyond the limits of a given field. Our culture is dominated by the visual, so that mass-distribution image-makers influence what political issues we as a society discuss. They are a key factor in why our culture talks so much about crime, for instance, and so little about a harder-to-picture issue like future overpopulation. Viewed in this context, I feel designers outside teaching institutions have visual editorializing power that too often has gone unrecognized and undeveloped. It's not that the tradition of modernist corporate design like Paul Rand's for IBM has been anti-democratic, but in its emphasis on creating a clean envelope to cover messier, more complex realities, it has often whitewashed questions for debate instead of foregrounding them. In contrast, a designer like Levant de Bretteville, with her installation projects that highlight local oral history, helps to bring diverse neighborhood issues into a public space for discussion.

Issues about the fate and look of private expressions in public forms inevitably raise questions about design and the Internet. On the Web, will we continue to express ourselves and talk to others with full displays of peacock feathers, unruly emotions, difficult politics, broad humor, keen elegance, information overload, and bad taste? Will graphic design contribute by revealing complexity or by reducing for clarity or both? Will communication remain kaleidoscopic? Or will all of this creative, transformative mess become increasingly filtered and clean?

With my writing on design, I aim to stir discussion that encourages or provokes those of us in communications, designers, writers, etc., to recognize and deal creatively with the cultural power we do, in fact, have. I'm interested, too, in design's operations in a broader social and cultural context: Design is a key marker in the historical shifts of institutions of funding, distribution, competitive reception, and audience. For example, design history needs to acknowledge the increased difficulty in publishing visual editorials today as compared to the twenties when the mass media was less monopolized. Design criticism could also focus more on how design functions to help formulate our norms and even the speed with which those norms are constantly recast, much as corporate identities and publicly aired individual identities are now rapidly retooled.

I see design—in its usual forms—as a hamstrung power in visual culture, but also a practice whose potential reach has remained largely unacknowledged by the critical field that set out to analyze it. Design history and criticism is a very young field—it has only existed as a regular presence in universities and art schools since the 1970s. Most writing on design has been preoccupied with analyzing design products, compiling designer biographies, and developing a historical narrative of style influences. There is, on the one hand, a desire to catalog basic information about design, which itself is quite young as a pervasive practice, born as a largely unacknowledged technique in advertising in the nineteenth century, with a growth spurt and recognition as a profession in the 1920s, and not really burgeoning until its widespread corporate sponsorship after World War II. On the other hand, creating a style lexicon and a design canon also fits with the service mentality of how design is usually practiced: such writing is useful in the marketplace as resource material for designers.

As necessary as such writing may be, design criticism needs to do more than this—to approach design from the broader field of visual culture criticism and ask ambitious questions about power and communication. Design criticism itself needs to be editorializing and polemical. This approach comes at a particularly exciting point in the evolution of design history and also design practice. Design historians and critics have begun to open their writing to interdisciplinary approaches, thus acknowledging the multifaceted face of design, and not coincidentally expanding its audience and discourse. Curator and designer Ellen Lupton did this with her 1993 Cooper-Hewitt exhibition "Mechanical Brides: Women and Machines from Home to Office," where she brought together issues of product and graphic design with women's history. Lupton continues to cross boundaries in her more recent work. Recently for the designer, professional competition and technological diversity have encouraged a multitasking role.

Typically, today's designer might provide a corporation with a visual identity, a mission statement, a Web site, a brochure, other advertising, and a trade exhibition presence—in short, a visual persona in the market. This diversity may still mean that the designer is curtailed in what he or she can say in a given corporate context, but it sets a pattern for a wide-ranging cultural involvement that the designer can pursue in his or her own work. Today design sits at the intersection of cottage-industry cultural production, corporate sponsorship, and mass-distribution systems, such as magazines or the Internet, which are heavily visual. It papers our world and its paper trail tells us much about how our culture is funded and disseminated.

Design critics need to ask questions about economics, power, and democracy as well as questions about style. I'm interested in enacting these questions, not just analyzing them. I've thought of my own writing trajectory as building a multitasked critical practice, one that aims to be sensitive to different audiences, morphing aesthetics, publishing economics, and evolving political debates—as well as simply my own pleasure in writing. In many ways, my writing practice parallels that of multitasking designers, and has in fact been stimulated by the examples of designers such as Levrant de Bretteville and McCarty. In other words, I try to practice what I preach. As a writer and cultural critic, I've published in a wide variety of venues, and my selection process of different forums has been motivated sometimes by love, sometimes by money, sometimes by both. My own span of cultural production—writing for large-audience, print-publishing companies like Hachette and small Internet servers like Cyborganic, the publisher of the cyberdrama *The Couch*—mirrors the practices of many designers as well as other writers and other cultural producers today. So it is with the intensity of personal engagement as well as a sense of cultural timeliness and political necessity that I ask as a cultural critic about democratic, creative, personal, and profitable possibilities for speech in design and elsewhere. Using images and words, I want to explore for designers, writers, and others, who gets to say what to whom and how to expand the pleasure, democracy, and messiness of communication.

Notes

1. Mildred Friedman, *Graphic Design in America* (Walker Art Center and Abrams, 1989), 9.
2. See *Inform* (AIGA Chicago), "Manifestos: The 'isms' Issue," *13*, no. 1.

Editor's note: The preceding was a revised excerpt from Clean New World: Culture, Politics, and Graphic Design, *by Maud Lavin, published by MIT Press in 2001.*

Typographica Mea Culpa
Unethical Downloading
Steven Heller

When I collected stamps as a kid, I sent away for "approval" packs with the proviso that I'd return what I did not pay for in five days. Needless to say, I broke the covenant, and I felt exhilarated the first time I kept all the stamps without paying for them. During the course of my mail-order crime spree, I accumulated a drawer-full of "bill me later" subscription invoices to magazines and ignored the futile collection letters. I later graduated to newspaper honor boxes. (How many of you have taken more than one? I did, until I realized that I only really needed one paper.) That's when I had an epiphany. I was speeding down the road to perdition. I changed my evil ways and have been upstanding ever since. Well, almost . . .

This near-religious experience did not extend to type fonts. In fact, until recently I always discarded the licensing agreements that come with type because the words "Read Me" had an onerous ring. By not reading the large print I chose not to acknowledge the muddy ethical waters in which I was about to wade. Through ignorance or malice, or the malice that comes from voluntary ignorance, many designers that I know simply ignore type licenses and, therefore, cavalierly trade or transfer entire fonts to fellow designers, service bureaus, mechanical artists, printers, lovers, or in-laws. The digital age has made this easy, but, as I realized, it does not make it right. Illicit type sharing betrays an honor system that can only work if we are all honorable.

The fact is, design is an honorable profession. We are not the cutthroat garment industry where styles and fabrics are routinely stolen by both big and small. Designers tend to respect one another's intellectual property, and do not as a rule engage in extreme larceny. And yet we have a skewed sense of entitlement when it comes to type. Perhaps because type is the most common means of written communication we assume the license to usurp it at will and without ramification as though it were decoupage.

The computer put the means of production into our hands and, in doing so, it implied freedom from vendors. Before, the computer type was bought directly from type-shops. We received a proof or filmstrip of type and paid our money. It was a clear-cut transaction. But even then I said to myself: "If only I had my own PhotoTypositor (remember them?) I would make my own fonts and never have to pay for type again." Then I actually got my own Typositor and found that making custom film fonts was even more expensive than buying them. So I reasoned that the only explanation for paying for them was convenience, and secretly longed for the day that type was made readily available. Hey, what about a box on my desk? Then I'll never pay for type again. And lo and behold, the Macintosh was invented and type was available in a box on my desk. And you know something? It was (and is) easy to get some fonts without paying for them.

Well, not the really good ones. So, for those faces unavailable through shareware (or a share-buddy), I paid my money and got the font. What I did not know, however, because as I said I never read the licensing agreements, was the limitations imposed on my "ownership." I reckoned that whenever I used a legitimately purchased font, it was mine to do with as I pleased and that I had the right to pass it along to anyone on the production assembly line that needed to work with my particular document and with the particular face(s). Therefore, I copied the font and sent it to them. I wasn't even consciously stealing because I presumed this was my eminent domain.

I was dead wrong. Type sharing is akin to tapping into cable TV. In fact, as it turns out, I was technically engaging in copyright infringement. All font software is protected by copyright and some typeface designs are protected by patents, which provides foundries with legal recourse. Some foundries have successfully gone to court over these issues, and in a few cases the FBI (the same body that never came after me for pilfering stamps) has been involved. I am told that this happened with someone who posted hundreds of fonts from dozens of foundries on the Internet for anybody to download (functioning somewhat like Napster). The FBI impounded his computers and the case is currently awaiting trial.

"All typefaces, from almost every foundry (from Adobe to House), are automatically licensed for a specific number of output devices and CPU's at one location. It is an industry standard," explains Rudy Vanderlans, founder of Emigre Fonts. "If you gave the font to someone else to carry through the designs, that means that they now have a free, illegally obtained copy on their computer. Most likely they will use it for another design job sometime in the future without remembering or being concerned where that font originally came from. It's a scenario we come across nearly every single day."

In the face of this, my mea culpa may sound disingenuous. After all, I work with and have written about type designers. I thought I knew their concerns, and Vanderlans is not alone. Every digital type founder that I have since spoken to complains of sharing abuses. Not surprisingly, many designers I've contacted admit to sharing because they "didn't know it was wrong." To this Vanderlans rebukes, "[They] simply didn't read the license agreement that comes with the font. Like the Church Lady used to say: 'Isn't that conveeeenient.'"

He's right. I would not use a font without paying for it, yet, once installed, I have readily shared with others. Ignorance is no excuse. Type vendors have gone to great lengths and expense to publicize these issues, yet designers have either not heard or ignored them for reasons that are endemic to unrealistic notions of entitlement. Why do we feel we have a right to unlimited access to digital fonts? Is it because in the digital realm ownership is still fuzzy? Or are we lulled into lackadaisical ethical behavior because in the digital realm it is so easy to download images and text? Or is it simply a primal need to get the proverbial free lunch that H. L. Mencken admonished did not really exist?

As fundamental as it is to visual communication, type is not considered sacrosanct in the same way as, say, a photograph or illustration. The principle of "one-time usage" or "one-person licensee" seems foreign when it comes to type. Vanderlans says that when this is brought to violators' attention "people usually admit their error and pay for the fonts." But some designers resent any strictures. "I bought a font for use in a book," explains a designer that I know. "It never occurred to me that I could not give it to my mechanical person, and from him to the printer. Isn't it enough that I paid for it? Do the foundries have to bleed me for an additional fee each time I use it on a job?" Vanderlans counters that he does not charge anybody an additional fee for each use. "Once you purchase a copy, users can use the font on as many jobs for as long as they want. And there is a way to hand your design job to a service bureau without breaching the font license. You can supply your documents as EPS files or Adobe Acrobat files with fonts embedded so you don't have to give the service bureau a copy of the font(s). Or users can buy a special license that allows them to take a font to their service bureau."

Nonetheless, veterans who are unfamiliar with the new or are used to the old methods may be confused by current procedures and, therefore, take the line of least resistance. It's easy to copy fonts, so they copy away. Younger designers, who are used to downloading shareware and other freebees may be spoiled by the bounty of entitlements (the Napster ethic). The education process continues.

Fontographer made it possible for anyone with skill to design a typeface. Some ethically challenged type vendors have pilfered original designs from the leading digital foundries, changed the name of the type, and sold them at cut-rate prices. This is obviously wrong, and Vanderlans notes that "most have been taken to court and lost, or settled by paying large sums of money, and ultimately discontinued their pirate ways." Yet it should not take a lot of additional soul-searching to conclude that violating the "industry standard" licensing agreement is also unfair to the people who have worked hard to make the type that we all use.

For years I have allowed designers working for me to infringe the agreement that I have failed to read. Forget about legality: Without adherence to the fundamental principal, we place our colleagues in financial jeopardy and we become much less ethical in the bargain.

Responsibility Answers Absurdity

Michael Schmidt

Absurdity

Let's start with a short quiz. Which scenario(s) is/are true?

1. McDonald's debuts in Johannesburg, South Africa, with an American-style parade and local youth chanting "Viva Big Mac! Viva Big Mac!"

2. Chick Fillet decides to take advantage of India's sacred cows by tossing sandwich boards over their backs that read "Eat Mor Chikin." The ad space costs significantly more than a billboard, but ad execs declare that "slow but mobile" is the next big thing.

3. Avon saleswomen aggressively attempt to sell beauty products door to door in rural Brazil to impoverished and aging wives, widows, and mothers with the promise of age-defying beauty.

Answers:

If you guessed 1 and 3 are correct, you're the winner. Number 2 is a product of my sick sense of humor but, given the competition, not that unreasonable a possibility. If you got number 1 wrong, don't feel bad. South Africans chanting the Spanish verb "viva" is a bit of a curve ball; chalk it up to Elvis's B-movies.[1] If you got number 3 wrong, you have obviously never met an Avon sales rep.[2]

Responsibility

So now, dear reader, you may be asking, given the theme of this book, if I'm implying that graphic designers share responsibility for such absurdity and corporate arrogance? And, if so, how has this come to be? What are the repercussions? What is the depth and position of our complicity and, therefore, our transnational responsibilities? Like Avon ladies trudging hopefully yet haplessly through the Brazilian night, you are relentless, and so I will do my best to answer your questions.

History, or Brief Pause for Station Identification

Dichotomies, and other opposed forces which may seem irreconcilable, abound in society, foreign policy, commerce, and—if we have the nerve to admit it—within our own belief systems. Hence the absurdity. What route can we take through absurdity? Nobody has all the answers. But the path I cut in this essay is determined to offer some manner of lucidity: an alternative to the "natural" state of confusion and seemingly inevitable uses of design we rarely stop to consider, let alone critique.

With that said, criticism isn't hard to write, it's hard to deliver. When design educators write or make statements critical of the design field, practitioners decry their ignorance of the "real world." When practitioners, like Tibor Kalman, offer up critique, graphic designers of all stripes denounce their complicity. And when design educators and practitioners unite in a common cause, designers of butt-toner labels lament the revived critical dimension of a field they could always rely on for its comfortable passivity.

Systemic Problems

Our society has a unique means of dealing with complex problems: we make bumper stickers. If the issue can be reduced to a bumper sticker, it can be resolved: "Shit Happens," "Welcome to the South, Now Go Home," "United We Stand," "Rush is Right," "Charlton Heston is My President," "My Kid Beat Up Your Honor Student," and so on and so forth. Like our constituents, we designers like to have a firm grasp on communication. We analyze our methods, materials, aesthetics, precedents, and trendsetters. But how much of this dialogue really provides a better grasp of the systemic problems swimming in and around graphic design? I'm specifically questioning the graphic designer's role in globalization, largely in the form of branding initiatives for transnational corporations. Yes, many designers do create informative and educational materials, but corporate branding, on the whole, and in all its ancillary manifestations, consumes the greatest amount of talent and time from our field's practitioners.[3]

Property

The most important piece of property in the globalization race is the brand. In 1996, the International Trademark Association (INTA) testified to the House Judiciary Committee that the value of Coca-Cola's mark was $39 billion, IBM's was $17 billion, and Kodak's was $11 billion.[4] For clarity, these are not valuations of real capital assets, but the "worth" of brand identities alone. Put another way, purchase price minus corporate assets equals brand equity (also termed brand valuation). Brand equity is further defined as business "good will," or the monetary value positive public perception ascribes the corporate entity. It's completely intangible.

What does brand equity/valuation actually do for a corporation? Well, as INTA explains, corporations need brand valuation to secure loans, encourage investors, attract new buyers, and rally joint ventures. Brand valuation is also a useful tool in planning mergers and acquisitions, litigation, tax strategies, marketing budgets, and new product and market development. The corporation exists off this intangible asset.[5]

True to the nature and concept of property, brands seek to be maintained; and they desire permanence and growth. Brands therefore rely on an estimation of long-term profits. Transnational corporations want every assurance that their brand equity will not be adversely affected by "foreign" competition.

Graphic design, through its overemphasis on corporate servitude, is very much involved in this power play for permanence. Ironic, since we generate so much ephemera. This power play maintains the status quo in order to preserve the lifestyles of the world's wealthiest residents: those growing fat off free trade.

Free trade drains natural resources from developing nations by heavily favoring extraction over conservation. Free trade also places little to no restrictions on corporate raiders, monopolies, and partnerships that lock out competition. It mandates, through coercive powers of the World Trade Organization and the World Bank, that nations set aside higher health standards, environmental regulations, and local investors in favor of WTO import/export standards and international investors. Importantly, Free Trade is free from public accountability, also thanks to the World Trade Organization.

The alternative concept of fair trade seeks equal opportunities for local and international interests. But the individual nation-state would maintain control over its health standards and natural resources. Fair trade could also facilitate higher-paying, higher-skilled jobs in developing nations by equitably managing import/export quotas.[6]

In late August of 2001, INTA lent its voice to the latest free trade proposal: Free Trade Area of the Americas (FTAA). Speaking specifically to intellectual property rights, INTA wrote suggested revisions to the FTAA plans. INTA argues that signs and symbols belonging to indigenous peoples, local communities, and African-Americans should not be entitled to any form of intellectual property protection. Quoting their report: "[INTA] has also expressed concerns regarding proposed protection for the words and symbols of New Zealand's indigenous people, the Maori." INTA spokespeople cite the undesirability of such protection partially on the grounds that "The terms 'indigenous' or 'afro-American' communities would require careful definition, and would be subject to great potential controversy. The term 'local community' is such a broad and indefinite term that it has the potential to allow almost any city, village, or group to claim rights in signs that may have been used commercially for years, by others."[7]

Once co-opted, always co-opted. Obviously the groundwork is laid for greater corporate colonialism, further enhancing corporate dominance over ethnic majorities and developing nations. And the "legitimating" factor: the brand, the trademark, the very symbol of our field's "professionalization."

Again with the absurdity! I can't wait to see Kwanzaa Korn Puffs, Earl Grey's Aboriginal Dream Time Tea, Maori Tattoo Barbie, or McDonald's Bacon McHopi Biscuits. Despite my injection of humor (such as it is), INTA is a serious and powerful organization. Its statements—whether testimonials before Congress or *amicus curiae* (friend of the court) briefings in civil lawsuits—carry tremendous weight.

As their name implies, the INTA membership of thirty-nine hundred is largely made up of transnational corporations who want to "protect" their interests around the globe. INTA maintains status reports related to trademark legislation on nearly every developing nation in the world. Each brief summation is written strictly from INTA's perspective, never taking into consideration the indigenous methods of exchange, valuation, communication, or conceptions of property rights.[8]

In reference to indigenous property rights, INTA states, "We urge the rejection of this or any other proposal that provides special 'interest' protection."[9] Compare this statement to the fact that trademarks, under U.S. law and World Trade Organization multilateral agreements, may last indefinitely. INTA's goal—akin to that of free trade globalization—is to form a centralized and homogenized system where trademarks and positive brand recognition—and World Trade Organization multilateral policy thereunto—take precedence over language, custom, and culture.[10]

Inevitability

Free Trade, the mechanism of choice for globalization, purports to be a natural state of progress. It promises material wealth and economic prosperity for all. Never mind that Third World deprivation is owed to colonialism and unforgiven World Bank debt. In other words, we still need a route that will get us out of this vicious circle of conquer-colonize-deprive-conquer. . . . You get the idea.

In the dominant Euro-American establishment, the proponents of globalization are seen as heroic visionaries with an enviable fortune. Meanwhile, the media—which is owned by this establishment—portrays anti-globalization protestors as fringe anarchists.

Truth is, the Anti-Globalization Movement, or the Fair Trade Movement, or the Pro-Democracy Movement, or the Living Democracy Movement, or whatever the heck you want to call it, does not advocate anarchy or mass fornication at nearby intersections. Their influential members are highly respected and educated people with plenty of ideas about fair trade. Furthermore, millions of people have protested free trade from France to Thailand and from Switzerland to Brazil before and after "The Battle of Seattle."[11] This may very well be the biggest humanitarian movement our new millennium will see. Where are the heated debates of the ilk we knew in the late 1980s and early 1990s? Graphic design is once again faced with unprecedented quandaries that deserve attention.

It is accurate, as Loretta Staples points out in a letter to *Emigre*, that designers tend to shy away from political discussions: that we instead personalize our work.[12] On the whole, corporate design is discussed in relation to project briefs and client satisfaction. Johanna Drucker also conveys the need for designers to question their complicity in the "nexus of corporate power" in her writings on design education.[13] As well, I respect Ellen Lupton and her contributions to the field. Her exhibition and book, *Mixing Messages*, is a terrific visual vessel, yet the vapid comments from the featured designers disturb me.[14]

Somewhere in the 1990s graphic design lost its thirst for ideological debate. Globalization, on the other hand, is replete with ideological riptides. We need to start navigating these currents before our students' futures truly are defined by inevitable free trade corporate servitude. This is not to say corporations will rule our every outlet—though expert predictions lean that direction—rather corporate propaganda will only strengthen as globalization gains greater ground in developing nations. The repercussions will manifest as design curricula and professional hallmarks that exude corporate transnational ideology. Is this what we want? How will textbooks read five to ten years from now?

Only through an enhanced understanding of the mechanisms that control and utilize graphic design and graphic designers can we hope to change the course. Debate will be key; more of us need to come to the table.

Ideology

Globalization subscribes to the ideology of competition and greed. Americans are told that this is capitalism, and that capitalism is our way of our life. Globalization is global capitalism, free of many of the tax burdens and legal restrictions faced domestically. Globalization, it may seem, is the sharing of our country's success and freedom. But in actuality it erodes indigenous property rights and restricts developing nations—through threat of legal action and sanctions—to accept a foreign system of values.[15]

The designer's ideology is, to detrimental ends, all too often that of the client and the client's network. In this way we become part of the dominant system and are complicit in its dealings.

So what is the viability of individual and unique cultural, political, or religious ideology in this mix? These intangibles are negligible factors in the sphere of brand and corporate hegemony.

In his novel, *Immortality*, Milan Kundera questions the reader by asking her "Are you objecting that advertising and propaganda cannot be compared, because one serves commerce and the other ideology? You understand nothing."[16] He goes on to explain that the rise of Marxism is owed to propaganda: simplifications upon simplifications of Marx's ideas until nothing but a small collection of unrelated slogans remained. This byproduct, Kundera maintains, can hardly be called an ideology. Instead he terms it "imagology" and demonstrates that the same process applied to Marx's theories is applied by advertising in its depictions of our "reality." Imagology therefore supersedes both ideology and reality. Imagology is, in short, our brand reality: an ontology which is becoming decidedly more difficult to tell apart from "The Real Thing." "IT" is just it. "Coke Adds Life." "Soylent Green is People."

Propaganda

Propaganda comes in different shades. During World War I, the Wilson administration established the Criel Commission (formally known as the Committee on Public Information) to motivate public support for America's entry into armed combat. The Commission's successful propaganda mechanisms provided the cornerstones for what we know today as public relations.[17]

Propaganda is also a key component of psychological warfare (PsyWar). Every branch of the military and several government agencies were involved in PsyWar leading up to the Korean War. Central control over PsyWar initiatives became a priority under President Truman, reaching still greater executive command under President Eisenhower.[18]

Striking parallels exist between the history and nature of PsyWar and the history and nature of U.S., and global, commerce, particularly where the protections for intellectual property rights are concerned. PsyWar is about convincing the enemy to behave differently, do the things you wish, see from your perspective and yours alone. Of course psychological warfare involves more than just these simple objectives. Strategies, the theory, and tactics, the implementation of theory, form a system of ever-changing objectives and applications.

The overarching mechanism pulling all of the various initiatives together is centralization of control: consolidation. After World War II, this mechanism was once again turned on "mainstream" America in an attempt to educate a post-war class of consumers who, it was hoped, would now identify more with brands than with ethnic origins or Depression-era experiences.

In our present-day scenario of globalization, it is once again hoped that cultural differences will be overcome by the power of the brand. In fact, distinctive local cultures are considered a barrier to free trade. As David Korten—former Harvard professor and lauded humanitarian—explains, "The need to respect local tastes and cultural differences as a condition of gaining consumer acceptance greatly complicates global marketing campaigns. The dream of corporate marketers is a globalized consumer culture united around brand-name loyalties that will allow a company to sell its products with the same advertising copy in Bangkok as in Paris or New York."[19]

INTA's global strategy is identical in nature to that of psychological warfare, as evidenced in this U.S. PsyWar textbook lesson describing post-combat consolidation:

The conquered people are left in the private, humble enjoyment of their old beliefs and folkways; but all participation in public life, whether political, cultural, or economic, is conditioned on the acceptance of the new faith. In this manner, all up-rising members of the society will move in a few generations over to the new faith in the progress of becoming rich, powerful, or learned; what is left of the old faith will be gutter superstition, possessing neither power nor majesty.[20]

Andrew Blauvelt, in *Emigre* 33, attributes global consolidation to the "traffic in signs." "The corporation's identity is protected through its status as a registered trademark as it makes its way through the global marketplace asserting its uniqueness, its difference, in the face of utter homogenization—illustrating a basic premise of consumer promotion, the first principle of advertising: how to be a unique individual while being like everybody else."[21] Blauvelt then goes a step further to admit that graphic design's existence—in large measure—is indebted to dominant interests.

Andrew's latter point is proven accurate by Plumb Line Enterprises Company, LTD. Based in Hong Kong and offering a cornucopia of graphic design and promotion services, Plumb Line states on its Web site " . . . call us right now and be a part of the march towards full globalization." Plumb Line's 200 mainland China factory laborers will place your brand name on just about any trinket you can imagine.[22]

In a much different league from Plumb Line, "enterprise architects" offer "globalization strategies" as part of their service package. Globalization is now a service offering! Well, freeze my head; Disney was right, it is a small world af-ter a-l-l. These businesses provide the organizational structure, the proprietary systems, the branding, and the globalization strategies required to form a transnational corporation.[23]

Control

Powerful groups of people, none of whom hold public office, strongly influence the Legislature, Judiciary, Presidency, the United Nations, and the World Trade Organization on matters of free trade and brand enforcement. The drive to psychologically control an audience, and the singularity of perspective applied, as well as the growing centralization of control empowering these individuals and corporations, has never been stronger.

Principal, but not popularly known, among this group of free trade and brand enforcers is the aforementioned International Trademark Association (INTA).[24] INTA's history is closely tied to post-World War II consumerism. The organization was instrumental in obtaining passage of the Trademark Act of 1946, more commonly referred to as the Lanham Act. The Lanham Act still provides the judicial backing for brand valuation. This is a crucial point because without the rapid accrual of debt by businesses and consumers, and brand-equity-instigated investment, the U.S. economy could not have grown by the leaps and bounds demanded in the Cold War race for economic superiority.

Setting the stage for postwar consumerism, the U.S. Supreme Court wrote the following statement in 1942:

The protection of trademarks is the law's recognition of the psychological function of symbols. If it is true that we live by symbols, it is no less true that we purchase goods by them. A trademark is a merchandising short-cut which induces a purchaser to select what he wants, or what he has been led to believe he wants. The owner of a mark exploits this human propensity by making every effort to impregnate the atmosphere of the market with the drawing power of a congenial symbol. Whatever the means employed, the aim is the same—to convey through the mark, in the minds of potential customers, the desirability of the commodity upon which it appears. Once this is attained, the trademark owner has something of value.[25]

Defenders of graphic design's integrity argue that design is about informing, not persuading. Under media, judicial, and transnational corporate control, how can we find the line between information and persuasion? Persuasion masquerades as information in both propaganda and corporate branding. The complicity and interdependence of design and advertising are clear. The line between persuader and informer—the division that supposedly distinguishes graphic design from advertising—becomes moot on this topic of brand hegemony and globalization. And if we could successfully proclaim that corporate graphic design is about informing, should this assessment shield our information products from critique? Would, if it were true, the fact that we are informers dismiss our complicity? The informer/persuader distinction is merely academic in this, the context, of our field's largest segment of production.

Trademarks were also originally intended to inform by distinguishing a company's products from those of an unscrupulous competitor. Trademark law protected the consumer from harm or fraud. By the mid-1900s, as we can see from the Supreme Court narrative however, the shift from guarding consumers to protecting corporations—so prevalent today—was fully initiated. This inequity plays out on the Web as well, where corporations hire "watching services," ostensibly to protect their trademarks from competitors and market confusion, to search for "virtual" infractions.

The Web is now patrolled by private "police" who search for actual or potential trademark infringements. While it is certainly valid for corporations to protect their trademarks from unscrupulous competitors, these domain name and metatag searches can also net corporate critics who should have just as much right to "market" their dissent but legally do not.[26] Corporations are protected at the expense of our civil liberties. Corporate proponents could counter my argument by saying that the protection of brand equity is the provision of job security. From this corporate standpoint it is OK to mute criticism and free speech for the sake of perceived security and financial gain. I agree that cyber squatting is a problem; but until provisions for dissent and parody are amended to trademark laws, corporate freedoms will continue to far outweigh legal mechanisms for critique, First and Fourteenth Amendments notwithstanding.

Democracy

Beyond the matter of corporate control are the multilateral institutions that represent, and further empower, corporate hegemony. Founded by representatives of forty-four nations who met in Bretton Woods, New Hampshire, in 1944, the three organizations are referred to as the Bretton Woods institutions. They are the World Bank, the International Monetary Fund (IMF), and the General Agreement on Tariffs and Trade (GATT)—established at a separate meeting and renamed the World Trade Organization (WTO) in 1995. They are "special agencies" of the UN, but they function independently from it—and from public view.

The objective of the 1944 meeting was to establish a mechanism for global prosperity that would dissuade future armed conflict. U.S. global economic leadership development, facilitated by the country's access to the world's markets and raw materials, is a key component of Bretton Woods.[27]

That our citizenry, or any other populace, was not offered a referendum in the Bretton Woods agglomeration was not unprecedented. Labor movements before and during the Great Depression became, for our "democratic" leadership, further affirmation that public assembly and the "common man's" intelligence were not to be trusted. This was an unfortunate conclusion, but not a new opinion by any means.[28] The very fact that the World Trade Organization, an institution responsible for global trade—and as such affects the lives of every citizen as it erodes the relevance of nation-states—can shut out the public from its meetings is uncontainable. We have an absurd form of democracy—predicated on the superiority of wealth—that carries only the image of egalitarianism. This is not news. But the effect of this condition must be considered as a determinate factor in our field's apolitical stance and dependence on corrupt corporations. In other words, I believe we consider ourselves powerless as designers because we feel powerless as citizens: revisionist history tells us so.

So we must remember that our clients, particularly transnational corporations, are not part of a democracy. The people and organizations with decision-making authority to enforce the brands we create were not elected by any citizenry, and certainly not by the world's poor.[29]

Poverty

Globalization, as described by its proponents, will save the Third World by sharing the wealth of developed nations through unlimited and unfettered trade. As wealth spreads, so too better living and working conditions for the world's poor. "They" will—the free traders hope—become more like "us."

Michael Kelly, editor of the *Atlantic Monthly* and columnist for the *Washington Post Writers Group,* declares the promise of global wealth-sharing a "fat herring of the reddest hue." Kelly maintains that globalization, nearly synonymous with free trade, is not about democracy and justice for all, but about profits. In a recent news article, Kelly discusses George W. Bush's unscripted perspective on Free Trade of the Americas: ". . . Bush said the agreement certainly must not contain 'codicils to destroy the spirit of free trade.' He added: 'While I understand that some unionists are interested in making sure there's labor protections, I don't want those labor protections to be used to destroy the free trade agreement.'"[30] Well I guess as long as we're not protecting indigenous rights we as may as well not protect indigent laborers working in sweatshops.

Kelly goes on to point out that this is a problem for U.S. laborers too. As higher-paying jobs migrate to lower-paying markets—through mergers, downsizing, and job exportation—the cost to the nation in unemployment may be severe.

The odds, however, least favor developing nations. The World Trade Organization exerts the tremendous coercive force of financial penalties and trade sanctions over the third world. This is a cost that developing nations, heavily indebted to the World Bank, can ill afford. Brand enforcement, as outlined and promulgated by INTA, comes with the consequences of these WTO penalties. Korten states, "Cases may also be brought against countries that attempt to give preferential treatment to local over foreign investors or that fail to protect the intellectual property rights (patents and copyrights) of foreign companies. Local interests are no longer a valid basis for local laws under the new WTO regime. The interests of international trade, which are primarily the interests of transnational corporations, take priority."[31]

The WTO does not prevent monopolies, corporate takeovers, or require higher safety or quality standards in exports/imports. The WTO only enacted more stringent intellection property agreements.[32]

Beyond and Behind

Graphic designers have argued convincingly for our field's continued relevance in the wake of the Macintosh and the World Wide Web. But the alliances we formed before, during, and after these "crises" warrant closer analysis and debate. There are various co-requisites to this agenda. For instance, we need to stop "greening-up" polluters, putting a socially conscious face on sweatshop owners, and using healthy-looking images for chemically preserved and/or genetically engineered foods. Our audience is more than just a target market. Hopefully our discussions will examine the socio-cultural milieus that surround our practice. Such initiatives will enable us to see beyond and behind the client.

I am not saying, however, that we need to step out of the realm of doing business with corporations. I'm saying we need to know that these transnationals will do business fairly. We can ensure this goal by supporting corporate and small business advocates of fair trade. We can also look for new outlets: alternative entrepreneurial ventures and programs for civil society entities, e.g., non-profits. Adversarial design is also coming to the fore in curatorial ventures, like Kenneth Fitzgerald's recent traveling exhibition, *Adversary*, which features new voices of dissent within the field.[33] While I laud these efforts, many more strategies for effecting change reside outside our purview. Members of the Pro-Democracy Movement, such as David Korten and contributors to *New Internationalist* magazine, take great pains to not only describe the problems but suggest specific, peaceful methods for their resolution. Your local Peace and Justice Center will also have this information. Graphic design does, however, possess problem posing and solving strategies that can be used to establish new responses in conjunction with anti-globalization initiatives.

Social activism now equals global responsibility. What we do as designers is becoming more and more a global act: whether we're talking about Web or brand design for transnational corporations. Importantly, our productions are not limited to the bounds of any one given nation-state or cultural milieu. We can tell ourselves that we're just one small piece of the puzzle; in which case we need a good look at the picture on the box.

Rick Poyner, in *Emigre* 51, discusses a prior call to question the use of design skills for brand development: the First Things First manifesto, originally published in 1963. He points out that Ken Garland, the manifesto's author, admittedly was not trying to change "the underlying political and economic system."[34] Garland did not see this as a feasible task. Obviously, though, we cannot successfully change our position within the system without analyzing systemic problems and advocating for their abolition. Just like the advertising industry censured by Garland and his fellow signatories, there is nothing "natural" about globalization, and hence there is nothing inevitable about it either. Likewise, there's nothing natural about our servitude to questionable corporations, and there's nothing inevitable about it either.

Incidentally, Poyner mentions that the First Things First manifesto debuted at a point of increased confidence in graphic design's growing professionalization.[35] Its re-issuance, by Rudy Vanderlans over three years ago, came at a time of design's strengthening global reach.

Our students need to be critical thinkers more than ever. They should consider, as Johanna Drucker so aptly states, "In whose interest and to what ends."[36] They need the skills to uncover the gears behind the curtain. And they need the self-determination, confidence, and non-fatalistic vision to choose the best-tailored career.

When opposing interests, viewpoints, and ideologies come into contact, absurd things occur. One side of the dichotomy, for instance, may not even be aware of the other to any meaningful extent. Peacefully and equitably acquainting opposing forces is not something the human race does well. We tend to get that one wrong more times than not. Through responsible and reasoned attention to such absurdities, we might just be able to make some sense.

Notes

1. News item selected from Suzanne Leclerc-Madlala, "Here's the Beef," *New Internationalist*, no. 280 (1996): *www.oneworld.org/ni/issue280/endpiece.htm*.

2. News item selected from David C. Korten, *When Corporations Rule the World* (San Francisco: Berrett-Koehler Publishers, Inc. and Kumarian Press, 2001), 156–157.

3. Rick Poynor, "First Things First Revisited," *Emigre* 51 (summer 1999): 3.

4. U.S. House Committee on the Judiciary, *The Patent and Trademark Office Corporation Act and the United States Intellectual Property Organization*, report prepared by The International Trademark Association, 8 March 1996. Visit *www.house.gov/judiciary/406.htm* to view the document.

5. International Trademark Association (INTA), *TM Basics: Brand Valuation* (2001): *www.inta.org/basics/ip/valuation/shtml*.

6. Tony Clarke, "Rewriting the Rules," *New Internationalist*, no. 320 (2000): *www.oneworld.org/ni/issue320/rules.htm*.

7. INTA, *Free Trade of the Americas Draft Agreement: Chapter on Intellectual Property Rights*, prepared by the FTAA Subcommittee (2001): 6–9.

8. INTA, *Developing Countries: Compliance with the TRIPS Agreement*, prepared by the TRIPS 2000 Subcommittee, Treaty Analysis Committee (1999): 8–19.

9. INTA, *Federal Trade Area of The Americas Draft Agreement*, prepared by the FTAA Subcommittee (2001): 10.

10. Trademark laws also pose serious threats to U.S. civil liberties. For an excellent and succinct discussion of the problem, see Jennifer B. Reiter, *Trademark Anti-Dilution Laws as Cultural Censorship* (2001): *www.fed-soc.org/ip010203.htm*. See also Michael Schmidt, "Operation Snowstorm: How Brands Ate the World," *News of the Whirled*, no. 3 (2001): 60–67. If you can't find a copy, call me and I'll mail you one.

11. Korten, 4–5.

12. Loretta Staples, The Readers Respond "Less is More 2000 Or Who Needs 'Design'?" *Emigre* 52 (fall 1999).

13. Johanna Drucker, "Talking Theory/Teaching Practice," in *The Education of a Graphic Designer*, ed. Steven Heller (New York: Allworth Press, 1998), 85.

14. Ellen Lupton, *Mixing Messages: Graphic Design in Contemporary Culture* (New York: Princeton Architectural Press, 1996).

15. Korten, 167.

16. Milan Kundera, *Immortality* (New York: Grove Press, Inc., 1991), 113.

17. Noam Chomsky, *Media Control: The Spectacular Achievements of Propaganda*, ed. Greg Ruggiero and Stuart Sahulka, The Open Media Pamphlet Series (New York: Seven Stories Press), 7–9 & 17–18.

18. William E. Daugherty and Morris Janowitz, *A Psychological Warfare Casebook* (Baltimore: The Johns Hopkins Press, 1958), 138.

19. Korten, 155.

20. Paul M. A. Linebarger, *Psychological Warfare*, International Propaganda and Communications Series (New York: Arno Press, 1972), 13.

21. Andrew Blauvelt, *Emigre* 33 (winter 1995): 5.

22. Plumb Line Enterprises Company, LTD., *www.plumbline-ent.com*.

23. See *www.sapient.com*.

24. In 1979 the World Intellectual Property Organization (WIPO)—a specialized agency of the United Nations—made INTA a non-governmental observer. According to INTA literature (INTA, *History* [*www.inta.org/about/history.shtml*]) "This status has allowed INTA to participate in diplomatic conferences and meetings of committees of experts as well as smaller, less formal meetings. More recently, INTA has taken a more active role in WIPO studies and activities in order to significantly influence WIPO's trademark-related initiatives."

    Year 2000 INTA board members were from Shell Oil Company, Warner Brothers, and Kraft. Year 2001 officer listings were pulled from their Web site at the date of this writing. INTA reinforced its influence in 1999 by officially deciding to declare itself a U.S. Political Action Committee.

25. Mishawaka Rubber & Woolen Mfg. Co. v. S.S. Kresge Co., 316 U.S. 203 (1942). This passage was used in one of INTA's 1996 statements to the Committee on the Judiciary of the U.S. House of Representatives. House Committee on the Judiciary, *Trademark Provisions Act: Hearings on H.R. 2740*, 1996. The case docket is available at *www.supremecourtus.gov/opinions/casefinder/casefinder_1926-1948.html*. To review testimonies before the House Judiciary by INTA and other like-minded organizations, see *www.house.gov/judiciary/4.htm*.

26. Law firm of Graham & Dunn, PC. *www.grahamdunn.com/whatsnew/articles/4a/right.htm*.

27. Korten, 161–162.

28. Chomsky, 17–18.

29. While the WTO may operate in secrecy, trade advisory groups, like the International Trade Association, must make their dealings with WTO public due to the Federal Advisory Committee Act of 1972 (Korten, 169). By walking through a few back doors, it is possible to learn a great deal about WTO initiatives.

30. Michael Kelly, "Secret is Out: Globalization is about profits, not democracy," *The (Memphis) Commercial Appeal*, 26 April 2001, 9(A).

31. Korten, 168.

32. Korten, 172.

33. Daniela Marx and Tuan Phan, recent graduates from CalArts, are included in the *Adversary* exhibition. Their work is both parasitic and virulent in its attack of unscrupulous corporations. They have also constructed course curricula for socially conscious design. Daniela Marx and Tuan Phan, interview by author, Memphis, TN, spring 2001.

34. Poynor, 3.

35. Poynor, 2.

36. Drucker, 85.

Usability Expert
Steven Heller Interviews Don Norman

Don Norman is a technology enthusiast annoyed by the unnecessary complexity of today's products. His goal is to humanize technology, to make it disappear from sight, replaced by a human-centered, activity-based family of information appliances that are easy to learn, easy to use. He argues that the technological problems today are sociological and organizational as much as technical. In this new age of portable, powerful, fully communicating tools, it is ever more important to develop a humane technology, one that takes into account the needs and capabilities of people. Norman is not merely an advocate, he is a feisty agitator. This professor emeritus at the University of California and former Apple executive is currently leading a "distributed-learning company (Unext.com), the goal of which is to create powerful learning communities that marry the world's most respected academic scholars and institutions with the global reach and interactive capabilities of the Internet." He also consults with The Nielson Norman Group, to help industry change its ways. Norman's books, *The Design of Everyday Things* and *Things That Make Us Smart*, should be required reading in this age of over-complexity and redundancy. During the Florida ballot fiasco Norman was called upon as an expert witness on why so many things do not work. In this interview he explains his mission as he waves the red flag.

SH: How did you become a usability expert?

DN: I was a cognitive scientist at the University of California, San Diego, studying, among other things, human error. As a result I was called in to look at some accidents [nuclear power and aviation]. I soon realized that the accidents were the result of bad design—if the designers had wanted to cause human error, they could not have done better.

This led me on a quest to understand why design fails the people who must use it. Thus, when I look at the curriculum of noted schools of design, it is rare to find anything at all about how to understand the people who will use, read, or otherwise make use of the designs. See, for example, *http://design.schoolofvisualarts. edu/curr_program.html.*

Why do people make errors? That is a nonsensical question. Human error is an entirely invented term. In the real world, we don't err. We approximate. Language and motor skills are wonderful at adapting to changes, to getting closer and closer to the desired outcome. Do we err when we walk along a weaving path? Of course not—that is how people walk. It is only when engineers and designers require us to walk in straight lines that we call the behavior erroneous—so too with almost every place where people err.

Do we err at arithmetic? Of course. Arithmetic is an artificial skill, not one well suited for the human mind (that's why I champion calculators to do the arithmetic for us). Do we err at precision? Of course. That's not a biological necessity—it is only an engineered and designed necessity.

Society has invented machines and designs that require inhuman acts. We require precise numerical precision from the human body that did not evolve with precision. We create fanciful print displays that are delightful and fun—especially for the designer—but that are difficult or impossible to read.

How did I become a usability expert? I rebelled against the arbitrary nature of engineering, of design. I determined it was time to put the human foremost into the equation. That is why I have written my books, taught my students, and championed human-centered design. I am now a trustee of the Institute of Design in Chicago. Maybe I can have an impact in design curricula. Hurrah hurrah.

SH: Design came to the fore of America's consciousness with the 2000 election butterfly ballot. Tell me, why are such problematic things designed in the first place? Is someone asleep at the wheel? Or is the design done by nondesigners?

DN: No it didn't. Design has long been in our consciousness. Look at automobiles, look at architecture, look at furniture. Industrial design has long been considered to be essential to product success—look at the annual *Business Week* awards.

The butterfly ballot simply points out what happens when you neglect human psychology. The ballot was designed by well-meaning amateurs who never considered testing the resulting ballots (and probably didn't know how to do such a test). The ballot machinery was designed to save money, not to maximize accuracy.

Is the design done by nondesigners? Yes. But, most designers would do worse. Designers learn about aesthetics. They seldom learn about human psychology, about the need to do iterative design with a repeated cycle of watching people at work, determining requirements, doing a rough prototype, testing the rough prototype, then refining the design by watching, predetermining requirements, doing a new prototype, and retesting. The cycle can be done in one day. Any design schools teach this? I thought not.

Most designers are just as guilty as nondesigners. It is not their fault—it is the fault of the design schools.

SH: You are right, design schools are lax about addressing the end-user and examining how products work in society. There are very few classes that I know about, including my own (which you cite above) that overtly and intensely do what you do, and what you propose. But isn't usability and functionality implicit in any design program where the goal is indeed utility? How can this be taught better?

DN: In my experience, an item does not receive the proper attention and concern unless it is explicit, unless conscious attention is paid to the issue. Things that are not conscious— that are "implicit"—are things ignored. If you want to do something right, you have to attend to it. Can design be taught? Of course. Can design for usability be taught? Of course. Can design that emphasizes functionality be taught? Of course. Note, however, these are three different things. Emphasis on usability does not mean that the result provides anything of value. Emphasis on functionality does not mean that the result is usable. Emphasis on usability and functionality does not mean that the result is aesthetically pleasing, or manufacturable, or cost-effective. Every dimension is important. Each must be considered explicitly and consciously. Each must be taught explicitly and consciously.

SH: The butterfly ballot is not the only poorly designed ballot. We have quality standards for so many things, why can't our most valuable right be protected?

DN: Alas, the prevailing opinion is that if someone uses a piece of equipment or software improperly, it is the person's fault. So the designer walks away smugly saying, "Well, if you can't use it right, you shouldn't be using it." Bad attitude is the real culprit.

Note how many people said that those who voted wrongly in Florida were just stupid voters.

Bad attitude and a lack of consideration for people is the major culprit.

Probably you do the same. When you turn on the wrong burner on your stove, you probably blame yourself. In fact, it is the bad design of the stove controls that should be blamed.

SH: You are an advocate of good design. But what is the definition of good design when applied to everyday things? Is good design a priori simple design?

DN: Is good design a priori simple? Of course not. In fact, the simplest looking designs are often the most complex to produce. I own a Michael Graves "Nana" teapot. It isn't simple, it is bizarre. I love it—it is great design.

SH: What do you mean by "design"? Aesthetics? Practicality? Manufacturability? Usability? Cost?

DN: All are part of design.

SH: Can good design be governmentally legislated?

DN: Of course it can. You can mandate anything: good sex, good food, good books, good baseball. It's silly, but governments often do silly things.

If usability and functionality are to be legislated, it should be in the form of performance requirements. Thus, the proper way is not to force design guidelines that unnaturally constrain the designers. Instead they should force performance requirements, such as: 99 percent of people should be able to perform the task with less than two minutes instruction, with an error rate less than X. I favor performance specifications for situations that are critical. I favor hands-off for the rest.

SH: My design school teaches students to be aware of what the public needs and doesn't need. Do they test their products on real people? Not often. Does this process start in school or should it start elsewhere?

DN: Although this process should clearly start in school, I am bothered by having someone else determine what I need or don't need. Do I need the Graves Nana teapot? Of course not. Do I like it? Yup. Do I need reality shows on television? Of course not. Do I get it? Yup.

SH: In advocating good design as a solution to unnecessary mistakes, where in your equation is user fallibility?

DN: On the side of the angels. Humans are fallible. Learn that. Cherish that. It is a fact of life. We people are creative, exciting, adventurous, imaginative, artistic, emotional, musical. And fallible.

Design for people as they are, not as you would have them be. Design for inefficient users. Design for fallible users. Design for creative, imaginative people who will do things with your design that you never dreamed of, things both good and horrid. Design for people who are tired and stressed, cranky and irritable, sloppy and inattentive. In other words, design for real people.

SH: Can good design actually be infallible enough to mitigate the human element?

DN: Of course.

SH: Do you believe, as I do, that the designers of instruction manuals make confounding guides? In other words, are there built-in handicaps for usability, and, if so, why?

DN: Those who write instruction manuals know what it is like to be in hell. They are given unusable objects and told to write clear, intelligible instructions. And, of course, they must also heed the legal warnings. They have an impossible job.

Want to know what designers of manuals should do? They should design and write the manual before the product is designed. Make the manual simple and elegant. Then insist that the designers build it the way they have described it. Then we might actually get usable products. And simple manuals.

The best-designed products won't even need manuals.

SH: When we talk about poor usability we refer to windows that don't open, VCRs that are too complex, toys that have too many parts. Other than the butterfly ballot, in your experience, what graphic designs would you say are user-unfriendly?

DN: What graphic designs are user-unfriendly? Almost any graphic design that wins a prize. Any graphic design that is intended to impress design colleagues and design judges rather than to be used by people.

SH: This raises the issue of Web site and interface design. In the past, a poster or brochure performed two tasks, to attract the eye (style, aesthetics) and convey a message. Of course, as you imply, sometimes these are at odds in overly designed graphics. Today, on the one hand, designers are applying a lot of quirky typographic styles to Web pages. But on the other, many Web pages (i.e., Excite.com, Amazon.com, Inside.com) are packed with text. What is desirable? What is most useable? How can the Web be made more efficient?

DN: I don't want to judge a Web site unless I know the goal of that site. Quirky typographic styles have their place. Yes, they are hard to read, yes, they are hard to use, but they display interesting design ethics. They are part of the exploration of art, to push the boundaries of what is possible, to cause people to think anew, to view the world differently.

But if the site is for a business, trying to attract customers, then the rules differ. First of all, we don't need to attract the eye in quite the same way as in a poster. With a poster, you want someone to look at it. With a Web page, well, the person is already there. Presumably they went there voluntarily. So you don't need to attract their attention—you already have it. Now is the time to provide real value. To answer questions, to make the trip worthwhile. Excite, Amazon, Inside, Yahoo have all discovered that packing the Web site with lots of information is what their viewers want, just as newspapers cram multiple stories onto page one. Is this ugly? Perhaps. Is this desirable? It all depends upon the audience you are trying to work with, to keep happy, to cause them to return. Is it efficient? Who cares? People are not efficient, so I do not know what it means to want an efficient Web site. Mind you, I do want one that does not waste my time, that delivers what I want. But mind you, sometimes what I want is fun, excitement, art, or entertainment.

Exercise: Go back to that Web site for the design school: *http://design. schoolofvisualarts.edu/curr_program.html*. Does this excite you, answer your questions, and make it obvious why you are there and what you will learn? Nope. The designers of this Web site may know about visual design but they do not understand people.

How can we make a Web site better? Design for the people who will be using it.

SH: If you had all the power in the world to effect universal usability, how would you wield it?

DN: I would train designers, engineers, and computer scientists differently. This way, we might solve the problems right at the source.

Designers and Architects
Cheryl Towler Weese Interviews Stanley Tigerman

Stanley Tigerman is an architect and partner at Tigerman McCurry Architects, and an educator and the director of Archeworks. The following is an excerpt from a conversation about the responsibilities of designers and architects held in July 2000.

CTW: I'd like to frame this interview as a call to action—your manifesto, let's say, on ethics and morality. What would you say the designer's moral obligations are? To him or herself, to the client, to the user, to society?

ST: What a huge question!

I think that you're obligated to everyone—to yourself, your client, the user, and society—and particularly to society. The problem comes up when there's a conflict between these groups. I don't want to overstate architecture's noble state, which is not so noble anymore, but architecture's about conflict resolution. Let me give you an example. When I went to graduate school, to Yale, I didn't apply to Columbia but I read their application. This is 1958—the time of Batista in Cuba, pre-Castro—and Columbia's application had three unusual questions.

The first question was, "Would you design a weekend house for Batista?" Interesting question. The second was, "If a municipality asked you to design housing in the inner city at an unreasonable density, would you do it?" And the third was, "Would you design a concentration camp?" Given the state of the American Institute of Architects today, they would say yes to all three questions—because they're into marketing.[1]

What do you do when somebody asks you to do something you know is wrong? (This happens all the time.) When I worked at Skidmore, Owings & Merrill, I moonlit at night. My first wife's brother was a homebuilder, and he asked me to do the drawings for some bullshit project, and I did. And he—this is an incredible story, actually—he didn't want to put rigid insulation in the foundation wall below grade because it couldn't be seen by the buyer. But architecture's supposed to be an ethical enterprise. Otherwise, why wouldn't you go to a builder? What the hell do you need an architect for? Isn't the architect supposed to protect you from that sort of behavior? And if the architect doesn't, what on earth is his or her role?

I think the idea of an ethical enterprise—architecture as a moral proposition— is key. First of all, the rest doesn't sustain you: the *business* of architecture is bull-shit. Sure, you have to pay rent—money is a necessary priority in a capitalist society. But money won't sustain your interest for more than half a century. Sure, there are architects that practice for that reason. But if you want to go into business, like my son who's a rich investment banker, you should go into something that will earn you tons of money.

Then there's the *profession* of architecture. What's so great about that? The word "profession" is etymologically problematic. "Pro"-fession means that you're doing it for a return: if you're a professional athlete, you get paid. The etymology of the word "amateur," where you do something for love, is better.

Then there's the *art* of architecture, going up the rungs of the ladder. The art of architecture has been a problem for decades. It's increasingly arcane; it's only for the cognoscenti. At one level that's fabulous—but at another level "art" becomes laden with jargon and is consciously off-putting, and keeps people out.

So what are you left with? The *discipline* of architecture, like a monastic discipline. That's where you practice the way a Benedictine or Jesuit monk or Talmudic scholar would. At yeshivas, schools for studying the Torah, the saying goes, "It's sufficient to read the Torah." You never have to *do* anything about it; just reading it is sufficient. That's interesting to me—just practicing the piano, or "practicing" architecture is sufficient. And that, for me, is the highest calling: the discipline of architecture.

There are monks, the Cistercian monks that Umberto Eco describes in *The Name of the Rose*, that sit there and copy the Bible. But they know they will err. You can't copy the whole Bible and not make an error—you have to have a total, Tiger Woods kind of concentration on one thing. That's the *discipline* of architecture. That's what makes it great. *Focus.*

And that's where morality and ethics come into play. Obviously, moral issues in the business of architecture aren't worth spit, and in the profession of architecture aren't worth a lot more, because the AIA has dropped its ethics laws. Isn't that interesting? And then, there's the art of architecture, which is so arcane; you know morality doesn't come into play.

CTW: Why don't aesthetics and morality overlap? Or why can't they?

ST: Well, they can, but not when they become hermetic, and so are only for the seventeen other people who understand what you're talking about. . . . I'll you a great story; it's absolutely germane. Years ago I worked on a number of projects in what was East Pakistan, now Bangladesh. There was a war of liberation in 1971: The Betsy Ross of East Pakistan sewed a flag, and the opposition leader proclaimed that they were free. Repression ensued, supported by the United States and Pakistan, in an attempt to keep the people down and kill off the intelligentsia. And I was designing projects there. One of my guys in the field was killed, others were beaten, and I had basically had it—I was going to resign the commission.

The night before I left, Bruce Graham (formerly the head of Skidmore, Owings & Merrill) and I met at a party in Lake Forest, and he asked, "What are you working on?" I said, "I'm going to Dhaka tomorrow to resign a commission because of everything that's happened there." And he said, "That's the most stupid thing I've ever heard—they're only going to hire somebody worse than you. You have to stay; you're an architect." It's very hard to argue with Bruce, who's deterministic, shall we say. So I bowed my head, and went the next day to Dhaka to resign. A few months passed, the Bengalis won the war, but the World Bank was furious with me for abandoning the commission. The Bengalis wanted to reinstate me, but the World Bank refused. Then the Bengalis said, "No, you don't understand. We want him back"—and the World Bank eventually capitulated. So I returned, and finished the project.

Another six months passed, and I saw Bruce Graham at a party (this is an incredible story; this'll tell you something about architecture). He said, "Now, aren't you glad that you paid attention and did what I told you to do?" He appropriated what I did—which was exactly the reverse of what he had said—as his own idea. In other words, the end justifies the means; the bottom line counts. Right? But when there are conflicts, you can't just cave to every client's whim. How do you say no and still get it built? Perhaps that's as good a definition of architecture as anything else.

John Entenza, the first director of the Graham Foundation, once introduced Mies van der Rohe by saying, "Here is an architect who has to will his buildings into existence." He had to work against the status quo, an inertia that didn't consider skeletal frames to be finished buildings. How did Mies do that? He had to have a resolute core to persuade people.

CTW: That idea of a resolute core is related to personal expression. Can personal expression and ethics collide in a positive way?

ST: Well, they can collide or they can merge. If they collide, we're back to conflict resolution. Artists engage in the same crap as the rest of the civilian population—their morality can give way to other needs that obsess them. How do you lead a balanced life? And if you do have to make a Solomonic decision—a wise choice— what is it based upon? I would submit that it's not rooted in artistic, professional, or business decision making. I think it's based on higher values. For example, the idea of building well; not building with crap, drywall, and two-by-fours. You've got to build well, because building well is building ethically.

There's a wonderful rabbi I know named Jose Faür, who teaches at a yeshiva in Jerusalem opposite the West Wall. We were having lunch after a lecture at the Spertus when he said, "You know, I really like what you're doing in Archeworks.[2] I like architecture when it's thought about well," he said; "it's the only way we have of communicating with God."

At that point I wondered, What is he talking about? I thought Judaism was rooted in the oral and written word, and that the debate between humankind and the divine being was rooted there. And he said, "No, the slipperiness of language is no longer sufficient evidence of moral behavior. You have to make something, and make it well in order to communicate with God."

I've got to tell you, Cheryl, I was blown away. I think that making things really well, uncompromisingly, is very hard to do. Jesus Christ, it's hard to build at all. Even a crappy building is hard to build, because it flies in the face of inertia. You take a primal site that's never been built upon. The neighbors have appropriated it as communal land. You could build a really lousy building and it would create a huge fight. To build a good building is only harder.

CTW: So what does it mean to build well?

ST: To make sure the buildings—I'm going to say some stupid-sounding things—don't leak, don't torque, don't act strangely. They should last; they should look good many years later. That's building well.

CTW: They should function, and should be made with care.

ST: Making something with care—that's more impressive than making beauty out of crap, because you can make beautiful things that will fail. It's very hard to make something well, because clients always want more than they can afford. Always. How do you persuade them to build less and build well? I don't have an answer to that.

CTW: Does it have to do with who you choose to work for? And can you tell when a client is immoral?

ST: Well, I'm an old guy now. As you age, you're supposed to hone your insight and intuition. The question is, do you use those abilities, or do you bury your head in the sand? You have to look carefully, as you and I are looking at each other now. Doesn't guarantee that you'll make the right choices, but there's a pretty good chance of it, because as you get older you're supposed to know that stuff.

CTW: Are there architects or designers who exemplify ethical practice?

ST: Endless numbers. John Hejduk, who was the dean at Cooper Union and recently died, was absolutely an ethical being, and he operated in a discreet, moral way. I'd also say, with the exception of the way Mies treated women, Mies van der Rohe. The way Mies treated his profession, the discipline of architecture, was exemplary.

CTW: What made it exemplary?

ST: Well, he built well. We live in 910 Lake Shore Drive, in a Mies building built in 1955. It looks brand new—it's impeccable. What architect can say their work looks impeccable forty-five years later?

CTW: Now Hejduk and Mies, you could argue, are both theoreticians. Do theory and ethics overlap?

ST: Sure. I think you have to have an attitude, a goal, a strategy. You have to ask, "What can I make of myself?" Most people just go to work, take down a salary, and go bowling, metaphorically speaking. How do you choose personal goals, and how do you manifest those goals? Tiger Woods is exemplary, because he focuses on one shot at a time. Total focus. Do you know how many decisions—well, graphic design is like architecture—how many decisions designers make every day?

CTW: A million.

ST: An endless number. You don't just design; you cull and pick. A number of factors help you design: what you're doing and why you're doing it, the project's budget, location, and context. But those don't add up to 100 percent. There are two unstated influences: the eye of the beholder, the client, and the eye of the author, the designer. Both count.

I treat clients and employees the same way. My process is simple: I only hire staff I like and clients I like. If I don't like a client and accept a commission, there's going to be trouble. And if I hire somebody just because they're talented, there's going to be trouble.

You can determine a client's pretensions quickly. I don't always choose the right clients. And when I choose the wrong ones, I don't want to fire them, because I'm the one that made the mistake. So I behave badly, and cause them to fire me. Then they feel better: "I got rid of that sonavubitch." (You know my reputation in any case, Cheryl; I'm not an easy guy.) But you have to use your intuition, and hone it all the time. And you do hone it as you make decisions.

CTW: But don't you also have to have a personal compass, a personal theory?

ST: Ethical beliefs.

CTW: But do those translate into design values? Values that dictate how you should approach design?

ST: Sure. I don't have a magical formula, because although I believe in building well, everything has a finite lifespan. The problem occurs when you pander to that condition of mortality. In other words, if you accept a client who wants more than what they can afford, they're going to build less well. That's a problem. But I don't want to just focus this on building well. I think decisions about who to work for are equally critical.

Back to those three questions from Columbia's architectural application: Who will you work for, and do you ever say no? Are you just, as Frank Lloyd Wright called himself while working for Louis Sullivan, another person's "pencil?" Are you simply the client's tool?

There's a book by Elaine Hochman called *Architects of Fortune: Mies van der Rohe and the Third Reich* that describes how Mies wanted to displace Albert Speer, Hitler's chief architect.

CTW: Wait—how does Mies then qualify as a moral architect?

ST: Because mortal beings are complex . . . Mies read everything. When he lived in Germany, he was said to have had a library of thousands of books. When he left to come to IIT in '37, the SS allowed him to bring thirty books. These were thirty really serious books. They weren't picture books—they were books by St. Augustine and St. Thomas Aquinas, among others. If you know your theology, Augustine and Aquinas are contrapuntal. St. Thomas Aquinas got into a lot of trouble in twelfth-century Paris because he interpreted and challenged faith. St. Augustine believed in pure faith, which is what Christianity is about. You see both belief systems in Mies's work. His lack of resolution at the corner of a building is about interpretation, right? And his continuous use of the golden section is about faith. The problem is, you're supposed to be modest—and Mies was not. He knew he was the best living architect in Germany, and that Speer was nowhere near as qualified, so he felt he should be Hitler's architect. He only moved to the U.S. when he finally, grudgingly, accepted that Hitler wouldn't hire him. But within the discipline of architecture, he was an entirely moral man.

Mies's books are the basis of a book I'm writing about ethics and morality in architecture. George Moore, in England, wrote about the "good," and asked: Is "good" intrinsic, or is it separate from the subject it addresses? Moore believed good is absolutely of itself; that it's axiomatic. And using that logic, I think Mies was an exemplary figure because he thought deeply about issues of faith. Now, did that make him a perfect being? Hardly. But the fact that he thought about those issues separates him from 99.9 percent of all architects, who don't ever think or read about those things.

CTW: Are there authors, philosophers, or theologians you would recommend particularly?

ST: In Western theology, I'd read Saints Thomas Aquinas and Augustine, because they represent polar positions of faith and interpretation. At any given moment, we all act according to one or the other of those positions—and one is always best seen in view of the other, as black is perceived best in the presence of white. I would add Jacques Derrida, Jacques Lacan, and Julia Kristeva, who write about issues of our time. And I'd include contemporary spiritual leaders like Jose Faür, who's brilliant.

I have a library of six thousand books, but it's been fifteen years since I attempted to buy an architecture book. I simply don't read them any longer. Instead, I began reading philosophy, which segued into reading theology. And that's what I do now. The architecture library I might as well sell.

CTW: What's wrong with contemporary design and architecture, and what would a more ethical approach improve?

ST: Well, I would separate design and architecture. I don't find as much wrong with industrial and graphic design—and I'm not pandering to you because you're a graphic designer. You don't have as much baggage as architects do. Architects have the burden of history, language, and precedent. The problem with history is that it confers legitimacy. An architect like Robert Stern uses history to legitimize his work. It was done before, so therefore . . .

CTW: Happens in graphic design, too.

ST: I'm sure—designers and architect share the same schizophrenia. In 1923, Mies said that architecture is the will of an age translated into space. That means that you're bound to represent your time. But there's an equal and opposing theory that says architects are supposed to show you a better way.

CTW: And both are true?

ST: Yes. You are obligated to reflect your time, and you are equally obligated to show a better way.

CTW: But historicism doesn't play into either theory.

ST: No—when your work reflects its time, historicism is always present. There's no question that history, and the theory emanating from history, are of value. You're placed on the planet, Cheryl, only to find a better way? There is no precedent? I don't think so. But are you only there to extend precedent infinitesimally? Again, I don't think so. How do you come to grips with these two mutually exclusive ideals? You have to have a value system. And that value system must be informed by moral and ethical truths, or it becomes insubstantial.

CTW: So that would be your charge to young designers?

ST: My charge to young designers . . . Make no mistake, I'm all for beautiful things. Archeworks makes beautiful things for those who need it most, for those who never get good design. But beauty is, as one is reminded, in the eye of the beholder. What is more substantial than beauty? The larger reason you should work with people in need is self-explanatory: I think one is never too young to give back. You, and people of your generation, if you're trying to get body and soul together to buy a house, that's just about you, you, and you. You still can give back, though most people don't do shit. If you want to give back, you need to think of the commonweal, and where you can help most.

CTW: Does doing good require self-examination—figuring out what you're good at?

ST: Yes. At Archeworks, we deal with heart-rending subjects, and it's easy as a designer—because you're also a human being—to be overwhelmed by them, which hampers your abilities. You need to contribute your education and expertise. Shoemakers make shoes; I don't know how to make shoes.

In yesterday's *Tribune* I read about a young couple who are plastic surgeons: they do cleft palates, and so on, free for three weeks, a couple times a year. Fabulous, fabulous—just imagine if every plastic surgeon did that. Imagine what would happen if graphic designers worked with their communities. Archeworks did a graphic program for the West Humboldt Park Development Corporation to make them look good and feel good about themselves. Now that's a great project. They could sit down with a banker and wouldn't look like a poor, struggling community organization, of which there are zillions. It provided collective self-esteem, and Jesus Christ, that's important. Why don't you do some of that—you specifically, personally? In tandem with this interview, why doesn't your editorial group do that? Why isn't it one of the AIGA's primary focuses, to go out and do that?

CTW: The AIGA actually does help serve the disadvantaged . . .

ST: But you see what I'm saying.

CTW: So what would that do for the world?

ST: Oh, God. It would be a much better place—*if* we used our expertise, preferably in tandem with others. Now, you can question like crazy not just what gets done, but the process by which it comes about. This is an interactive time, I'll give you that. But sometimes it's difficult talking to other people—things get deferred, and decisions aren't made. Don't be held hostage to indecision, or engage in endless foreplay: get going. Figure it out. Do something.

I don't want to sound like the heroic figure who has all the answers; I don't have better answers than any other guy. I just think you've got to figure out what the questions are, have a moral program, and act accordingly.

Notes

1. See Tigerman's op-ed article in the June 2000 issue of *Architectural Record*, which is co-published by the AIA.

2. Tigerman is cofounder and director of Archeworks, which he describes as "alternative education, with no prerequisites and no tenure. It's a one-year post-professional course for practicing architects, for interior, graphic, and industrial designers, and others (though credit is occasionally given to students from other institutions). The student body is broken into three teams who work on actual, useful projects, rather than academic ones. Last year, for example, one team worked on Alzheimer's, another on affordable, accessible housing, and a third worked with Illinois's Department of Human Services to rethink the image they project." Eva Maddox is Archeworks's cofounder and the school's project and program director.

*Originally published in the volume 13, number 2, 2001 issue of in*Form, *the journal of the Chicago chapter of the American Institute of Graphic Arts.*

Part III

Artistic Responsibility

"Beautility"
Good Design Has Utility
Tucker Viemeister

Design is about two things: creating beauty and fulfilling our destiny as humans to make things better. Trying to make our environment more pleasant than it is *naturally* drives human *progress*.

Good (or bad) design is what separates humans from all other forms of life. Design is *premeditated action*. Dogs or monkeys may act like designers, but they don't really plan ahead, think in abstract concepts, dress themselves, move the furniture around, or create new economic initiatives. Humans realized a long time ago that things happen either by choice or by chance, and that if they were smart enough (or strong enough) they could tip events to their favor. With forethought, we make better choices and avoid accidents. What homo sapiens have been doing for the last 500,000 years (or so) is hopefully making things turn out better, i.e., work better, look better, feel better for everyone. It takes so long because of two problems: 1) one person's idea of "better" is not necessarily someone else's; and 2) unforeseen consequences. No matter what happens to the environment, we'll continue changing things, making things, doing things, and trying to fix the mistakes.

The union of what we *think* and making it *real* is design. We try to make things work better and look better. But why think of utility and beauty separately? It's the combination that's powerful. I have now reunited them in the term "beautility"—

the convergence of ethics and aesthetics. Putting a name to this concept allows people to talk about it and it makes it easier for them to appreciate the value.

Americans make beauty a second-class priority. Clear the forest, put up a barn, build the highway, "Eat your dinner, *then* you can have dessert." The Puritan in us keeps saying, "Beauty is a luxury." Beauty is called shallow and superficial; we don't want to admit publicly that beauty is important. Beautility is a new way of moving beauty away from the frivolous, to something that serves a function, and that, in turn, elevates it to the bottom line (where things really count in America!).

Beauty has utility. It makes us feel good. It serves a practical purpose in our lives. Being around something that is beautiful stimulates us intellectually, emotionally, and sensually—a multimedia experience! It is the fuel that keeps humanity moving ahead.

Maslow created his hierarchy of human needs a long time ago and didn't take into consideration the needs and desires of modern Americans. So I've made a new one. It's 2002: Imagine the suburbanite at the base level "surviving" in a house, with a refrigerator, and a car. To reach the next level he needs to get comfortable in a La-Z-Boy recliner, a beer, and a remote controller—Bingo! You've reached Level 2: convenience. America is the land of comfort and convenience—the masters of the entertainment delivery system—all in the pursuit of happiness! OXO Good Grips make peeling potatoes "fun"! "Are we having fun yet?" If the answer is YES! you've almost reached the top of the pyramid. Although it's nice to have fun at work, and everyone likes to escape into a Hollywood film experience, I can't believe that fun is the ultimate goal of life. At the top of Maslow's pyramid, people aspire to something that transcends their own selves. But nirvana is not just spiritual, it's physical and intellectual too. Beauty is seeing the connection of the biggest ideas and richest sensual feelings—it's the supreme goal of life. Seeing, feeling, contemplating, enjoying a beautiful composition, painting, landscape, etc.—these are peak Mihaly Csikszentmihalyi "flow" moments. Although fleeting and ever expanding, beauty is satisfying, and making beauty is the ultimate experience (it's off the charts).

While attending Pratt, I learned to understand the structure of visual relationships and how to manipulate forms. I learned how to critique form and how to create a good one. We polished our talents for making things work well and look beautiful, combining the intellectual with the sensual. My teacher, and one of the founders of Pratt's industrial design program, Rowena Reed Kostellow, told us: "Pure, unadulterated beauty should be the goal of civilization."

Beautility is the number-one criteria for good design. Designers are experts in the utility of beauty. We have the talent and training to improve form and function. Designers may do a lot of other things (research, strategy, branding, marketing, etc.), but in the development cycle, designers are the *only ones* with the ability and expertise to make things look good. Designers are key players in the beauty business. Besides plastic surgeons (maybe), design professionals are the only ones whose *job* it is to create beautility!

Today we have much more time, energy, and technology to make our lives comfortable and fulfilling than the cavemen had. It's the designer's charge to sync up usability, "look and feel," and economy to satisfy our customers. But it's our obligation to our civilization and, indeed, to all living things to do better design! Beautility is the basis of good design. The more we learn about the consequences of our lifestyle, the more critical beautility is to sustaining a healthy planet.

What's Wrong with Plagiarism?

Gunnar Swanson

A few years back I sent out a questionnaire that started with two simple questions: "What does 'plagiarism' mean?" and "What's wrong with it?" They may seem like stupid questions (and I was told as much by at least one person I sent it to)[1] but I don't believe most designers and artists have good answers.

It seems clear to most of us that plagiarism is wrong. I believe that the nature of the wrong seems evident to most: It seems to be a particular form of theft. I started looking at plagiarism and designers' views of plagiarism to find out more about what we value in design. (I'm less interested in property rights than in how we understand the nature of the "property.") The more I looked at the issues, the less either theft or the very notion of "intellectual property" made sense. But before I get to that, let's look at a few explanations of the crime of plagiarism.

The Word of God Argument

Although the role of God is normally played by an associate professor or a favorite art teacher, this might be the most commonly accepted explanation. Only one reply to my highly unscientific survey directly invoked the Word of God argument. While others asked rhetorical questions like "What's wrong with stealing cars?" to indicate disdain for the line of questioning, Lou Danzinger left the section with items that might make plagiarism bad blank, writing "All of this is irrelevant—it is dishonest, immoral, and for anyone who has any sense of ethics it requires no further elaboration—it is simply wrong—period!"

Although the statement that plagiarism is bad because it violates our ethics may seem tautological, it is in some ways the most satisfying argument. Defining ethics as a cultural construct that needs to be swallowed whole is not the same thing as claiming morality to be arbitrary. Plagiarism is an ethical question, and not necessarily a moral one.

I need to pause for a moment to define some terms. I cannot find commonly used terms for a distinction I need to make so I've adapted two nearly synonymous words. The distinction I wish to make is between what I will call a moral question and an ethical one. Although there is significant overlap, I use "morality" to describe what can be considered at least to aspire to a universal scope, where by "ethics" I mean the conduct code of a specific group such as a profession.

Even when similar principles apply, the ethical code varies greatly from group to group. Aside from tax implications, there is nothing wrong with a graphic designer trading services with a carpenter—a brochure for some kitchen cabinets, say. For a psychologist, the same trade would be considered a dual relationship and would be seen as clearly unethical. Martin Luther King's plagiarism in his doctoral thesis was, in an academic setting, serious and cannot be explained away either as naïveté or as others' petty attack on a great man.[2] The same borrowing of phrases without attribution would probably not have been an ethical problem in a sermon, however. (If you think the difference is just oral versus written presentation, I suggest you ask Joe Biden about his speeches.[3])

Whether divine command or collective intuition, much discussion of the "It is simply wrong" explanation would necessarily open up a Pandora's box of questions of theology and ethnocentrism. Ultimately the Word of God theory suffers because we want to ask, "Why does He say that?" To explain that plagiarism is wrong because it violates our ethics dodges the questions of *why* it is a violation of our ethics, how our ethics change or evolve and why. Even if ethical codes are historical, there must be a historical logic to them. The historical logic behind legal protection of creations of various sorts falls largely into the encouragement of such creativity and the protection of property rights. Most designers talking about plagiarism seem to concentrate on the latter.

Property Rights/Plagiarism as Thievery

The majority of people I polled tended to state the problem of plagiarism as one of property and theft. I believe that the majority of designers, writers, photographers, and artists agree. It would be a mistake to assume that all discussions of morality and/or ethics should concentrate on a search for the victim, but the victim certainly must be a major issue when discussing property rights and theft.

One *could* argue that the greatest harm caused by shoplifting or burglary is not the loss of the property stolen, but the damage to the self-development, karma, or soul of the thief, or to the unwitting receiver of the stolen goods who has been duped into participation in crime, or to society as a whole. Crime also forces us to spend resources on burglar alarms and security guards, and robs us of the chance to lead life free of fear. Somehow, though, the stance that the harm to the owner of property stolen is not central to the nature of theft seems a bit perverse. Certainly we can state that stealing from a billionaire "who wouldn't miss it" is as much stealing as is stealing from someone poor, but does anyone believe that taking a couple of pencils home from your work at a large corporation is the *exact* equivalent of taking pencils from a blind man selling them on the street?

As a society we get around this contradiction by taking a wider view—if *anyone* is to be really secure, we say, then we *all* must be. Thus "wouldn't miss it" is beside the point. But it is still the collective possibility of *individual* harm that is at issue. Petty theft is punished less severely than grand theft, for instance: It is not just the act of thievery we abhor, but the loss of property. We do, as a society, factor in the extent of the harm.

So how do we view harm and the victim when we treat plagiarism as theft? Unless dead people's work is in an estate or public trust, does it become "fair game?" Do people automatically own their imagery whether they want to or not? Are we violating the property rights of people who don't believe in such property rights if we use a motif of another culture, or does the "property" only exist if those rights are asserted?

The notion of theft is based on the idea of ownership and property rights. People from many non-Western cultures would find this entire discussion quite curious, since in much of the world the idea of collective accretion of ideas and form is dominant, and the construct of individual creativity that dominates in the United States and Europe is not emphasized. The idea of ownership of form even begins to fade as we leave the world of art, design, and related commerce here in the United States. The thought that someone was first to create an "I ❤ someplace-or-something" bumper sticker has probably never occurred to most owners of "I ❤ someplace-or-something" bumper stickers. Even if the original and its originator were pointed out, the idea that their "I ❤ someplace-or-something else" bumper sticker steals something from Milton Glaser[4] would probably seem quite foreign. The exclusive right to profit from an invention by means of ownership of rights to the invention is widespread in our culture; I'm not sure the same idea applied to aesthetic or communicative configuration is.

Another pause for definition. The term "rights" has a range of meaning including the freedoms we reserve for all people: human rights, those we reserve for all people in a given society: civil rights, and those that are less permanent and more case specific: other legal rights. It is proper to say that the vehicle code gives one the right to drive at a given speed but that "right" is revocable in a way that we do not consider the right to free speech to be. Referring to these lesser and more specific rights as "rights" can confuse an argument. This is my reason for making a distinction between "rights"—i.e., moral rights—and "interests"—i.e., purely legal rights.

We need to reconsider authorship and the way we regard the author. If we correctly speak of property *rights* (as opposed to, say, property *interests*), we must assign to those rights inherent nature. We believe rights exist even if not asserted or even known by the holder of the rights. When a designer appropriates a form or a visual idea from the work of another designer, we deem it plagiarism. When designers appropriate forms from "fine artists," the reaction is mixed. When designers appropriate forms from non-designers/non-artists, it is called "recognition of the vernacular." If our property rights to our work are, indeed, rights, they must exist inherently. By making the "vernacular" fair game, we are stating that there are rights that we accrue by the fact of our being professional designers. Signs painted in the windows of grocery stores do not just appear; they are created by people every bit as much as fancy paper promotions are. Their authors are real, but because graphic designers do not know the authors we pretend they do not exist.

Designers seem to think of themselves as part of a privileged elite. We think that we should be able to borrow freely from the work of non-designers, yet should be able to defend our own work from such use by others. This is either pure hypocrisy or we must assume there is something in the origin or intent of work that makes it plagerizable or not.[5]

If we consider that plagiarism is a special case of theft—the stealing of something that can only be possessed by a special category of people—then we must either be specific about what makes that category of people special or risk being assumed to be another "special interest group" like mining or oil companies claiming their "right" to the minerals below public lands, or agribusiness corporations claiming their "right" to crop subsidies.

Even if designers' self-appointed position as the owners of form is valid, plagiarism-as-theft runs counter to the rhetoric and the interests of designers. Most designers will claim that design is not a commodity and should not be treated as such. We are hurt and mystified that bureaucrats are so stupid and unfeeling that they wish us to collect sales tax on our work, as if our work were a product. Our work, we insist, is not a product but rather it is a process. (If that is true, wouldn't real plagiarism be the copying of someone's working method rather than the copying of someone's work?[6])

The legal basis for the protection of intellectual property under U.S. law is not that someone has the *right* to the "sweat of his brow," but that it is to society's benefit to have people invent things. Giving profit from an invention to the inventor encourages more invention. When we extend legal privilege and label it "moral rights," we must be careful to avoid mistaking a privilege we covet for a right denied us.

U.S. copyright law does not protect ideas; it protects the expression of ideas. This is because the law is designed to encourage invention. The owning of ideas is contrary to that end, whereas receiving benefit from specific use of ideas works toward that end by rewarding creators but minimizing the impact on other potential creators.

The plagiarism-as-theft argument that doesn't smack of self-interest is the idea that the owner of design is the culture,[7] and that the theft is of the unique cultural significance of the original object. Doesn't valid improvement on the original (thus not a plagiarism) diminish the original's unique cultural significance in much the same way? Doesn't this really come down to a problem of a muddling of the historical record—not theft but dishonesty?[8]

One objection to theft is that it deprives a rightful owner of the use or the sale of the thing stolen. That fails to address theft of intangibles such as software piracy. The assumption of typeface designers is that if unauthorized copies of fonts weren't made, authorized copies would be paid for (and type design would become a more viable business). That dubious proposition is beside the point for those who see theft as a basic wrong, but for many the question of who is harmed will always be central. Although one might assume that the entity that would lose the most by plagiarism is a client who paid good money for original work only to have it hijacked by an unscrupulous competitor, "Harm to the original artist's client" ranked very low in my poll results. It seems clear to most that the thing being stolen belongs to the originator and isn't transferred with the payment of an invoice.[9] And it's not strictly the diminishment of the value of the originator's craft that's at stake. If the client never knows the work was copied, that doesn't seem to diminish the damage. I have managed to find few who would argue that unnoticed plagiarism is even relatively benign. It seems that knowledge of the act (by other than the plagiarizer) is not the primary problem and the obvious direct injuries might seem to require knowledge.

One property-like construct where the property stays with the designer rather than transferring to a client assumes that the important factor is the advancement of a creator's career and the "property" is a style or tendency that crosses many works for many clients. I suspect that this is one of the most commonly held views about what makes plagiarism bad. If we expect society at large to care about this (rather than it being a "code of honor" known only to a few designers), then we need to explain how our innovations differ from those in any other line of work. Would we accept a bricklayer's or stockbroker's refusal to work in a better manner on the basis of the improved practice being someone else's innovation?

There is some parallel to legal practice in the idea of a sort of *meta*-property. Unless specifically transferred in writing, U.S. copyright does stay with the original author even when the object of the copyright is sold. Singers Bette Midler and Tom Waits have each successfully enjoined advertisers' uses of impersonations that made it seem that they had released their recordings for television commercials. The advertisers' ruses were clearly dishonest, using false implications as well as usurping any legal rights to self-promotion, bringing us to another way of looking at plagiarism and related problems.

Plagiarism as an Assault on the Collective Good/Lies and Fraud

Plagiarism as a lie is probably the definition with the fewest problems: Lying can have victims and result in specific harm, but most of us believe that lying is wrong even if no victim other than the liar is identifiable. And, after all, no matter how you feel about issues of property, ownership, cultural value, there is no doubt that presenting someone else's work and claiming it as your own is lying. When a lie is told for the purpose of gain it becomes fraud. We can assume that most design presented by professional designers is for the purpose of gain, so the term generally applies to designers' plagiarism.

Plagiarism can also be seen as a violation of a general prohibition against freeloading. It is wrong, under this theory, for anyone to act in a manner that would threaten society if we all acted that way.[10] Applying this to design is a problem, however. The idea that everybody should do original work because otherwise there wouldn't be anything left to plagiarize is interesting but strikes me as a dead end.

Designers discussing plagiarism usually distinguish it from homage, appropriation, quotation, or eclecticism. There are no clear boundaries between these modes of use and plagiarism. Judgments are often made not on the basis of the work, but on the basis of the respect one has for the author of the "copy." Once in a class I took a fellow student was looking for graphic illustrations of the word "appropriation" and I suggested he look at some of Picasso's compositions that I described as "ripped from Goya." The instructor was angered by the use of the term "ripped" because, he said, "Picasso was a great artist." My use of the word "ripped" in that instance was deliberately obtuse and provocative, but I don't believe I'm being either by asking now whether Picasso's status as an artist had anything to do with it. Bad work by a lousy artist approached with the same intent as Picasso might not have been as important a tribute to Goya, but would it have been any closer to being plagiarism? If so, aren't we back to a privileged elite who are not subject to the constraints of the common folk?

In addition to the homage, appropriation, et al. problem, the very nature of design makes attribution a stickier problem than it is with painting or sculpture. Design is generally a collaborative process. Many people work on it and contributions and improvements upon those contributions are made freely.

When a designer speaks before an art directors' club or AIGA meeting and shows work, there is the implicit statement that what we are seeing is *that* designer's work. I can count on one hand (with fingers left over) the number of times I've heard a designer say "this piece was designed by my assistant so-and-so" or "this page was put together by freelancer what's-her-name." The argument in the favor of our hypothetical speaker is that our hypothetical audience knows how design goes together and thus suffers no illusion that anyone does *all* of the work that comes out of a design firm. Following this argument one might expect a designer showing a piece involving photography to point out that it was *stock* photography. After all, our audience knows how design goes together and would falsely assume the designer's participation in art direction of the photos.

The assumption of a level of knowledge and the intent to confuse the truth are, of course, central to the question of implicit lying and this definition of plagiarism. If we generally assume the best of people, we will minimize our assumption that there was an actual attempt to defraud, but is plagiarism (or lying, for that matter) necessarily a willful act? We do not call misinformed people who make statements believing them to be true "liars." We *do* speak of unconscious plagiarizers, however. This makes it clear that the act of plagiarizing and the lie of presenting the work as "original" are not exactly one and the same. (This may be a linguistic problem, where there is an intersection of the definitions of "plagiarism" and "lie," but each is inadequate to describe the other. It is also possible, though I think unlikely, that it is merely one of those language quirks like *pants* being plural while *shirt* is singular.)

It is equally clear that the physical act of copying is not the plagiarism. If copies are made for analysis, practice, or legitimate use involving no fraud, we do not consider them to be plagiarized. (Please note that violation of copyright and plagiarism are not synonymous. Copying this article on a photocopy machine without permission may be a violation of copyright, but it is not likely to be plagiarism.)

It is some combination of the copy and the lie that add up to plagiarism. But what if the potential plagiarizer doesn't know that a falsehood is being understood? Is a joke told when there is someone in the room without a sense of humor a lie? Is a parody plagiarism if someone isn't familiar with the work being parodied?

There was quite a bit of complaint about Paula Scher's Swatch ads based on Herbert Matter's 1930s Swiss tourism posters as examples of plagiarism. The claim was that confusion was created over authorship. My assumption has always been that Scher assumed that either people would recognize Matter in the ads, know that *that* work was from before Scher's time, and know that Matter had died before the ads were produced, or they were outside the world that cared to make judgments about authorship and thus it wasn't important. While some considered the Matter + Scher attribution deception, I saw it as an homage combined with a joke. (The fact that Scher had permission from Mercedes Matter, Herbert Matter's widow, and paid a royalty for the use of the form removes any "property rights" arguments from this discussion.)

Design is also usually about clear communication and thus it dwells primarily in the realm of the cultural norm. Every metaphor, cliché, and standard phrase had an original author. At some point each becomes "part of the language" and the original author need not be acknowledged. How do you sort out what is quotation and what is just plain talking?

Does the great Swatch plagiarism case hinge on whether the audience knew Herbert Matter's work? If so, can one become a plagiarizer by overestimating people? Is work shown in one venue proper quotation and in another plagiarized? Does the fact that Herbert Matter is both a great and important designer and dead make him a part of the culture and thus part of the language, or does the fact that Herbert Matter is both a great and important designer and dead make him a part of the culture and thus precious and to be protected against commercial encroachment? Again, is the harm caused by plagiarism's lie a collective harm?

Another form of dishonesty closely related to fraud is cheating. It differs from theft in that it does not require the existence of property or ownership. Although cheating can harm a real or would-be winner directly, everyone is harmed by cheating. By unjustly rewarding a dishonest individual, cheating shakes everyone's faith in the fairness of the system, making everyone less able to compete. Does the metaphor or reality of competition apply to design, and is that the way we wish to judge ourselves and our work? Even if competition is not important in design, we can decry an atmosphere of *unfair* competition. Cheating, like the other forms of dishonesty I've discussed, can do great damage to the cheater, creating the illusion that a simple trick can make life or our work easy. It can do similar damage to the rest of us by leaving the impression that the cheater might be right about that.

A Need for Further Examination

I don't offer any of this as a general rule of plagiarism. It may be that we might more properly talk about plagiarisms, or related acts that are not quite defined the same way. The differences in attitudes about authorship and individuality make it hard to consider borrowing a phrase in a blues or folk song the same way we might consider borrowing a phrase in a doctoral thesis or a poem. Perhaps it's not just the context or the localized rules of plagiarisms that are different but the natures of the acts. Most of my arguments apply, I believe, in most instances of plagiarism, but I cannot say for sure.

It is the other side of the theft argument that I think needs real examination—the notion of intellectual property. Perhaps the phrase started out as a metaphor but it is usually taken literally. The difference in legal origin (the Fifth Amendment protection of a "natural right" against usurpation by tyrants versus a utilitarian move to "promote the Progress of Science and Useful Arts") was once important but now too often the right to such supposed property is regarded as every bit as real and natural as any other ownership.[11]

The Sonny Bono Copyright Extension Act[12] put a strain on the Constitutional justification—"to encourage the practical arts." One could hardly believe that Mickey Mouse entering the public domain after so many years would have discouraged future cartoonists.[13] Copyright is, for society, a balancing act between rewarding authorship, and thus encouraging more such production, and restricting use, thus discouraging authorship based on past work. By most descriptions our culture is accelerating and its artifacts are becoming more quickly disposable. There is some dissonance in the fact that copyright has been extended even as its utility for encouragement would seem to have been compressed.[14]

I believe that many of the problems with the notion of plagiarism as theft come from the acceptance of noncorporeal manifestations of creativity as "stuff" that is indistinguishable from, say, a home or farm. The very real (and very sticky) problem we face is the issue of ownership of increasingly unreal "stuff" in our lives.

Plagiarism and Computer Technology

Advances in technology have brought old questions to a new light. There is a grand tradition in the arts of the appropriation of previous material. In the plastic arts this has taken the form of formal elements having been digested by artists and re-presented. Thus the "copying" was made by reforming by hand the work of the copying artist.

In collage, found elements were reused in their original form but with new context. This practice escapes the claim of fraud in that the source is evident. A casual viewer would not tend to assume that a collage artist had created the elements, cut them out, and glued them together (although this has occasionally been the case.) A collage seems to be a collection of borrowed elements.

In music the announcement of assemblage is not as clear. The crafts of composition and performance tend to integrate material, leaving the impression of an original whole. When symphonies quoted folk songs the humble, public domain nature of the quoted material may have been a legal saving grace; the ethical questions are slightly murkier. Jazz riffing off of popular tunes often made a show of the original and its transformation. To the extent that this was not the fact, the original tune was beside the point of the major creative activities. If craft and performance elements are of prime concern, the performance can stand on its own even when somehow derived from a previous performance. (For a Charlie Parker fan, Bird's debt to the authors of "Back Home Again in Indiana" or "Cherokee" were negligible or, at least, beside the point. "Donna Lee" and "Ko Ko" were the genius and Parker was no dwarf, whether on the shoulders of giants or not.)

This is also a factor in the visual collage. When a collage artist cuts out a bit of a photograph to reuse in an illustration, it may or may not be a copyright law violation but it can hardly be condemned as plagiarism. In "Little Photoshop of Horrors," a panel discussion in *Print* magazine, photo collage artist Stephen Kroniger made the apt comparison of his use of a baseball cap cut out of someone else's photograph to the photographer's presentation of the logo on the cap. The photographer cannot be expected to have originated all of the form in the photo. Logo design is beside the point of where we see the originality of the photograph; cap photography is beside the point of collage making.[15]

This argument extended is the defense for the sampling and reworking of existing material, two staples of hip-hop culture. The sampling ethos has been absorbed by the visual culture, at least that portion that is below the legal radar. Rave flyers and much of the Web are classic examples.

Technological advances allow a relatively unskilled Web designer to combine code from one Web site and images from others and end up with something that does not scream "borrowed elements recombined," like a collage of magazine clippings. Digital collage techniques allow the combination of elements in a seamless fashion and also remove the natural disclaimer of cut edges. Music sampling can create "new" works derivative of previous performance that are not reperformed. The derivative work makes collages of sound, seemingly claiming preexisting form as somehow original—falsely so by previous standards of originality.

Although defenders of hip-hop aesthetics and ethics have argued that old standards were in need of reassessment in the face of this new creative form, legal realities seem to be prevailing. Current practice is for samples to be credited and paid for.

Conclusions/Confusion

In an earlier draft of this article I tried to explain why I would recommend against engaging in plagiarism. The best answer I came up with is "It's no damned fun."

Like many ethical problems, my main objection to plagiarism may not be my moral outrage but my disgust at stupidity. British graphic designer James Souttar put it well: "I'd always thought that graphic design was like cooking in this respect. A plagiarist is someone who buys a meal from a smart restaurant, takes it home and serves it up to his guests. He could do it every night—even put a sign outside the door, advertising the food—but it would be a sorry way to make a living (especially since it's likely to be cold and congealed by the time he serves it up). Especially when the same amount of effort could be put into convincing the chef to show him how it's done."[16]

My strongest objection to plagiarism isn't my being served congealed food. It's the thought of the poor wretch in that metaphoric kitchen. Most things plagiarizable might be likened to a random drug test.[17] Whether a final exam, a work of art, a piece of design, a speech, or an article, the object says "This is a fair sample of who I am" as much as a drug-free urine sample might say "This is representative of my drug-free life." There is significant disagreement over the validity, importance, fairness, and legality of random drug testing. The message of buying a tube of certified drug-free urine might be protest against invasion of privacy or a statement that drug use is not an important describer of our characters. The message of buying a term paper or copying a poster design must be less viable as objection to tyranny.

Design is a voluntary act, so plagiarism as protest seems unlikely. Whether theft, lie, fraud, freeloading, deafness to the voice of God, cultural vandalism, or whatever combination, plagiarism is a falsification of self.

I'm not one who defines design as primarily self-expression but clearly there is something of the designer in the design. That's why most designers choose to design. For many of us, the important part is the part that is a small sample of our souls. My naïveté may be showing but I don't understand the desire to falsify an affirmation of self. It seems like a losing game. Not only is the act of plagiarism a negative reflection of character, but plagiarized work robs the designer/copyist of one more precious chance to reach out with the very thing we design for—to connect directly with other human beings. It makes a spiritual act mechanical.[18]

Notes

1. In 1990 I mailed a questionnaire to designers, design educators, a law professor, and several others whom I suspected would have something interesting to say. After the first two questions I asked for a rating of importance of various items that might make plagiarism bad: "Its effect on the original artist (i.e., person plagiarized)," "Harm to the original artist's client," "Its effect on the plagiarizer," "Its fraud against the plagiarizer's client," "Its degradation of the design profession," "Its insult to creative autonomy and the artistic spirit," and "Other (please specify)." I also asked for the most significant aspect or damage attributable to the most important item from that list.

2. King received his doctorate from Boston University in the 1950s. In the early 1990s researchers discovered apparent plagiarism in his thesis. BU provost Jon Westling appointed a committee of three professors in the BU School of Theology and one from American University. They recommended that a letter be attached to King's dissertation in the university library, noting that numerous passages lacked appropriate quotations and citations of sources. The committee said that "no thought should be given to the revocation of Dr. King's doctoral degree from Boston University" and the assertion that despite its flaws, the dissertation "makes an intelligent contribution to scholarship." "Panel confirms plagiarism by King at BU," Charles A. Radin, *Boston Globe*, October 11, 1991.

3. Biden's presidential aspirations were derailed when an opponent's aides delivered a video-tape to journalists that suggested that Biden had plagiarized some of his comments from British Labor Party leader Neil Kinnock. "Plagiarism Suggestion Angers Biden's Aides; British Politician Given Credit, Senator Says," Eleanor Randolph, *Washington Post*, September 13, 1987.

4. Glaser's "I ❤ NY" campaign's translation into bumper stickers ranging from "Yo [Amo] Oaxaca" to "I [Love] My [Dog Head]" is thought to have inspired the designer/illustrator's many talks on inspiration and plagiarism.

5. If we define plagiarism as a lie or a lie combined with other acts (as I believe we should—see later in this essay) then one can argue that much of "retro" design is not plagiarized since its form clearly announces its relationship to past vernacular work. It should be noted, however, that the same argument applies to any obvious copying. Just because many acts of piracy do not fit the definition of plagiarism, one need not conclude that they are somehow acceptable or honorable, of course.

6. I thank Ed McDonald for this insight from the margin of his questionnaire.

7. This is not entirely an academic construct or some bit of New Age gee-whizness. The legal basis of copyright in U.S. law is that works are owned by society and copyright is *awarded* to the authors to encourage the creativity that will benefit society at large.

8. The "muddling of the record" is one of the best arguments against plagiarism (and for full and specific footnotes) in academic writing. If academics are part of a wider activity of knowledge building, keeping the record clear is vital to their pursuit. Plagiarism confuses the history of ideas and expression of the ideas, distorting the knowledge that is academia's purpose. (Speaking of knowledge and a clear record, I've long thought that journalism would be greatly improved by newspapers using footnotes.)

9. Although one could argue that such damage to the original creator's client is a separate ill of unfair business practices not covered under the problem of plagiarism, nobody made that argument.

10. My thanks to Dr. David "Doc" Mayo of the philosophy department at University of Minnesota Duluth for this insight and his many comments on a draft of an earlier article on this subject.

11. For an excellent introduction to the philosophy and history of copyright and a full argument against the intellectual property approach, see *Copyrights and Copywrongs: The Rise of Intellectual Property and How It Threatens Creativity*, Siva Vaidhyanathan, New York University Press, 2001.

12. See "Legal Affairs: Tad Crawford and Laura Mankin Review the Sonny Bono Copyright Term Extension Act," *Communication Arts* 41, no. 2, 1999.

13. Bono, the law's congressional sponsor, personally believed in perpetual copyright.

14. When I first began writing and talking about the implications of the Sonny Bono Copyright Term Extension Act, I had several copyright attorneys stare at me like I was a moron for suggesting a First Amendment basis for limiting congressional power to extend copyright. Since then, the Supreme Court has heard arguments on *Eldred v. Ashcroft* ("Justices Hear Challenge to Copyright Law Extensions Stifle Access, Opponents Say; Government Claims Congressional Prerogative," Charles Lane, *Washington Post*, October 10, 2002.) The case turned on issues of constitutionally delineated congressional power. Unfortunately for copyright policy (but perhaps fortunately for judicial restraint), seven

justices declared that they should not second guess "the First Branch" and upheld the copyright extension. They expressed their skepticism about the wisdom of Congress's action, however ("Protecting Mickey Mouse at Art's Expense," Lawrence Lessig, The *New York Times*, January 18, 2003.)

15. "Little Photoshop of Horrors: The Ethics of Manipulating Journalistic Imagery," Janet Abrams, *Print* 49, no. 6, 1995.

16. Message to *Graphics* e-mail list.

17. My thanks to Dr. David Cole of the philosophy department at the University of Minnesota Duluth for this delightfully bizarre metaphor.

18. I would like to thank Dr. Robert Evans of the philosophy department at the University of Minnesota Duluth for his comments on plagiarism and character, as well as the whole UMD philosophy department and everyone else who attended my colloquium on this subject at UMD in April 1996. Finally I wish to thank Katie Salen and Rosemary Swanson for their work in editing the first version of this article. That version appeared in *Zed3*.

The Designer as Producer
Working Outside Mainstream Manufacturing
Victor Margolin

More than ten years ago at a small interdisciplinary conference entitled "Discovering Design," held at the University of Illinois at Chicago, I presented a paper in which I proposed a concept called the "product milieu." In a subsequent essay based on the paper, I characterized this milieu as "the aggregate of objects, activities, services, and environments that fills the lifeworld."[1] My argument in the paper and in the essay that followed was that human beings depend on products in order to live their lives, or, as the phenomenologists Alfred Schutz and Thomas Luckmann put it, to transform their consciousness into projects.

At the time, I was attempting to add a new dimension to the sociological and philosophical discussions of action that tend to focus on human intention rather than on the instruments or tools (to use a term favored by Ivan Illich) that people require to act in the social world. My concept of the product milieu was similar to that which many people have of the Internet today. I envisioned this milieu as a medium within which people move and which they activate as they find specific products to meet their needs. Humans build their own collections of things that they use repeatedly and they maintain internal and external references to products they might want to use in the future.

Because my original concern was with human action as social scientists and philosophers consider it, the product milieu paper focused more on how people use existing products than on how they create new ones. I did, however, note that designers also utilize products since they depend on existing equipment and materials to accomplish their own projects of making things for use.

Goods in the product milieu are turning over at an accelerating pace because of rapid advances in technology. The major implication of these advances for design is that designers who are so inclined can now produce and distribute finished products, whether these be books, bicycles, or furniture, far more easily than previously. This new situation is due to several factors: the dematerialization and reduced cost of the equipment needed to make products; the dematerialization of many products themselves, i.e., software and Web sites, but also hard goods that are made with more compact but stronger materials; the possibility to create electronic product prototypes that can be used to solicit financial support and stimulate public discussion; and the opportunity to market products inexpensively through electronic means.[2] The development of faster and less-expensive chips has allowed manufacturers to pack more intelligence into compact and cheap computers. These machines enable small businesses to run bookkeeping, accounting, and inventory control programs at fairly low costs. Advances in computing mean that in the long run many factories will function with less-expensive equipment, making it possible to produce material objects with far less capital outlay.

An emerging global marketing structure is also changing the way that goods are sold. A manufacturer can now build a network of interested consumers who are widely distributed in space rather than located in a specific geographic area. Through the Internet, one can reach people scattered around the globe without having to target a particular location with printed material, billboards, and the like. This enhances the opportunity for innovation. Many new products can reach the market in ways they never could before. Production can be based on small batches of goods that are distributed to individuals or selected retailers, and, in fact, a producer can create a special community for a particular product. A number of years ago, Everett Rogers and other anthropologists devoted considerable attention to the diffusion of cultural and technical innovations in nonindustrialized cultures. Today their work can serve as a good basis for better understanding the dissemination of innovative new products in societies that are technologically advanced.

New technologies enable us to redefine the traditional notion of a cottage industry. No longer associated specifically with the crafts and limited to local distribution, a contemporary cottage industry can use the most advanced technology and reach a worldwide market. We see this now with any number of products, such as clothing, food, music, and software. Innovative marketing has, for example, long been a mainstay of the bicycle industry, where high-end cycles, produced in small numbers, are marketed through customized channels. Given the new networking approach to the production of goods and services, where resources, both human and material, are brought together for specific projects, small manufacturers can lease production facilities or services for particular projects, just as a small-press entrepreneur goes to a printer.

A New Practice for Designers

Designers today have the opportunity to produce and distribute new things, whether type fonts, software, or material goods of all kinds, to worldwide markets at low costs. In the realm of dematerialized products like digital typography, new typefaces are being produced in hundreds of small font shops similar to the diffuse way bicycles and automobiles were fabricated a century ago. With the development and distribution costs for these typefaces being fairly low, there is nothing to prevent a young typographer from becoming an entrepreneur. We already have numerous examples. The proliferation of fonts has changed the way designers think about typography, and there is more experimentation than in the past because the choice of faces is so large and their use so inexpensive.

The plethora of products that has resulted from these new conditions of production and distribution is also evident in the arts, and interested designers can learn from artists who have used advanced technologies for both the production and distribution of their work. Writers are starting their own electronic publishing companies and producing books online; composers are creating orchestral compositions without orchestras; and filmmakers are presenting new films on the Web. Film equipment has also dematerialized. Today small video cameras can generate broadcast or theater-quality footage, and independent filmmakers can shoot their films with such cameras and edit them on computers. They are able to control the entire production process with a cash outlay that is only a fraction of what it once cost to make a film. By contrast, I can recall my days as an apprentice film editor many years ago when we depended on heavy, expensive moviolas and costly processes of making workprints. Shooting was done either with 16mm cameras or very expensive 35mm apparatuses that required additional equipment to support and move them.

Just as those artists who are using technology to produce and distribute their work constitute only a small percentage of the larger community of writers, painters, filmmakers, and so forth, so too designers who choose to become manufacturers as well are unlikely to become more than a small minority of the design profession. Large companies still dominate the market and will continue to be the primary clients for design services. But designers who get involved with the production and distribution of products they conceive themselves have the possibility to change the market, even in small ways, and open up new product sectors that might even become beacons for larger manufacturers to follow.

I don't want to claim any particular moral or socially responsible high ground for designer/entrepreneurs but, in fact, there is a better chance for a small company to innovate in socially responsible ways than there is for a large organization that must work against many constraints—shareholder concerns, competing visions of corporate purpose, and aversions to small-scale innovations, for example.

The Social Potential of Design/Entrepreneurship

One area where this new decentralized and dematerialized production system can make a mark is in the sector of sustainable products. Since the Industrial

Revolution, large companies have had a near monopoly on the production system, and because of this the necessary shift to a culture of sustainable production has been slow to materialize. Now, those designers with ideas for sustainable products have a better chance than ever to create prototypes or finished goods and bring them to the market in a new way. With possibilities to reach a receptive consumption community that is not bounded by material geography, a sustainable product culture may begin to emerge.

A number of sustainable products have already been created by designer/entrepreneurs such as Ross Evans, Wendy Brawer, Dean Kamen, and Vogt + Weizenegger. Evans, for example, has developed new kinds of cargo-carrying bicycles. His Xtracycle Access Foundation makes cheap, reliable bikes for developing countries, while his Xtracycle manufacturing company markets a higher-tech cargo bike as an alternative to motorized transport. In addition, he organizes workshops to help poor communities design and build bikes themselves. Wendy Brawer has used the Internet to create a Green Map System, a global network of green maps which indicate a city's cultural and sustainable resources, while Dean Kamen, through his company DEKA Research and Development Corp., designed and markets a revised version of a wheelchair that can do far more than the original version, such as climb stairs and maneuver in tight spaces. Oliver Vogt and Hermann Weizenegger, worked with Berlin's Institute for the Blind to manufacturer well-designed brushes and household accessories that were sold from a catalogue. They also developed a line of furniture called Blaupause, which was offered only as 1:1 blueprints from which buyers assembled the pieces themselves.[3] While such products do not have an effect on the world comparable to the launch of a mass-produced object, they do begin to change the product milieu in an incremental fashion.

Authors such as Paul Hawken have written extensively about working with corporations to develop a kind of "green capitalism."[4] While many large companies do make contributions to a culture of sustainability, significant breakthroughs in sustainable product development are beginning to come from smaller designer/entrepreneurs such as those described above. Ross Evans and Dean Kamen have established their own foundations to fund the research, design, and production of innovative products on a modest scale and to promote their adoption. This, I want to argue, is a new model for the designer, one that holds great promise for changing the global product culture. I am not presenting this model as a universal one; rather, it is one that responds to a particular set of circumstances.

The Historical Context

In the past, we have had few examples of designers who were also manufacturers and distributors. In fact, the very notion of a product designer, as the profession was conceived historically, is of a Christopher Dresser, a Peter Behrens, or a Raymond Loewy, all of whom created drawings and models for others to turn into finished goods. Historically, the expense of tooling up to manufacture and distribute products discouraged most designers from becoming producers. But, as indicated, conditions now enable a graphic designer or product designer to think seriously about becoming a product developer and manufacturer as well.

There are actually precedents in the Arts and Crafts movement of the late nineteenth century for the establishment of design firms that produce products for the market according to a new paradigm. Morris, Marshall, Faulkner & Co., the firm in which William Morris was a principal, sought to challenge the prevailing British taste in home furnishings as well as the harsh division of labor in British factories. The firm was able to create a range of products, from furniture and tiles to wallpaper and tapestries, that were highly innovative in a formal sense and were produced to some extent according to a workshop model. Other Arts and Crafts firms such as the Century Guild and the Guild of Handicraft were created to achieve similar ends. While they all faced the contradiction of using craft-based practices to produce for a new enlarged market, they nonetheless became examples of design firms that sought to challenge the dominant production paradigm.

Today designer/entrepreneurs can do more than challenge the system of industrial production; they can establish their own niches in it. The market is ready for a resurgence of small designer/entrepreneurs who work outside mainstream manufacturing, just as the Arts and Crafts designers sought to do. But today, the focus of such a practice is based neither on the handicraft production of the nineteenth century nor on the concepts of intermediate technology of the 1960s and 1970s. On the contrary, designer/entrepreneurs are likely to make use of the most advanced technology for modeling, prototyping, manufacturing, and distributing new products. Desktop manufacturing systems for producing cheap prototypes have been around for a decade. Other trends suggest that reductions in technological costs will enable small manufacturers to follow the examples of large automobile companies who transmit design files from one part of the world to another and send messages to prototyping machines thousands of miles away. This is already done easily and cheaply by designer/manufacturers of dematerialized products such as type fonts and software, but eventually the cost of doing it for hard goods as well should come down. Eventually, it may be possible to make products on demand and distribute them globally by downloading them to local manufacturing facilities.

The Future of the Product Milieu

Design schools, which have historically prepared designers to serve manufacturers rather than become entrepreneurs themselves, should pay more attention to these conditions and create new programs for designer/entrepreneurs who have to understand technology, marketing, and management as well as design itself. The possibility exists in many universities to bring this type of knowledge together but the leadership and vision of design educators is required to get such programs off the ground.

Designer/entrepreneurs should be able to create business plans, identify niches for new products within the emerging global marketplace, and seek appropriate venture capital. Such training is already provided in business schools, but without the design ability to actually create new products. For this emerging practice, there should be a master's degree in design entrepreneurship, tailored to designers who want to be both product innovators and manufacturers.

The Internet has spawned an active and powerful worldwide citizen's movement that is challenging the ability of governments to manage their political affairs
in traditional ways. There is now a configuration of new technologies and dematerialized product forms that can facilitate a similar kind of civil action in the realm of
material culture. We badly need new products to address pressing social needs that
are not being met by large manufacturers. Highest on the agenda are products that
address issues of ecological sustainability, but there are other urgent needs in sectors
related to health, children, communication, the aged, and those with disabilities.

Until now, users have engaged more flexibly than producers with the product
milieu. Now designer/entrepreneurs have the opportunity to create a much more
inventive and spontaneous product culture than we have ever had in the past. They
can subvert the near monopolies of large companies in many product sectors and
create products for needs that have yet to be met. Their impact is already evident
in sectors such as digital typography and software design. With vision and initiative,
the product milieu can spread far more widely.

Notes

1. Victor Margolin, "The Product Milieu and Social Action," in *Discovering Design: Explorations
   in Design Studies*, Richard Buchanan and Victor Margolin, eds. (Chicago: University of
   Chicago Press, 1995), 122.

2. On dematerialization, see the special number of *Design Issues* on "Designing the Immaterial
   Society," *Design Issues* 4, nos. 1 and 2 (1988) and *Neue Technologien und Design: Das
   Vershwinden der Dinge*, Arnica-Verena Langenmaier, ed. (Munich: Design Zentrum
   München, 1993).

3. These projects and others are described in a special issue of *I.D.* magazine, edited by
   Christopher Mount, entitled "The I.D. Forty: Socially Conscious Design" (February 2001).

4. See Paul Hawken, *The Ecology of Commerce: A Declaration of Sustainability* (New York:
   HarperCollins, 1993).

I Was Thinking the Other Day about One Possible Scenario for a Collective Future

The Open Source Software Movement

David Reinfurt

April 15, 2001—Shortly after returning from ten days in East Berlin, I find myself considering a new future for graphic design. Spring is here, the economy is shorting out, real estate is going vacant, and designers are out of jobs. It seems that now is a good time for a new working method. Building on the free-formed, distributed, and collaborative model of the Open Source Software movement, which produced recent successes Linux operating system and Netscape 6.0, graphic designers might openly copy, share, and modify each others' work—all for the common good. What follows in five sections of travelogue and speculation is one possible scenario for a collective future.

Part 1. The Dotconomy and Karl-Marx-Allee

Found on CNBC.com (some bad news) . . .

April 12, 2001, 10:30 A.M.—Weaker-than-expected economic data brought another round of recession fears to the market. Still, market watchers hoped the limp data would spur the Federal Reserve to cut interest rates. Shortly after the opening bell, the tech-heavy Nasdaq composite dropped 25 to 1,874, the Dow Jones industrial average dropped 70 points to

9,942, and the broader S&P 500 was off 7 at 1,159. Retail sales for March fell 0.2 percent, lower than the flat rate economists predicted and the upwardly revised flat rate in the year-ago period. Excluding automobile sales, sales dropped 0.1 percent, much lower than the 0.2 percent rise that was forecast. The figure had slipped 0.2 percent in the previous month. In addition, the number of people initially filing for unemployment rose 9,000 to 392,000 for the week ending April 7. This paints a much more dire unemployment picture than economists expected. They had called for the figure to drop by 3,000.

I arrived in Berlin at 9:00 the morning after an overnight flight from New York. To kill time before checking in, I walked east down Karl-Marx-Allee from Alexanderplatz. Karl-Marx-Allee was built in 1951 as the principal symbolic promenade of the newly formed German Democratic Republic. On this very straight and very wide boulevard, the will of the new socialist government was written in architecture. Following in the footsteps of Pope Sixtus V in Rome and Baron von Haussmann in Paris, the new government inserted a ceremonial avenue that terminated in the Communist Party headquarters. Along Karl-Marx-Allee, principles of the culture were mirrored in the architecture. The avenue is wide enough to accommodate the May Day military parades and it is lined by similar soviet modernist apartment buildings, which served as worker housing. Karl-Marx-Allee is a showcase for socialism. Each eight-to-ten-story building is meant as a model of society with categories of workers assigned to specific floors. Writers and artists were given the top floors.

Figure 1. Karl-Marx-Allee from the Fernsehturm observation deck

From: Bob Bernard (CEO of MarchFIRST, Inc.)
Sent: Monday, November 13, 2000, 3:49 PM
To: All Employees
Subject: IMPORTANT ANNOUNCEMENT

To all MarchFIRST professionals:
We are in a situation where business needs necessitate reduction throughout the organization.

Karl-Marx-Allee was originally named Stalinallee, though that name didn't stick. The workers riots of June 17, 1953 happened on this street. In response to a loss of workers to the West, the GDR enforced a 10 percent increase in the required number of hours and daily output for each worker. This didn't go over so well and building workers led a massive strike on Stalinallee. The crowd marched down Stalinallee to the Communist Party offices, tearing down flags and demanding to speak with the government. Later that day, the government called in Soviet tanks to Stalinallee to quiet the crowd. The tanks were met by angry workers throwing stones. In the end, between twenty-three and 200 people were killed and over four thousand arrested. The name was changed to Karl-Marx-Allee in 1954. Today, after the fall of the GDR, the graffitied and abandoned pavilions that line the avenue are used as locations for *Wallpaper* magazine photo shoots and as temporary venues for moving parties.

"Look for the market to trend lower today and trading to peter out, analysts say, as investors take off early for the three-day weekend."

The dotconomy suffered a fate similar to that of Karl-Marx-Allee. Poised to change everything about the way we live, love, and spend our money, the Internet economy also attempted to give a form to its ideology. Instead of architecture, the instrument of this new social order was graphic design. From Amazon to Zoo.com, e-companies employed a relentlessly similar graphic language to identify themselves as part of this new social and economic order. A partial lozenge encircling the name set in bold, italic, sans-serif typeface was standard. Orange and baby-blue were the officially sanctioned colors of the new society. Clever names were dressed in designer graphics that were moderately sophisticated and absolutely familiar. Things would never be the same again.

Figure 2. Collective.com logotype

It didn't last, either, of course. Instead of empty buildings, the dotconomy's collapse left in its wake a vast collection of perfectly serviceable logos, with no companies to attach them to, as well as a surplus of graphic designers, suddenly finding themselves too numerous for the few commercial graphic design jobs now available. Perhaps these extra graphics and extra graphic designers could be reemployed in a new way. The logos could be reused, taken apart, and repurposed. The graphic designers could choose to not be offended by this.

Figure 3. Peace.com mark

Kozmo.com to Shut Down, Lay Off 1,100
Online convenience store Kozmo will cease operations, lay off 1,100 workers, and begin liquidating assets. Said financial analyst Vern Keenan, "This seemed like a dumb idea from the beginning."

Part 2. Emerging Futures

I saw groups of job trailers on construction sites all over Berlin. Inside each trailer there was an identical set of furnishings: one Steelcase-like desk, a padded office chair on casters, one neatly stacked pile of papers, a beige file cabinet, a twelve-inch wall clock and one pin-up calendar. And wherever one trailer appears, seven or twenty-seven more soon join it. The trailers are often stacked one on top of the other to form mini trailer-cities, endlessly forming and re-forming in construction sites across Berlin.

Figure 4. Trailers at a construction site in Mitte

Spontaneously forming construction trailer-cities is not a unique phenomenon. When vacancies exist in an otherwise dense situation, patterns will emerge to fill in the gap. As the economy tightens up, as more and more jobs go away, now is a natural time for designers to come together.

Author and former *Wired* magazine editor Kevin Kelley has described a range of emerging systems whose collective power is greater than the sum of its parts. In "Out of Control: The New Biology of Machines, Social Systems and the Economic World," Kelley discusses systems from the collective consciousness of a beehive to the globally connected reality of the Internet that emerge from complex and loosely organized collections.

Further, Kelley has described three states of copying that have particular relevance to graphic design. The first stage of copying is perfection. This is possible when available technology can produce

Figure 5. Individual decision and collective will

copies that are indistinguishable from the original (printing press). The second stage is freeness. In a digital environment, the perfect and costless reproduction of copies is possible (desktop publishing). The third and final stage is fluidity. Duplication is perfect, free, and ubiquitous. The copy can be instantly modified, reformed, reconnected, and even redistributed. Fluid duplication, facilitated by globally networked computers exchanging digital data (World Wide Web), presents a sympathetic, productive environment for a collective and nonproprietary graphic design practice.

This is an e-mail from a recently terminated employee to the CEO of Saltmine.com.

——*Original Message*——
Mr. Jarmon:

Since you preach an open door/open e-mail type of management style, I figured I would take this opportunity to take you up on that! You see, since this is my last day with this disorganization, I decided to air my issues and opinions that typically would be aired out in an exit interview, out in the open. That way, all HR will need to do is print this e-mail and enclose it in my employee file. I mean what are you going to do, FIRE ME! And in the spirit of open communication, I kept it all in the family, coming from a lowly, exiting Business Analyst who has no clout in the organization. What kind of influence do I have?

Part 3. Flipper

I took the photograph below in Berlin on Monday, March 12, 2001 at about 11:30 A.M. I was walking somewhere on Torstrasse in Mitte, not far from where I was staying. It was the beginning of my week in Berlin. I had no idea what went on inside this storefront, what Flipper meant, who made this sign, or how long it had been there. I just thought it looked really good. So I made a slide.

On my last night in Berlin, I was set to go to an occasional, not-quite-legal bar that my American German-speaking friend knew of. The place is run by a graphic designer named Anja Lutz. Anja had started the sometimes bar on Friday nights in a disused storefront. It is called Flipper. I was surprised and amused that it was the place that I had taken a picture of at the beginning of the week.

Once inside, I asked about the Flipper sign that I had photographed

Figure 6. Flipper

earlier in the week and received a lengthy explanation:

While vacationing in Sicily, Anja had seen modular plastic systems used to shade and protect storefronts and shops. She thought these plastic pieces would be easy to track down. Not quite. She was sent from storeowner to storeowner trying to find the plastic clips, with each shopkeeper saying he didn't have any, but he knew this other shop that certainly did. After being sent from one place to another, she was told that she could definitely get them from a certain shop across the water. It was getting late in the day, and she had to take a ferry to get there. When she arrived, the shop owner had some, but only in green, yellow, and white. That was fine and she loaded up. He told her the last ferry would be leaving in ten minutes, and otherwise she would have to spend the night. The shop owner drove her to the dock and she just made the boat as it left. Returning to Berlin, she combined the individual plastic pieces to make the Flipper sign, without a clear purpose in mind. Later, when the possibility to use this empty space came up, she adjusted the Flipper sign to fit the window, and opened a bar.

In addition to running Flipper, Anja Lutz publishes and art-directs a collaborative magazine project called *Shift!* The thirteen issues of this always-changing magazine project seems to embody the spirit of a nonproprietary and openly collaborative graphic design practice. Issue number 12, "Doubletake," is particularly appropriate.

Figure 7. Cover and spread from Shift!, no. 12, "Doubletake"

Shift! number 12, "Doubletake," is a "photographic experiment combining the convenience of global communication with happy snapping. The contained images are the result of recording the day, by shooting thirty-six shots, one every twenty minutes from morning to night, then rewinding the film and mailing it to a distant friend who is asked to repeat the process. Over one hundred individuals from around the world exposed around 1,800 frames." Doubletake asks the contributors to consider their contribution as nothing more than an incremental step that will be altered and maybe improved by the next contributor.

Can you imagine graphic design employing this method in wider practice? I can. But it'll require a fundamental change in designers' mindsets. No longer will the designer be the sole author of a unique solution for a discrete problem, but instead, we will be free to explicitly adopt other designers' works to fit our own needs. And we won't even need to conceal this reality. Conversely, we have to accept that what we have done is subject to modification by any other designer. Can we stand it? I think so.

Part 4. Open Source Software and Sharing

The Open Source Software movement provides a solid model for a future practice of graphic design. Open Source Software preaches a gospel of open collaboration and sharing for the collective good. The basic premise is that software can be made by a group of dispersed collaborative individuals more effectively than it can be by an individual or tight team. And, that free software is inherently better than the commercial alternative.

When a consumer buys a piece of commercial software, what he is getting is only a license to use it. Consumers might be surprised to find out that they don't own the source code that determines how the software works. Technically sophisticated users want access to modify, fix, or add to the software. They want access to the technology, because that is where the power resides. This is like buying a car with the hood sealed shut. Writing in the September 24, 2000 *New York Times*, Peter Wayner compares the individual altering his or her Linux operating system to a concrete precedent. "They're using the source code in much the same way that Bo and Luke Duke welded a few enhancements to their car in the television show *The Dukes of Hazzard*."

The Linux operating system is one of the best-known and most successful examples of Open Source Software engineering. In developing Linux, the many distributed participants adhered to the following four rules (posted on *www.GNU.org*.)

Figure 8. Peace, Love, and Linux logo from a recent IBM ad campaign

The principles of Open Source Software are listed as "Four Freedoms."

1. The freedom to run the program, for any purpose.

2. The freedom to study how the program works, and adapt it to your needs.

3. The freedom to redistribute copies so you can help your neighbor.

4. The freedom to improve the program, and release your improvements to the public, so that the whole community benefits.

Could this actually be a model for a different type of graphic design practice? An open-source design where ownership and authorship are explicitly negotiated and shared?

An open-source model for graphic design gets its power from the collective. And like any collective, the only way to enact it is through the individual. The decision to embrace an open and nonproprietary method of working, perhaps allowing your brilliant and original ideas to be marginalized in the context of a collaborative product, can be balanced by the possibility of developing someone else's ideas without the added burden of cloaking them in your unique style.

Berlin-based graphic designer Prem Krishnamurthy has employed a similar method in his Berlin Berlin (Daily Tourism) project. Prem invited willing Berliners to become tourists in their own city. He outlined a simple task expressed as two instructions: (1) Shoot a roll of 24-exposure film on a single day in Berlin; (2) Include six pictures, each of a letter that fills the frame. These pictures may be spread throughout the roll, but must consist of the following six letters in this order: B-E-R-L-I-N.

Figure 9. Contact sheets from Prem Krishnamurthy's Berlin Berlin (Daily Tourism)

Each roll of 24-exposure film printed directly to a contact sheet records one person's day spent photographing the letters. By relinquishing control over the set of artifacts (contact sheets), the designer has opened up possibilities and dialogues within a clearly prescribed framework. The resulting contact sheets begin to make legible multiple experiences of B-E-R-L-I-N.

Graphic designers are already largely their own best audience for the work of graphic design. Designers have a rabid interest in the work and details of other designers. The idea of open-source design would be to harness this interest to bring the whole of graphic design to a completely new place. Designers copy each others work all the time anyway. Why not use this for the collective good?

I am not suggesting a radical realignment of the entire profession. This would be antithetical to the spirit of the Open Source movement. Rather, it must be a personal decision to regard your own work as not proprietary, then to proactively and unabashedly copy other designers' work. But in copying the work, the ideas, even the style of the original, it is then your responsibility to improve upon it, add to it, or shift its meaning. Then, with luck, another designer might see your work and copy it as well. Perhaps, the design might even return to be used by you later in a much altered form on a different project. And, in evaluating work, it becomes the open-source designer's responsibility to gauge the work in the context of all or some of the others from which it directly and explicitly borrowed partial or complete ideas.

Figure 10. GSW headquarters building facade in different states

During the week I spent walking around Berlin, the spirit of open collaboration and sharing was tangible. I saw the headquarters building of GSW, the former East German state housing authority. The facade of the building changes throughout the day, and with the weather, as each individual closes or opens their brightly colored louvres to create a collective pattern.

Part 5. A Model

On April 3, 2001, the *New York Times* reported that the Massachusetts Institute of Technology (MIT) was trying an open-source model with their course materials:

"Other universities may be striving to market their courses to the Internet masses in hopes of dot-com wealth. But the Massachusetts Institute of Technology has chosen the opposite path: to post virtually all its course materials on the Web, free to everybody. MIT plans on Wednesday to announce a ten-year initiative, apparently the biggest of its kind, that intends to create public Web sites for almost all of its 2,000 courses and to post materials like lecture notes, problem sets, syllabuses, exams, simulations, even video lectures."

MIT is a hotbed of the Open Source Software movement, so this makes sense. However, it is the only university that is attempting anything close to this model with their course materials and the Internet. "And ultimately," said the MIT representative, "there will probably be a lot of uses that will really surprise us and that we can't really predict."

Coincidentally, MIT has taken a similar approach to the graphic design of their main Web site (*www.mit.edu*). According to Suzana Lisanti, Director of Web Communications Services, "The home page reflects the diversity of interests in the MIT community with a changing header graphic." The main identifying MIT logo on the institution's home page is a graphic solicited openly from anyone in the extended community and it changes every day. It's hard to imagine a large corporation taking such a radical approach to its graphic identity, but this makes perfect sense at an institution deeply committed to Open Source.

MIT's constantly evolving, reconfigurable, and fluid logo is a prescient example of the possibilities for an open-source graphic design practice. On the Web page, Graphic Guidelines for the MIT Home Page, Ms. Lisanti provides a checklist for Web site logo submissions. This listing of practical concerns includes the following instruction, which describes the nature of an open and collaborative graphic design model concisely:

"Graphics should elicit surprise, laughter, or delight. (Other reactions may be equally acceptable.)"

A Life of Luxury

When Products Are Naughty But Nice

Hugh Aldersey-Williams

"Luxury," spits Graham Chapman in derision when Michael Palin tells him his family used to live "in't paper bag" in the Monty Python sketch on the inverted snobbery of Yorkshiremen. (Chapman grew up "in't hole in't road," so far as I recall.) The idea of *luxury* begins with property. No hotel is good enough unless it's a luxury hotel. To sell a vacation home, call it a luxury vacation home. We spend so much time in our cars these days that they count as luxury properties too, or at least the word is invoked when a brand name like Mercedes isn't there to do the job; for example, in the case of top-of-the-line Japanese models. But now the epithet extends to all manner of consumer goods.

It is easy to imagine that luxury might have had its origins in austerity that gave way to plenty during the 1950s. This may indeed be when the word began to appear in the branding of foods. But the history of the idea in Britain has its roots in the mercantilism and expansion of the middle class in the eighteenth century, which transformed the meaning of the word from sinfulness to licit self-indulgence, "from an essential, general element of moral theory to a minor, technical element of economic theory," according to John Sekora's *Luxury: The Concept in Western Thought, Eden to Smollett.*

Luxury was always bound to have a distinctive meaning at the heart of a protestant imperial power. Our luxury items—coffee and spices, silk and cotton—are obtained at not inconsiderable cost (to others) and are to be enjoyed only with some residual guilt. In an earlier career, Salman Rushdie peeled away the layers of tittering English ambivalence to sensual pleasure with forensic accuracy in order to put together the memorably concise copy line to sell cream cakes: "Naughty but nice."

Marks and Spencer now reinforces its position in the market as a food retailer a cut above the average with an abundance of "luxury" lines. Designers have reason to love "luxury," as was explained to me by Guy Douglass of FLB, a branding and packaging design agency based in Cheltenham. "You can really make the word look nice. The ascender of the *l* is balanced by the descender of the *y*, pivoted round the central *x*. It's much easier to make it look nice than 'sumptuous.'"

On one level, "luxury" is a synonym for "premium" or "superior"—other Latinate emblazonments of poshness. As if to confirm this correlation between higher-quality and foreign words, Marks has a range of products even more luxurious than "luxury," which it labels "connoisseur" (a connoisseur being one who exercises a certain discrimination in his consumption of luxuries). But "luxury" has an orotundity—not lost on the Pythons—whereas "prestige," "premium," and "superior" now sound mealy-mouthed through overuse. "Premium" has begun to be used for things like dog food. Eventually, "luxury" may begin to pall. New words will be needed.

"Luxury" is not simply an indicator of superiority, however. It has a secondary connotation of comfort, appropriate in its original commercial context of describing property, but now deemed fitting for any goods that come into body contact. So the idea of luxury motor oil or luxury computer software is meaningless. It is even impossible to conceive of a luxury dog food, unless perhaps it is one hand-prepared to a chef's recipe that you would be prepared to eat yourself. But soap and caviar and lingerie may be luxuries. It is no coincidence that the French, who understand these things, dominate the export of luxury goods. Louis Vuitton Möet Hennessy, the luggage-to-champagne conglomerate, calls itself "the world's leading luxury products group."

The indulgence of luxury offers a more private pleasure than conspicuous consumption. A luxury product does not just give you more of something, it gives you more than you have a right to expect, whether it's a thicker chocolate coating, more fruit, more alcohol, more supple leather, or a higher proportion of cashmere wool. So there are no luxury diet products. Neither must any preparation be required by the consumer: Labor is no part of luxury.

But this isn't the whole story. We also have luxury muesli, luxury toilet tissue, advertisements promising luxury camping holidays—all bowels and suffering. Here, "luxury" is no longer a promise of pleasure. The word has subtly metamorphosed in meaning again. Today's luxury is more precisely an assurance of reduced discomfort. What better evidence could one want that this is the true meaning of luxury than the existing classification of tampons as luxuries for the purposes of levying VAT?

Luxury has long been a quality of interest to economists who find a measure of the health of the consumer society in its propensity for luxury goods. From Adam Smith to Kenneth Galbraith, they have observed and welcomed the graduation of luxuries into necessities. Now the Chancellor Gordon Brown may follow in their footsteps by announcing in his budget next week that tampons are no longer luxuries. Meanwhile, the boffins in new product development offer them lists of new things to tax with every humdrum item that they choose to upgrade to luxury status.

Editor's note: The preceding piece originally appeared under the headline, "Luxury Rip-Off," in The New Statesman, *27 March 2000, pp 48–49.*

I ❤ NY More Than Ever

Steven Heller Interviews Milton Glaser

Two decades ago Milton Glaser designed the I ❤ NY logo to help the state of New York in its tourism campaign. It was a reasonable problem with a simple enough solution. Little did Glaser, or anyone for that matter, know how incredibly popular I ❤ NY would be. Not only did it quantifiably aid the fundamental campaign, it became an icon first for New York, and ultimately for virtually every city and town throughout the world. It is the most borrowed visual idea since Grant Wood's "American Gothic" or Saul Steinberg's *New Yorker* cover. But in the wake of the World Trade Center attack on September 11, I ❤ NY has taken on an entirely new, and unexpected, relevance. It has become the seal of a determined city and nation. Seeing this, within hours of the tragedy Glaser decided to add even greater emotion to this symbol: to I ❤ NY he added the words "more than ever" and bruised a corner of the heart. Although the state of New York, which owns the mark, objected to this alteration, in this interview Glaser talks about how and why this symbol—old and new—has become such an emotional touchstone.

SH: Before we talk about recent events, I've always wanted to know if you were surprised by the sudden universality of your I ❤ NY logo?

MG: I certainly was. It's hard to anticipate what part of one's work might enter into public awareness, but the universal acceptance and ongoing reinterpretation of the I ❤ NY logo continues to astonish me.

SH: Well, it certainly has been given added dimension in light of the attack on the World Trade Center on September 11. I've seen hundreds of people wearing and displaying the logo. And in response to the events, you went a step further. Why did you feel the need to alter your design, by wounding the heart and adding the words "more than ever?" Wasn't the original still valid?

MG: It depends on what you mean by valid. Something happened on September 11 that must be acknowledged. The first step toward healing is acknowledging that one has been hurt. In the same way that we feel more deeply toward a loved one who has been hurt, all of us suddenly realized how deeply we feel about this city. A confident giant is hard to love, a vulnerable one is not. The original I ❤ NY is a pledge of affection that has become banal. The pain has made us recommit to this now vulnerable, magnificent place.

SH: Your bruised heart demonstratively expresses the fact that New York did indeed suffer a terrible blow, but I understand that the State of New York objected to this new iteration. Why?

MG: The state has no interest in using this variation of the logo, feeling that anything that acknowledges the 9/11 event might be interpreted as a sign of weakness.

SH: I would think otherwise, and agree with you that we must acknowledge our hurt to deal with it. So, did you decide to make the change or did someone approach you to do so? And how did it become the front and back cover of the *New York Daily News?*

MG: Like all of us, I felt the need to respond to this incomprehensible tragedy. I woke up a day after the attack with the words and image completely formed in my mind. I e-mailed it to a good friend, Pete Hamill, who now is a reporter for the *Daily News,* to ask his opinion of the idea. He showed it to the editor, Ed Kosner, who called telling me he would run it inside the newspaper in two days. The following morning at 6:00 A.M. I was awakened by a call from a local-radio interview show asking me why I designed the logo. "How do you know anything about it?" I asked. "It's hard to avoid, it's on the front and back cover of the *Daily News,*" she replied. Evidently Kosner had decided to use it earlier and more dramatically than I could have imagined.

SH: It does resonate. I can almost hear the words "more than ever" coming from our collective hearts. But the slogan nonetheless raises a question. Do you feel that I ❤ NY is designed to be about exclusion or inclusion?

MG: Alas, the sad fact is that any claim for uniqueness that intends to build community pride, "I love New York," "Black is beautiful," "Jews are the chosen people," "Jesus saves," you name it, has within it the capacity to exclude and alienate others.

SH: How does this commercialism enter into the equation?

MG: I'm not sure what you mean by commercialism. The original I ❤ NY campaign intended to raise the spirits of our citizens as well as produce an atmosphere that would attract tourists and business to New York. It succeeded beyond anyone's expectations. The logo was freely distributed for about fifteen years to any enterprise that wished to use it. Later the state decided to trademark it and control its use. Like it or not, commerce is the engine that propels this country.

SH: Then, how do you feel about your transformed symbol? Should it be sold on t-shirts and buttons to commemorate this event, or should the logo and everything that it is printed on be free to all who want and need it?

MG: Whatever its application, I would want some part or all of the proceeds to go toward the city's restoration.

SH: Do you feel that any transformation is appropriate or that there is only one right way to revisit the symbol?

MG: I'm sure there are many ways to revise the symbol. A day hardly passes that I do not get an e-mail from someone suggesting I put an American flag or the two towers within the heart. I know that potent symbols can be made by combining clichés but they must seem inevitable, not predictable. Ideally the effect is poetic rather than logical. The phrase "more than ever" is explained and illuminated by the wounded heart. I can only judge its effect by the response of the first two people I sent it to—they both said the same thing: "It made me want to cry."

SH: How do you feel about the abundance of generic red, white, and blue, and flag imagery that has sprung up since the tragedy? Is using patriotic imagery the most effective way to bind us together, or does it somehow neutralize the experience?

MG: While driving home from the country last week, I was almost run off the road by a battered yellow Chevy sporting two flags and the words "Nuke the Bastards" written crudely across the trunk. This sort of ardent patriotism always makes me uneasy. On the other hand, at this moment we all desperately want to express our solidarity around a powerful symbol and as usual the nation's flag, because it is familiar and available, serves that purpose.

SH: Do you feel that there are any designs that can truly capture our sadness, fears, and hopes?

MG: Forgive me; I've not checked the AIGA site—not out of indifference, but simply because I've been using my time differently. Given the quality of professional practice in America, I'm sure there are many excellent ideas.

SH: Is there another symbol that you would like to do that further sums up your feelings, and by extension our feelings about the tragedy?

MG: Not so much about the tragedy but perhaps what we must do now to recover from it.

SH: Does that take the form of a symbol or is action or deed more effective in terms of recovery?

MG: Both are needed.

SH: What do you suggest that our profession, or for that matter artists in general, do to comfort victims and rebuild the city?

MG: That is the kind of question that can make you sound like a pompous idiot if you try to answer it. I'll try anyhow. The only comfort I can hope for is the possibility that this perception-changing event will make us realize how related we are to all the rest of the world. That our tragedies and dreams are theirs and theirs ours. Without that understanding, it will be very hard to ever come to terms with September 11, 2001.

Socialist Designers
Véronique Vienne Interviews Fabrizio Gilardino

Socialist Designers Manifesto

Socialist Designers is a collective of politically conscious graphic designers who have agreed to follow "an indisputable set of rules":

1. Design must be done on location. "Props and sets" (i.e., stock photographs and illustrations) must not be brought in.

2. Design must be done in spot colors. Four-color process and varnish are not acceptable.

3. Photoshop filters and any other filters are forbidden.

4. Design must not contain superficial elements.

5. Temporary and geographical alienation are forbidden (that is that design must take place here and now).

6. "Genre" design is not acceptable.
   —Montreal, Fall 2001

Fabrizio Gilardino is an Italian graphic designer currently based in Montreal, Canada. In October 2001, he founded the graphic design collective Socialist Designers.

Véronique Vienne: Who are you? How many people are there in your Socialist Designers collective?

Fabrizio Gilardino (chuckles): I knew you would ask that. Honestly? I am the main guy. Our collective is very loose and flexible. There are a few people gravitating around me but they're not involved as much as I am. In a certain way, it is a collective, but at the same time I'm the one maybe doing most of the work.

VV: Where did the ideas in your manifesto come from?

FG: The Socialist Designers' "Vows of Chastity" were inspired by the DOGME 95 manifesto written in 1995 by filmmaker Lars Von Trier, the director of *Dancer in the Dark*, and Thomas Vinterberg, another Danish film director. That was our main influence. What really attracted me to that particular manifesto was that it was a clear and strong statement against a certain made-in-Hollywood ideal. I was also attracted by this notion of it being a "manifesto"—a call for freedom within very strict rules—which is of course a contradiction. But there's nothing wrong with contradictions.

The DOGMA 95 manifesto has been very influential—mostly in the cinema milieu. Even though its vows of chastity are strict, there's room for humor. It's the same with my manifesto. I advocate not using stock photographs, stock illustrations, Photoshop filters, and superficial elements, for instance. But I also make reference to Situationist leader Guy Debord by signing all my letters with an insider's pun, "Vive Guy, d'abord."

VV: What is your connection with Guy Debord and the Situationists?

FG: There are no real connections. I am familiar with Debord's writing. He has been an influential thinker for me. More specifically, his critique of everyday life is still very relevant today.

But what really interests me and what I think we should point out is that at the beginning of their critique of everyday life, the Situationists thought that urban planning and architecture were the two disciplines that were the most compromised with the bureaucracy and what they called the "Society of the Spectacle." But it's important these days that we also think about the role played by graphic design and the advertising industry. I think that, today, those are the most compromised disciplines. Those are the fields that more than any other convey certain messages coming from the dictatorship of the market.

VV: For someone not familiar with Situationist ideals, your Socialist Designers Manifesto is totally obscure, arbitrary, dictatorial even. Do you find yourself having to explain what it all means, or do people who are part of your collective know what you're talking about?

FG: Yes, sometimes I do have to explain. People react in a funny way, asking, "Why should I follow those rules? I like Photoshop filters!" Or, "Why shouldn't I print in four-color process?"

VV: So, what do you say?

FG: My explanations are two-fold: First, there are political aspects—they're quite clear and obvious—but at the same time, I also have aesthetic concerns. I grew tired of seeing the same genre of graphic design over and over. The introduction of computers has played a major role in the homogenization of graphic design. I'm constantly exposed to things that all look the same—that bear certain common traits—slick stuff everywhere.

In our collective, we're tired of being dismissed as minor-league players just because a large amount of what we do is silk-screened, for instance. It's by choice that we tend to use two- or three-color spots and cheaper papers. Yet the reaction is like: "You don't run a big studio, you don't have the budget to do four-color process, that's why you advocate 'chastity.'"

Yet my clients are all smart—they come from the cultural sector. I'm working for quite a number of theater companies, dance companies, record labels, independent choreographers, and members of the new music community here in Montreal—composers and musicians.

VV: Can you make a living? I'm not even asking you if you are getting rich—but can you survive with those ideals?

FG: I know, I know . . . It has been a problem. It's getting a little bit better since last year, when I started to teach typography. But if I were to work only for those not-for-profit clients, it would be a lot more difficult.

I work alone, and with such small budgets it would be impossible for me to hire anybody else. Sometimes I'm working with illustrators or people on very specific projects. But most of the time I'm a one-man studio, or whatever you want to call it. I prefer the word "atelier."

I don't really see myself as a professional. I really have problems with that term, anyway. I'm more of a "craft" person. I prefer that term because "professional" almost immediately means someone who knows much more than he or she does.

VV: My last question is about the word "socialist." Does it make people uneasy? Do they even know what to talk about?

FG: Yeah, I know. We were kind of careful about that in the sense that . . . we are aware of the fact that this term could be used to create misunderstandings and problems. We are socialists but we are not attached to any institutions. It's our desire to act in the original sense of the word.

We are socialist because we have social concerns, because we are interested in a very specific way of thinking about life, about a better life. Being conscious of the fact—and I guess that's very European—that anything you do in a certain way is political. Every time you talk, every time you buy something, every time you apply certain principles (conscious or unconscious or whatever), you make a political statement.

I really have problems when graphic designers say, "I'm not into politics," or, "Politics bother me," or, "I'm not interested in it." That's so absurd to me. I can't relate to this way of seeing things.

Part IV
Raves and Rants

Responsible to Whom, I'd Like to Know?
Consorting with Clients to Con Shareholders
Ken Garland

In a previous existence, as it now seems, I would not infrequently find myself seated at boardroom tables in close conclave with CEOs and their cohorts as we debated the corporate images of their companies. With my features composed into what I hoped was a serious and attentive expression—nodding slowly with lips pursed was one of my favorites—I would make copious notes of my clients' sage remarks (or appeared to; in reality it was mostly scribble). Many's the time, toward the end of such conferences, that I would find myself about to break into mighty yawns. God only knows how I managed to abort them. Thoughts of the consultancy fees helped, I suppose; one careless, chasmal dropping of the jaw and I would have been ushered into commercial oblivion, blacklisted from every boardroom in the country.

Inevitably, at some point in the discussions, the words would crop up. The CEO or the sales director or, most probably, the finance director would say, "The thing we have to bear in mind, Garland, in all this vast expenditure on corporate identity, is our ultimate responsibility, our overriding responsibility, to our share-holders. Hope you've got that firmly in your mental conceptualization at this point in time, hmm?" Such strictures might well be accompanied by surreptitious glances at those parts of my appearance—long hair, lack of tie, trousers uncreased, wrong color of shirt, unpolished shoes—which might give rise to suspicions of incipient irresponsibility and which I would be well advised to attend to before the next meeting. In the meantime, my immediate response was a very slow nod, a very judicious pursing of the lips, and a very visible note, "over-rdg. resp. to sh'holders," underlined twice.

If I had comported myself properly during some of these boardroom colloquia and was decently attired, I might be invited afterward to lengthy lunches at ritzy restaurants. When much alcohol had loosened their tongues, some of the directors became a bit more revelatory on the subject of overriding responsibility to share-holders. During just such an occasion, when we had reached the brandy stage, one director said to me, "Thing about our bloody shareholders is, as long as they're assured of a reasonable return and have their chance to sound off a bit at the annual general meeting, we can get them to agree to anything we want to do. More brandy?" I'd heard politicians say much the same about voters and elections and was reminded about someone's definition of democracy as "a form of government in which you say what you like and do what you're told."

After I'd been incautious enough in 1964 to publish a rather provocative mani-festo with the title "First Things First," which cast aspersions at certain commercial practices, the sales director of one of my client companies at that time invited me to lunch, just the two of us. "Well, Ken," he said, "you're putting yourself about a bit, laddie, appearing on television and proclaiming manifestos. All good fun, of course, but I wonder if you're not being a bit, ah, irresponsible, if I may say so. Do hope this won't frighten off some of your clients, know what I mean?" I did indeed know what he meant. Fortunately, none of my client companies saw fit to sever rela-tions—except his, that is.

I suppose that all the rest of them were only too well aware of my opinions on these matters and thought to themselves, "Oh, that's Ken for you; every now and then he likes to sound off. Pay no attention and it'll wear off, like whooping cough." The most unpredictable reaction came from my bank manager, whom I had to confront the day after I had declaimed "First Things First" on a prime-time TV chat show, wearing a leather jacket and an incendiary expression. I had to ask him for a large loan and assumed I must have blown it; but quite the reverse. "Saw you on television last night," he said, with uncustomary cordiality. "Very impressive performance, if I may say so. I look forward to seeing more of you on the box. Now, about this loan: shouldn't be any difficulty at all, old chap. How much d'you want?"

Now, glad as I was to have the unexpected offer of a loan, I was rather miffed that the bank manager regarded my televised declaration as a "performance," rather as though I were the equivalent of a stand-up comedian. A more apt simile might be that of a court jester: licensed to be irresponsible. Not a role I had anticipated but one into which I appeared to have been thrust, though it never for one moment applied to anything I did as a graphic designer (the truth being that I continued to work in exactly the same way after "First Things First" as I had done before).

So there we have it. "Responsibility" means consorting with captains of industry in order to take appropriate action while conning the shareholders into letting it through on the nod. "Irresponsibility" means sounding off in public about anything you don't happen to like about The Way Things Are.

Taking one thing with another, I think I'm going to opt for irresponsibility. After all, at my time of life, what have I got to lose?

Note for the New Millennium

Is the Role of Design to Glorify Corporate Power?

Stuart Ewen

Entranced by the still-recent invention of photography, Oliver Wendell Holmes Sr. in 1859 prophesized that a new culture was about to take hold. The most prominent feature of this new way of life would be a profusion of mass-produced images, drawn from any source, applied to any thing. In the wake of this development, surface would overwhelm substance in the structure of meaning. "Every conceivable object of Nature and Art will soon scale off its surface for us," he said. "Men will hunt all curious, beautiful grand objects as they hunt cattle in South America, for their skins, and leave the carcasses as of little worth."

Looking at the endless vistas of mass-produced imagery today, we can appreciate the prescience of his insight. The ubiquitous power of the image is visible in products, packaging, and advertisement. It is an essential element in the construction of corporate and national identity. Increasingly, information—or disinformation—is graphically communicated, shaping common understanding of the truth. Mass imagery, in fact, is a powerful component of how we've come to understand and envision the meaning of democracy.

Images also influence the ways in which individuals establish a sense of personal identity. In the United States, where most people live anonymously as part of a mass audience, the prospect of being projected into the spectacle, of becoming an image, represents society's highest kind of acclaim. Mass-produced and disseminated images are even woven into the depths of human desire: For many, their first sexual experiences are essentially encounters with images.

Yet the pivotal position of design within contemporary culture traces back to the turn of this century, and its growth in importance is inextricably linked to the rise of industrial mass production. The modern phenomenon of design grew out of a simultaneous critique of the aristocratic style traditions of the past and of the flood of cheap, mass-produced images and bric-a-brac that swamped European and American markets from 1870 onward. Disgusted by the "degeneracy" of these two forces and awestruck by industrialism, designers claimed they could light the path to a new democratic society.

Designers during this period shared one fundamental belief: that design was alive with social implications. They felt that style was more than a matter of subjective taste. For the advocates of Arts and Crafts, Art Nouveau, industrial modernism, and other modern tendencies, these approaches inherently expressed social and political outlooks; styles aestheticized and communicated common assumptions. For many who entered into the debates over which style was appropriate to the industrial age, design held the fate of civilization in its hands. Conscientiously applied, it could transform social reality. It could help to bring about a utopian future, or, if misused, put a varnish on barbarism. Intrinsic to these notions was the conviction that designers must be involved in an ongoing evaluation of their work and of its implications for society.

Today such thinking is rare. Designers are primarily aware of their work as a selling device; there are few connections made to the socio-aesthetic tradition from which their profession was born. An aestheticism that separates images from social concerns dominates not only the thinking of practicing designers but also the curricula of most design schools. The understanding of design as a transmitter of values has vanished in favor of overarching ideas that "good design" is that which sells.

This kind of thinking is evident, for example, in an ad that was recently run in the *Wall Street Journal* by the Michael Peters/Duffy Design Group. Addressing potential corporate clients, the ad reads:

> Good design, we believe, can be the most profitable way to spend a marketing budget. . . . It can make your product disappear off the shelf, instead of disappearing into it. And as more and more competitive products become more and more alike, a good package can become a packaged good's best . . . point of difference.

The ad concludes by reassuring its audience:

> The good news is that you don't have to give a fig about understanding the design process to appreciate the beauty of its results.

Amid the acceptance of such thinking, the social and political significance of design remains, for the most part, neither understood nor addressed as a problem. There is a near universal amnesia regarding the issues that first propelled the field of design into being. Where an awareness of it exits at all, the early history of design is regarded as nothing more than an aesthetic warehouse, a pile of discarded "skins" from which to steal ideas.

This lack of systematic thought about the impact of design on social life is the intrinsic outcome of design having become a corporate profession. It is part of a general process by which systems of images, symbols, and meanings have over the past century become increasingly fused with the priorities of corporate merchandising and mass marketing. During this period, design has been called upon to establish corporate identities firmly in the public mind and to motivate the development of ever-hungry consumer markets. These design imperatives are now embedded within the routines of the job and thus appear natural: they are rarely thrown into question.

With the capture of the eye well established as the prime strategy of corporate marketing, design today speaks a visual language that continually reinforces the outlook and interests of business. Appealing to the emotions, and most often bypassing critical thinking on the part of consumers, design has become a particularly toxic form of communication, one that regularly masks destructive patterns within our society. In its day-to-day practice, with little or no self-examination, commercial design routinely aestheticizes, or renders beautiful, hazardous ideas about the use of environmental resources, about the nature and concentration of power, and about the ordering of the values by which we live. In the process, tendencies that threaten the interests of human survival are transformed into icons of "the good life."

At the heart of the environmental crisis is the fact that within a consumer society engineered waste and obsolescence are prime stimulants of "economic health." This reflects seventy-five years of American history, in which disposability has been key to merchandising. Within the entrenched strategies of planned product obsolescence, "new and improved" designs have become essential tools for encouraging waste—for making waste desirable.

Indeed, the desirability of waste is now a basic element in our definition of social prosperity. To some extent, this idea was already evident at the turn of the century, when Simon Patten, a prominent social theorist, approvingly observed a new standard of living that was taking hold in the United States. This "standard of life," he said, "is determined not so much by what a man has to enjoy as by the rapidity with which he tires of the pleasure. To have a high standard means to enjoy a pleasure intensely, and to tire of it quickly."

By 1930, this notion was essential to the practice of commercial design. Earnest Elmo Calkins, an American advertising man, described it this way: "The purpose is to make the customer discontented with his old type of fountain pen, kitchen utensil, bathroom, or motor car, because it is old-fashioned, out-of-date. . . . We no longer wait for things to wear out. We displace them with others that are not more effective but more attractive."

Since that time, merchandising has been propelled by a never-ending search for new images. Taken from any source, inspired by all forms of human expression, these images enter the skin trade as sales resources, only to leave it—once their economic value has been extracted—as garbage. And today the garbage pile grows higher and higher.

In the path of impending environmental disaster, the range of human possibility is being incrementally narrowed to that which is for sale. With nearly all forms of visual expression—even the fine arts—reduced to the status of commodities, our ability to learn from such expressions, to make sense of our world through them, is diminished. As our line of sight is drawn further into the market of images, democratic choice is reduced to window-shopping for disposable impressions. History itself is reduced to a consumable parade of visual clichés, and the social forces that drive it are rendered less and less comprehensible.

This is especially problematic at a time when society's most profitable growth lies in the commerce of pure representation: money, credit, information. Recent years have witnessed an explosion in the size of the symbolic economy, while those sectors concerned with the production of actual goods are in desperate health. As disembodied representation has come to dominate our culture, aesthetic values have become increasingly evanescent. The relation between image and power is an ancient one, but today the two have become interchangeable. And insofar as wealth itself has become pure representation, there now exits an equivalency between the nature of wealth and the nature of design.

A binge of insubstantiality is sweeping through the world of design. Invisibility, self-aggrandizing superficiality, and the elevation of immateriality are ruling aesthetic goals. Design has become a thing in and of itself. No longer a way of communicating something about a product or about its use, most design speaks of an ethic of pure packaging. Underlying this disembodied play of images lies an ongoing premise: Design is useful as an instrument for glorifying corporate power. In a global economy, where ownership and wealth operate on a transnational level, designers and other image-doctors celebrate and aestheticize colossal institutions that are for the most part entirely unresponsive to the needs of the broader human community.

Today this glorification of the corporation, so dominant within the practice of commercial design, has implications that affect the subjective experience of our lives. Notions of "prosperity" and "the good life" are announced and authenticated within the unverifiable choreography of commercial images, while the significant presence of squalor, deprivation, and loss of hope are, for the most part, left invisible. When suffering is seen within the spectacle, it is usually depicted as the natural plight of others. For us, it is best to invest our hopes in the imagery of prosperity. If designers at one time believed they could deliver humanity from social inequities and help to bring about a utopian future, designers today place a gloss on social inequity and limit utopia in the marketplace.

As we approach the new millennium, the design profession stands at a fateful juncture. Designers must come to reflect upon the functions they serve, and on the potentially hazardous implications of those functions. In the 1930s Walter Benjamin wrote that humankind's "self-alienation has reached such a degree that it can experience its own destruction as an aesthetic pleasure of the first order." When we consider the ways in which design serves to aestheticize and validate waste, anti-democratic forms of power and the primacy of surface over substance, Benjamin's words can only give us pause.

The terrible power of a culture to render even human destruction beautiful must begin to motivate self-reflection within the design profession. Only by critically confronting this concern and by integrating it into a conscious, ethical practice of design will meaningful alternatives be possible.

Originally published in ID: International Design, *March/April 1990.*

Brand You

Better Selling through Anthropology

Thomas Frank

"Advertising is a means of contributing meaning and values that are necessary and useful to people in structuring their lives, their social relationships, and their rituals."
—from a British pamphlet

Introducing Account Planning

It is an easy thing, I admit, even in this high noon of the bull market, to scoff at the dot-coms, the hedge funds, the silicon millionaires, the day traders, and all the other ephemera of prosperity. But beneath all the prodigious bubbling, counsel the wise, stands an institution as solid and reliable as U.S. Steel: the *Brand*. But the *brand* is a complex thing, not easily understood by the earthbound and the pessimistic. Its power is not a matter of simple force, of the workery brawn celebrated in WPA murals; nor does our faith in the *brand* resemble the naive patriotism of the early Cold War. The *brand*, correctly understood, is a relationship, a thing of nuance and complexity, of irony and coy evasiveness. We are at once skeptical of consumer culture and more ravenous consumers than ever, easily seeing through the clumsy sales pitches that convinced our parents and grandparents, and yet continuing to hum the Lite-Brite jingle to ourselves more than fifteen years after it ceased appearing on TV. *Brands* are special things to us Americans, interactive myths that earn our loyalty through endless repetition and constant adjustment by people of learning and subtlety.

I have spent some time in the company of those people, the individuals charged with overseeing the *brand* relationship. They call themselves "Account Planners," and although their field is a relatively new addition to the organizational flowcharts of Madison Avenue, account planning has already captured the imagination of "New Economy" enthusiasts everywhere. Its Stalinist-sounding name notwithstanding, planning is insurrectionary stuff. Not only is it identified with the sort of places where future-envisioning "change agents" are always making heroic revolution on the old rules, but its every advance hastens the achievement of full consumer democracy, that imagined free-market utopia wherein each empowered customer can make his or her voice heard in the great public agoras of shopping mall or Internet.

One of the first things I learned after arriving last July at Boston's Westin Hotel was that one did not come to gatherings of account planners dressed in a gray flannel suit. I had hoped to make myself inconspicuous by wearing the stereotypical adman's costume of the 1950s; I accomplished exactly the opposite. Not only were a majority of the planners female and a good number of them British, but I appeared to be the lone square in an auditorium full of high-budget hipsters. They had arrived at the Westin in white synthetic T-shirts stretched tightly over black brassieres, in those oblong spectacles favored by European intellectuals, in hair that had been bleached, bobbed, and barretted in Riot Grrl style. The men, for their part, wore four- and five-button leisure suits and sported corporate goatees and pierced noses. One group of planners periodically donned bright red fezzes; another set wandered around in camouflage. The sight of so much visible extremeness did what it no doubt was intended to do: It threw me, in my obsolete garb, into instant and compound self-doubt.

There were 750 people at the account planning conference, a number that seemed to startle everyone. The previous year's gathering was said to have been more "radical" but drew only around 500; a year before that it was an intimate affair of only 300. Planning has about it the air of a youth subculture that is on the cusp of going mainstream. It began in Britain in the corporate-revolutionary days of the 1960s and until quite recently had attracted only a handful of American initiates. But now, as talk of revolution once again blazes through the nation's office blocks, even the less tuned-in agencies are setting up planning departments, a fact that seemed vaguely to annoy several of the younger planners I spoke to. One of these actually warned me against "Fake Planners," agency opportunists who know no more about the mystery and the mission of planning than they do about Altaic verb conjugation. No one actually came right out and complained that planning's newfound popularity in the American hinterland meant that it had lost its edge or sold out to The Man, but the feeling was difficult to miss.

What has permitted planning to infiltrate the world of American business with so little notice, I suspect, is its name. The term "account planning" seems almost designed to disguise the profession as just another unremarkable component of the

"Fordist" order (a term that was actually used in one planner's presentation). But we live in an age of public skepticism and heightened sensitivity to every subtle shading of the advertising form, and it is not enough simply to dream up a pleasant-sounding jingle and a sleek-looking logo back at corporate headquarters. In a time when markets are routinely understood as the ultimate democratic form, as an almost perfectly transparent medium connecting the People with their corporations, planners function (or believe they function) as interpreters of and advocates for the popular will. Planning thus turns out to be virtually the opposite of what its name implies. I would hear again and again over the course of the weekend how advertising people must change their ways to acknowledge the fact of market democracy, how they must abandon their various fixed ideas, how they must "talk to consumers" and initiate an "agenda-free discussion" and "let consumers direct your plan." And to assist them in "uncovering the rational and emotional components of a product's *Brand* Essence," as one planner's job description read (yes, with caps in the original), planners enlist any number of audience-research techniques. I would hear about getting at the essence of the *brand* with the help of techniques such as "beeper studies," "fixed-camera analysis," "shadowing," "visual stories," brainstorming sessions with celebrities, and, of course, focus groups, which some planners seem to invest with an almost holy significance.

Account planning is postmodern cultural democracy come home to Madison Avenue complete with all its usual militancy against master narratives and hierarchical authority, its cheerleading for the marginalized, its breathless reverence for the wisdom of everyday people, and its claim to hear the revolutionary voice of the subaltern behind virtually any bit of mass-cultural detritus. Only one thing seems to be wrong: These enthusiastic, self-proclaimed vicars of the vox populi are also, almost to a person, paid agents of the Fortune 500.

The planners were addressed on the first day of their conference by Gerry Laybourne, the former head of Nickelodeon and occupant of the number twenty spot in *Fortune*'s list of the "Fifty Most Powerful Women in American Business," who was introduced as someone "known for creating incredibly profitable media *brands* by always putting the consumer first." A woman who confessed to having "epiphanies" during focus-group sessions and who referred to target demographics as "constituents" for whom she aimed to "make life better," Laybourne embodied account planning's combination of corporate power and effusive, hyperdemocratic populism. Perched on a tall stool and gently prompted by the solicitous questions of a planner associate, she described for us the bleak world of TV programming before the dawn of Laybourne, a time when her former employer "believed you should shout down a pipe" to reach your audience. At this the audience murmured scornfully: they knew it was all about listening, respect, dialogue, interactivity—and they knew what was coming next. Laybourne described the Nickelodeon focus group in which the revelation had come:

> [W]e asked kids a very innocuous question: "What do you like about being kids?" And in four different rooms, with these kids who were ten years old, we got a barrage of stuff back. "We're afraid of teenage suicide, we've heard about teenage drunk driving, we've heard about teenage pregnancy,

we're terrified about growing up, our parents have us programmed, we're
being hurried, we don't have a childhood."

So I stopped the research and I said, "Just go in and ask them what
Nickelodeon can do for them." And in all four groups: "Just give us back our
childhood.". . . And that became our battle cry. That became our platform.

Now, with childhood back in the hands of its rightful owners, with access to
Rugrats and *Bewitched* assured in perpetuity, the demographic battle lines had been
drawn and fortified.

"We were clearly on the side of kids," Laybourne continued, "clearly their
advocate, and we were never going to turn our backs on them."

But the work of empowerment-through-listening went on. There were other
demographics to liberate, and Laybourne told the planners how she and her new
organization, Oxygen Media, were preparing to launch a new "entertainment
brand" for women, a segment of the population that sounded just as lovable in
Laybourne's telling—as misunderstood, as monolithic, and as desperate for accurate
media representation—as the kids themselves. Although the exact nature of the
programming to which Laybourne's new *brand* was to be affixed remained mysterious throughout her talk, she did let drop that the ideal medium for it would be the
Internet, which she described as a living embodiment of her notion of democracy
through dialogue. Growing audibly indignant, Laybourne switched into protest
mode, railing against the arrogance of those who think that they can put a structure
on this thing. But the Internet is an organism, and they are trying to put mechanisms on top of an organism. It won't work. It's too powerful. Once people taste
freedom—this is the United States of America; we've got that in our blood. . . .
This is a revolution that will be led by kids . . . , and I hope women as well.

No revolution is complete without reactionaries, real or imagined, and so
Laybourne let us know where she and her new *brand* drew the line, stopped listening, and started excluding: namely at Southern Baptism, which had recently made
the subjection of women an official element of its credo. "I don't think that our
brand is going to appeal to those Southern Baptist men," she remarked tartly. The
ad execs erupted in laughter and applause.

But in the revolution against institutional hierarchy that continues to embroil
the republic of business, Laybourne was a moderate and slow-moving Girondin compared with the Jacobins of the British St. Luke's agency, which had dispatched Planner
Phil Teer to inspire his American comrades with tales of upheaval and progress at "the
agency of the future." St. Luke's was nothing less than a syndicalist agency, its ownership shared uniformly by each employee. Teer was said to have come to advertising
only after working as a critic of the tobacco industry, which bestowed upon him a credibility that not even Laybourne's focus-group epiphanies could match. His irreverent,
self-effacing way of talking won the instant enthusiasm of the audience. He showed us
slides that contained the word "fuckin'." He spoke in a working-class Scottish accent,
which, he acknowledged, made him difficult for Americans to understand but which
also demonstrated the progress of the revolution: "It used to be, a year ago, we always
sent nice, middle-class, Oxford-educated, public school boys to talk at conferences for
St. Luke's." Surely this was the real thing at last.

Teer did not disappoint. He passed the next hour alternately extolling the artistic idealism that burned at his agency and tersely proclaiming the slogans of the business revolution. "If we stop exploring, we'll die," he said. "Work is leisure," read one of his slides. "Transform people," insisted another, flashing on the screen while Teer told of the liberation of the admen: the story of the security guard who now "dances to jazz funk as he does his rounds," the former suit-wearing executive who is now "a shaven-headed DJ." Not only had St. Luke's freed its employees to participate in the subculture of their choice but it had also invented such boons to productivity as "hot desking," a system in which people worked wherever they wanted in the company's unstructured office. "Abolish private space, and you abolish ego," Teer proclaimed. Even agency performance reviews had been revolutionized (the chairman was reviewed by a receptionist), apparently along the lines of the criticism/self-criticism sessions once fashionable on the Maoist left. But the people of St. Luke's were less interested in smashing the state than in "killing cynicism."

Not surprisingly, the ads produced by syndicalist admen turned out to imagine the *brands* in question as the contested terrain of social conflict. For Ikea, St. Luke's had imagined a cultural revolution in which the women of England rise up against chintz, a symbol of the old order as loathsome as cold desks or middle-class public school boys. "Chuck out that chintz. Come on, do it today," ran the jingle, sung to acoustic guitar accompaniment. The planners boisterously endorsed the call for People's War on chintz with waves of enthusiastic cheering.

After the planners had talked enough chaos and revolution for one day, they descended on gleaming, polished escalators past the Palm steak restaurant, the elite pen shop, and the indoor waterfall, and were ferried by buses disguised as trolleys to the Massachusetts State House, where they were welcomed by a platoon of men dressed in Revolutionary War uniforms and ushered up to one of four or five open bars dispensing microbrews and Maker's Mark.

"Anyone can make an identical product," one adman told me as we relaxed in a gallery of patriotic artifacts from Boston's heroic period. "Why do we choose one over another?" I listened to assorted rumors about Red Spider, the mysterious Scottish planning consultancy whose representatives had conducted an extremely exclusive all-day training session at the conference. I was told by one planner that your company's check must clear the bank before Red Spider will even leave Scotland; by another, that Red Spider never distributes anything that has been written down; by a third, that their instruction is done in a mystical master-to-acolyte approach; by a fourth, that their instruction takes a simple fiction-writing-seminar approach; and by a fifth, that, in fact, Red Spider will distribute things that are written down, it's just that the guy who was supposed to bring the written materials got sick.

Many planners are former graduate students from the social sciences, a woman from a Chicago-area agency told me. It's "Margaret Mead meets the Marlboro Man." A man in bifocals from one of the more creative New York agencies informed me that planners are outsiders in a Peyton Place industry, both ethnically and institutionally.

"That's the mystique of the Swiss Army Knife," came an earnest voice from a nearby table. "Now, when you put that on a sweatshirt. . . ."

For me, the most telling fact about account planning is that its practitioners do not speak of it as a job or a workaday division of agency labor. Planners refer to what they do—and almost universally, it seems—as "the discipline." The academic pretensions that the word carries are intentional: Even casual talk at the conference, although not academic jargon per se, was often phrased so as to imply familiarity with academia, with other "disciplines," with realms of learning and expertise that lay far beyond the usual narrow purviews of Madison Avenue.

A number of senior planners, I was told, hold advanced degrees in various very sophisticated fields. One Planner related to me how "my insight on the meaning of [a *brand*] came from evolutionary psychology." Another compared the goings-on at his agency to the intellectual freedom and self-questioning that takes place at universities. Gerry Laybourne had told us that "this whole planning process" she was undertaking prior to launching Oxygen made her "feel like I've been in graduate school." And again and again I came across the word "ethnography," used sometimes to describe what is normally called "market research" and on other occasions as a handy, compact definition of the discipline itself.

The only bona fide Ph.D. I came across at the conference, however, was Rick Robinson, a social psychologist whose speech had introduced the planners to E-Lab, the Chicago-based consultancy he headed. Robinson littered his talk promiscuously with juicy bits of academese. He repeatedly reminded the assembled admen of his postgraduate credentials, implied that he spoke both German and ancient Greek, read a quote from anthropologist Clifford Geertz (in which Geertz himself quotes Max Weber), and asked us not to confuse a *book* he wrote with a similarly titled one by Aldous Huxley. He told us about "theories of narrative behavior" and prefaced one story by remarking, "If this is Perception 101, I apologize."

In some hotel ballroom in some distant city, perhaps, Babbittesque businessmen were still inspiring one another with exhortations to think positively and with crude pep talks evolved only slightly from the halftime originals. Maybe they were still cursing the "tenured radicals" who had distracted our youth from their rightful concerns with leaders and forward passes. Here, though, the arcana of cultural studies and anthropology were exactly what the planners had come to absorb. It was helpful to think of the *brand* as a myth, Robinson said, a primal tale of hero and archetype. Unfortunately, though, most *brands* were related to consumers haphazardly: "disparate" and "distributed" were the terms Robinson actually used, meaning that a company's thirty-second commercials didn't always dovetail with consumers' actual experiences of the product in question. And so planners, whose job it was to transform these bits and pieces into what Robinson called "a mythic whole," were sometimes forced to call in the heavy intellect to put things right.

Enter E-Lab, which, as its promotional literature puts it, "specializes in providing a deep understanding of everyday experience through a variety of innovative, ethnographic methods." Robinson described some of them for us: questioning people about products while they're actually using them, mounting cameras in stores or homes so that the ethnographers can observe exactly how we go about buying coffee or watching TV. As Robinson showed us slides from the latter operation, distorted and grainy like surveillance-camera views of convenience-store holdups, his language of benign academic understanding morphed into a language of imperial control. A *brand*'s myth is everyday experience for consumers, he noted, and "if you can understand experience, you can own it."

This rather startling remark was the closest anyone at the conference would come to the sort of sales-through-domination language that was once such a standard part of advertising-industry discourse. It had now been fully forty years since Vance Packard used a bookful of such manipulative talk to send the industry into the public-relations tailspin from which it has never really recovered. In those days, advertising executives were in the habit of comparing themselves to scientists: They were "engineers of consent," as one famous title had it, masters of applied psychology who were as certain of which sales pitches worked and which didn't as the lab-coated authorities who peopled their works. In the sixties, and partially in response to the tidal wave of doubt whipped up by Packard's accusations, admen changed their minds: Now they were artists, temperamental geniuses whose intolerance for order and hierarchy was shared by the insurgent consumers they imagined clamoring to purchase all those cars, cigarettes, and air conditioners. These days, with the media world grown as fragmented as the American demographic map, the sales fantasy du jour is anthropology.

It is important to distinguish this professional fiction of the planners from more standard corporate anthropology: all those practical efforts to increase productivity by studying shop-floor behavior, or to avoid "insensitivity" when building a new factory in some distant clime. Those varieties of corporate anthropology require real anthropologists, formally trained scholars who, the literature on the subject warns, tend to bring all sorts of troublesome "values" to the job with them. The admen here were as much anthropologists as their forebears were scientists when they donned white lab coats and sat for the cameras before a bookcase full of *Encyclopaedia Britannicas*. What they had taken from anthropology was attitude alone.

And for good reason. Anthropology allows advertising to do what it does in the democratic language of sensitivity and empowerment. To understand production and consumption as "rituals" is to remove them entirely from the great sweep of history and enlightenment, to place them beyond criticism. To understand demographic groups as "tribes," and admen as sympathetic observers, is both to celebrate the relationship and to ensure that any resulting exchange takes place in a rigorously circumscribed context. The business writer Tom Peters coined the phrase "the *brand* called you" to describe techniques for career building; applied to advertising, the phrase acquires a much creepier significance. What the planners are planning is, quite literally, you.

"Chaos" had been last year's planning buzzword, and this year it seemed to boast two discrete schools of elaboration. Adepts of a happy chaos foresaw opportunity everywhere, whereas those theorizing a pessimistic chaos believed that extinction lurked around every corner. Either way, account planning was being touted as a crucial navigating tool, a compass without which clients would either fail to profit from chaos or fail to avoid chaos's pitfalls.

Ted Nelson of the Mullen agency cleaved to the happy chaos camp. With a series of slides depicting fractals, the growth of musical genres, and a tangled landscape of strip-mall signs, he impressed upon a small audience in a hotel conference room the notion that "life is getting complicated." Clearly *brands* "based on consistency" were, like the master narratives invented by all those dead white males, in for some pretty rough debunking; meanwhile, *brands* that dared to acknowledge and accept chaos could prosper. As Nelson got carried away with his subject, "chaos" began to sound less like an unavoidable state of affairs and more like a rosy and ultra-democratic utopia that planners needed to work desperately to bring about. Until the day that planning was practiced as he had counseled, Nelson warned, "the existing paradigm will not be subverted."

Others understood "chaos" differently, as something closer to "evasion" or, simply, the "cynicism" denounced by so many of the conference's dominant paradigm subverters. And confronting that evasiveness, that cynicism, that towering doubt was, ultimately, what planners were charged with doing.

No *brand* had enjoyed more success over the years than Nike, with its ubiquitous swoosh and its creepy soft-totalitarian NikeTown shops in the big cities. At the same time, no *brand* had suffered as much for its accomplishments. In the wake of revelations about its labor practices and its unpleasant encounters with Michael Moore and *Doonesbury*, Nike had gone from signifying athletic excellence to symbolizing everything that was wrong with global capitalism: multi-millionaire athletes and starvation wages in Indonesia. So it was inevitable, perhaps, that as the account planning conference drew to a close, we should all have been brought together into one room to hear two dramatic accounts of Nike's recent travails and of the heroic work of the planners to whom the company had turned.

One day, Nike had decided to sell special shoes to skateboarders. But there was a problem. Not the obvious problem of whether or not skateboarders actually required special shoes but the problem of skater resistance. As Kelly Evans-Pfeifer of the Goodby, Silverstein agency spun the tale, the problem when Nike "decided to get into the skateboarding market" was that "skateboarders did not want them there." Skateboarding, it turned out, was "an alternative culture" populated with difficult people who "don't really like this attention they're getting from mainstream companies." The cultural task the planners faced was not to decide whether this hostility was deserved or warranted but to liquidate it:

> [T]he objective for the advertising was not to reach a certain sales goal but rather it had a more basic, grassroots task, which was that it needed to begin to start a relationship between Nike and skateboarders, and make skateboarders think that it wasn't such a bad thing that Nike was going to get involved.

Nike had wanted the agency to run commercials featuring superstar skaters doing tricks at skating arenas, but the planners at Goodby saw through that in an instant: The thing to do was to talk to "real" skaters, who do their tricks on the outdoor walkways, planters, and banisters of corporate America. And what the planners found was that skaters believe that they are the victims of a culture war all their own, that they are persecuted unjustly by intolerant cops and suburban city councils. The key to bringing skaters into the *brand*'s fold, then, was to transform Nike from an enemy into a sympathizer, "to acknowledge and harness all those feelings of persecution." The ads that resulted asked, amusingly, what it would look like if other athletes were harassed and fined the way skaters so routinely are. In focus groups done to test the commercials, Evans-Pfeifer told us, skaters "came in completely hostile to Nike: 'Nike's the man, they don't know anything.'" But, postviewing, "they said, 'God, man, that's totally coming from a skater's view. That's awesome that that's going to be out there.'" This was a campaign with "grassroots objectives," she reminded us, and it garnered "grassroots results." The Nike 800 number, ordinarily a conduit for complaints, she said, began to receive a shower of congratulations: Skaters asked for a copy of the commercials to show during their court dates. Then she displayed the cover of the May 1998 issue of *Big Brother*, a skateboarding magazine, and proudly related to us the campaign's crowning victory: In an issue denouncing "corporate infiltration" of the subculture, the publication had singled Nike out for praise.

Pamela Scott and Diana Kapp, another team of planners from the same agency, began their presentation by reminding us how "Nike has been stewing in a bit of negativity for the last couple of years." "We realized that there was a distance and certainly a disconnect that [young people] were experiencing with the *brand*," the planners told us. Again that dread cynicism was tearing people and their *brands* apart! The planners rolled up their sleeves and prepared to "address this negativity by re-injecting authenticity and credibility back into the *brand*." To make their advertisements effective, Scott and Kapp needed to find a sport as distant as possible from Nike's traditional advertising approach, discredited now with its excesses of money and celebrity. So they set about studying high school girls' basketball and packaging it into an elaborate pitch for the Nike *brand*. The two ad women told us how they embarked on an ethnographic fact-finding tour throughout the South, "inner-city Philly," and other regions where authenticity can be mined cheaply and plentifully. They narrated with the enthusiasm of a post-vacation slide show how they had encountered all manner of curious "rituals" among the girl athletes they found and how they had come across "the most unself-conscious laughter you've ever heard"; they played a recording of an exotic-sounding high school cheer and showed us black-and-white photos of serious-looking teenagers staring past the camera like Dust Bowl farmers in a Dorothea Lange picture. And then they told us how they went about putting that authenticity to work for Nike.

NCAA rules forbade the agency to film an actual high school team, so the agency invented a replica team to reenact the unsullied love of sport that the planners had witnessed on their tour. A group of high school–age girls was duly recruited and dispatched to basketball camp, where they were assigned to "build their own relationship, their own sisterhood, that we could reflect with great authenticity on film." The squad was dubbed the Charlestown Cougars and made the subject of intentionally low-budget-looking commercials that document the team's arduous, unsung road to a fictitious state championship. The commercials stretched to push all of our authenticity buttons: the timeless black-and-white imagery, the heroic slow motion at crucial points, the unpolished voice-overs, the women's voices humming church spirituals in the background. Consumers, the duo assured us, found the authenticity convincing. We heard of Web-site hits and plaintive messages from real-life high school girls. But the campaign wasn't to be judged in terms of Nike sales alone, the adwomen insisted, for the ads were about "raising consciousness" as well. They worked not merely commercially but "to build role models for young girls." The audience of planners erupted once more.

When I was in graduate school, it was a pedagogical given that the turn from studying the makers of culture to examining the way culture was received and experienced was a liberating development. Liberating not merely in the sense of scholarly opportunity, in that it was now permissible to study subjects that had formerly been considered unworthy; this stuff was politically liberating as well. Certainly the new pedagogies had all the right enemies: Southern Baptists; undersecretaries from the Reagan administration infuriated by textbooks' failure to pay homage to national heroes; newspaper columnists angered to derangement by the parade of sin at the MLA. As the culture wars got loudly underway, what was less frequently remarked upon were the sundry ways in which the rhetoric of cultural studies mirrored the new language of market research.

Today, though, it is impossible to overlook. What we are wandering into at this fin de siècle is not "culture war" but a strange cultural consensus between business and its putative opponents, a consensus in which both sides agree on the obsolescence of social class and heavy industry and in which both sides shamelessly abuse the language of popular consent. It is a consensus in which even the most stridently radical of disciplines feed evermore directly into the culture industry, in which it no longer surprises anyone when Ogilvy & Mather trawl for anthropology Ph.D.s who have "no ideological or moral objections to consumption/materialism." As is the way with all such things, it is a consensus that seems impossible to resist.

Prizes distributed, conference adjourned, and several hours still before my plane back to the Midwest, I walked out of the Westin Hotel and down Newbury Street. It was eighty degrees and sunny, a great day for being seen in a public place with a Penguin Classic. I wandered past the Boston Public Library and on into the magic landscape of sunglass boutiques, Au Bon Pains, record stores, and vegetarian restaurants, and the slow hum of Lexuses and BMWs. Before me lay that gorgeous parade of commerce where anthropology grad students mingled comfortably and understandingly with less-enlightened shoppers, where the old conflicts were as meaningless as the heavy, oxidizing statues of abolitionists on the next avenue over.

Even the Tufts-educated barman smiled. In fact, he was ecstatic at my presence. Next year he would be moving on to the state department, maybe, or Morgan Stanley. But this year was good enough for him. He complimented my choice of Famous Grouse over Dewar's. He meant to see to it that my Scotch-drinking experience was a peak one. Three times did the goateed counter guy at the Burger King (Boston University) inquire whether I had been provided sufficient salt. I floated down the street in my new green tie, past the Armani Exchange where the planners in fezzes were dining at a sidewalk cafe, giggling and gesturing, rocking backward and upward in crescendoing paroxysms. I could feel my journalistic cynicism fall from me like the unsubtle enthusiasms of my youth, and we were all of us as one under the empowering gaze of Ronaldo, exotic of the moment, who looked hopefully down on us from the windows of NikeTown.

Originally published in Harper's, *July 1999.*

Hysteria™
Intelligent Design, Not Clever Advertising
Mr. Keedy

To many, the word "design" is practically synonymous with commercial hype. You can't expect people to see a line between advertising and design when designers don't bother to draw one. But they had better draw one soon, because people are getting hysterical, and they're not after witches in Salem or commies in Hollywood. This time, they're after corporate tools like you.

In an era of inscrutable complexity, corporate marketing has become the one-cause-fits-all scapegoat for almost everything wrong with the world. Ecological chaos, racism, sexism, class warfare—you name it, you'll find it represented in corporate consumerism, because virtually everything today is connected to commerce. Best of all, marketing is an enemy that won't fight back; it needs you. No wonder designers are getting their Calvins in a knot. Who wants to be on the receiving end of all that rage?

As problem-solvers, many designers would no doubt like to be a part of the solution to the problems created in the wake of global capitalism. But can they honestly be part of the solution when they remain a large part of the problem? This September, a guerrilla army in Prada shoes toting Titanium PowerBooks will be checking their Tumi luggage in at the Marriot Hotel in Washington, D.C., to strategize their social and political engagement with capitalism. This revolution will not be televised, but it will have corporate sponsorship. At the annual AIGA conference, the designer-activists will no doubt accessorize their dissent with *Adbusters* magazine and a copy of Naomi Klein's *No Logo*, this fall's coolest anti-consumer consumables. At best, this designer insurrection is an honest attempt to "fight fire with fire"; at worst, it confirms social conscience and anti-consumerism as the latest cultural fad (next year: yoga).

In the context of graphic design, anti-consumerism is a radical idea precisely because it doesn't make much sense. The graphic designer as anti-consumerist is a lot like the liquor company promoting responsible drinking, or the tobacco company discouraging underage smoking—maybe they're sincere, but it's hard to believe. Perhaps the bursting of the e-commerce bubble and the sudden interest in anti-consumerist design is more than just a coincidence. Are the designers who lost their jobs designing Web sites for the home delivery of butt toners now designing Web sites about the butt toner industry's use of sweatshop labor?

Design as a practice doesn't have much of a conscience, even if individual designers do. Design organizations have rules of ethical practice, but is anyone ever busted for breaking them? For the most part, the pseudo-profession of graphic design does not require a license because it is satisfactorily regulated by the marketplace. Designers can draft codes of behavior, make proclamations, sign manifestos, and offer up ideas and solutions to any number of problems. In the end, somebody has to buy what they create, or none of it is going anywhere.

Some designers believe they have found a liberating alternative to commercial servitude in culture jamming and subverting. The idea is to topple existing power structures by subverting their messages, pulling pranks, and being a pain in the corporate ass. In the ensuing chaos and anarchy, artists and designers start running the show, which needless to say results in utopia. Wow! A world run by artists and designers. That's pretty close to my idea of hell, but that may just be me.

A typical example of this type of intervention is to sneak around at night and illegally paste your clever one-liner on top of an existing clever one-liner on an advertisement nobody likes. This demonstrates to the world (for free) that you are equally clever and morally superior to those advertising hacks, and you're not buying what it is they're selling, so they had better listen to you . . . I mean, us! It's a strategy that transforms the artist's or designer's personally motivated aesthetic self-indulgence into a selfless act of civic duty. It's a trick the art world invented in the late eighties so that artists' self-importance could compete on the corporate and institutional scale.

No doubt culture jamming is fun—it's like being a good terrorist; how cool is that? But is being even more obnoxious than the enemy really the best answer? Forget about trying to one-up the ad hacks (you can't). The question is, why are you playing the same creepy game? The idea that a design intervention can drive consumer reform is putting the designer cart in front of the horse—it looks good but it doesn't work. And design, unlike art, is supposed to work.

So when I signed "First Things First 2000," it wasn't because the world needs an anti-consumerist declaration of independence to encourage design shenanigans. If that was all I had read into the manifesto, I wouldn't have added my John Hancock.

Back in 1987, I gave a lecture entitled "Greasing the Wheels of Capitalism with Style and Taste," which I expanded into an essay for *Emigré* magazine in 1997. For the past fifteen years I have watched advertising-oriented values infiltrate the culture of design. With the arrival of *FTF 2000*, I could see that others had concerns along similar lines and that they wanted to open the issue up to a more general discussion. I have hoped that designers would establish their own ethics, free from commercial duplicity and without imitating art-world politics or pop-star platitudes. Maybe not a "new kind of meaning," but at least a new way of thinking. It was a good start to revisit the ideas behind the original 1964 "First Things First" manifesto, but I would add to that the ideas of other designers and critics like Christopher Jones, George Nelson, Otl Aicher, Eva Zeisel, and W. A. Dwiggins.

Ironically, designers can make their biggest social and political impact by not designing. After all, someone designs most of our ecological, social, and cultural nightmares before they are unleashed on the world. Yes, it's helpful to make a pretty poster for the Save the Kittens Coalition, but it's hardly essential—a less-fashionable choice of typeface or color won't jeopardize the cause. It's much more important to not stretch a magazine article into a five-hundred-page hardbound book, or design a hot Web site-of-the-week that makes corporate jackals look like giggling preteens.

In the past decade, advertising has gotten a lot hipper and cooler, due in large part to a handful of talented graphic designers handpicked from design annuals and magazines. They get to make a ton of money and work on big projects that otherwise would never come to them, while the ad agencies get the best talent and make more money still. This exchange has created a handful of design superstars, while turning the profession into an art ghetto where advertising "creatives" shop for cheap, disposable talent. Now there is an endless supply of young designers trying to get noticed—"Pick me, pick me next!"—because design conferences and magazines celebrate opportunist sellouts, as if they were doing us all a big favor. Gee, thanks!

Designers think of themselves as good people whose clients make them do bad things—the "I was only following orders" defense. This is usually followed by the "a person's got to make a living" defense, as if the only way a designer can make ends meet is by crafting insipid propaganda for multinational corporations. The debate about the designer's responsibility in society tends to get polarized between powerless complicity and social actualization. The vast majority of designers work somewhere in the middle, within subtle gradations, and it is in these gray areas that distinctions need to be made. That is, in the real world, not the theoretical extremities.

If you are a corporate tool, at least be a good one. Everyone knows the difference between engaging and deceptive messages. If you are doing work that you feel conflicted about, however, don't kid yourself that some *pro bono* work or anonymous culture jamming will even the score. It doesn't, and stop pretending you're an artist, because you're not.

Try to make less, and make it better; brands should be memorable because they are good, not because they are omnipresent. The difference between design and advertising used to be that design was informative, not persuasive; compelling, not intrusive; and intelligent, not just clever. What's the difference now? Truth in advertising is an oxymoron, but does it have to be in design as well? The increasingly personal and invasive presence of marketing and corporate control in people's lives has provoked global hysteria. Design has played a part in the problem, but, unlike advertising, design can also help offer an alternative—and this time, a real alternative.

Originally published in Adbusters, *September/October 2001.*

Culture Jamming, or Something Like It
Matt Soar

Contrary to the impression one might get from reading *Adbusters* magazine, "culture jamming"—or something like it—goes way, *way* back. Certainly before *The Journal of the Mental Environment* ran a cover story on it in 1993, and decades, even centuries, before the term was invented (in 1984) by Negativland, an experimental music group based in the United States. Even so, for many people, culture jamming has become practically synonymous with the persistent antics of the Vancouver-based Media Foundation, which, aside from publishing *Adbusters*, also promotes increasingly international events such as Buy Nothing Day and World Car Free Day.

As the term culture jamming has begun to wear on the ears (mine in particular), it is perhaps worth taking a moment to reflect on its historical precursors (not to mention its future potential as a galvanizing force for those disaffected souls who have come together to fight the good fight on several issues—the counter-democratic tendencies of the mass media) now largely in the hands of just six corporations: the petrochemical industries' renewed assault on the environment; the inhuman side-effects of the drive to globalize; and the pugnacious intransigence of an unelected U.S. government (to name but a few of many current flashpoints).

Choosing to screw around with received ideas about life, and how it should be lived, can of course be traced back to the activities of the Situationists—their notion of "detournement" being a favorite incantation of *Adbusters*. However, we can look back farther still to the proto-dadaist groups and performances of the late 1800s[1] and even the ancient, trans-historical figure of the trickster.[2] The factor that distinguishes contemporary American society from earlier periods in history, however, is that we now get most of our information (and entertainment) from the media, rather than the fireside, the town hall, or the village commons. We may feel rather more worldly than our ancestors, but we are also subject to the systematic and pervasive biases of a corporatized, advertising-supported media system that puts profit first every time (and uses the public airwaves to do so). In his profoundly important book, *Rich Media, Poor Democracy: Communication Politics in Dubious Times*, Robert W. McChesney has called this arrangement "a poison pill for democracy."[3]

Recognizing the urgency of many of these issues, Kalle Lasn, the editor of *Adbusters* (and cofounder of the Media Foundation), has recently put forward something of a political agenda, both in the magazine and in a recent book called *Culture Jam: The Uncooling of America*™.[4] It is through his elaborations of this strategy, and through his utilization of the "First Things First" manifesto, that Lasn continues to make overtures to both graphic designers and ad creatives to involve themselves in a culture jamming "revolution."[5]

Naomi Klein, in her best-selling book, *No Logo*, refers to culture jamming as "semiotic Robin Hoodism."[6] Having interviewed jammers in various cities across North America in the course of her research (many of whom have day jobs or careers as designers or ad creatives), Klein also notes that: "Ad culture has demonstrated its remarkable ability to absorb, accommodate and even profit from content critiques."[7] Klein discusses the creation of billboard ads in Australia (also for Nike) that are effectively "pre-jammed," that is, made to appear as if they have already been altered, or are otherwise couched in the rhetoric of dissent.[8] Klein continues: "It turns out that culture jamming—with its combination of hip-hop attitude, punk anti-authoritarianism and a well of visual gimmicks—has great sales potential."[9]

Klein remains hopeful that jamming is, at its best, an adept political force to be reckoned with. That said, with reference to *Adbusters*, and Kalle Lasn in particular, she says: "Adbusters are susceptible to a spiraling bravado and to a level of self-promotion that can be just plain silly. . . . There is a strong tendency to exaggerate the power of wheatpaste and a damn good joke."[10] Furthermore, Lasn's editorial strategy in *Adbusters* and elsewhere[11] suggests an enduring faith in a hybrid movement of his own making that seems to be devoid of any broader political vision. To insist, as Lasn does, on dramatizing a perceived schism between culture jamming on the one hand and feminism, environmentalism, and the Left on the other[12] strikes me as altogether counterproductive. At times, it actually seems that Lasn is at least as invested in jamming a long and venerable history of progressive social movements in the U.S. as he is in "uncooling" corporate America.

Given the fact that Lasn's agenda is high on graphic polish and bravado and low on intellectual substance, then the cautionary words of Janet Wolff seem particularly apt right now:

> The conditions under which art may be effective, politically and historically, are determined both by the nature of cultural production at that moment, and its possibilities, and by the nature of the contemporary society, and in

particular of its general ideology . . . any attempt at political intervention through cultural politics cannot be made in ignorance of these conditions, but must be based on an analysis of the specific relations of culture, ideology and society. *That is why sweeping demands for cultural activism are both meaningless and pointless.*[13]

While there are certainly resistive pleasures to be had with culture jamming—both for its inventive practitioners and its knowing audiences—the sneaky modification of corporate logos and ads, or postering in the dead of night, will never be a complete *substitute* for the kind of negotiated and cumulative critical insights that are typical of the social movements Lasn seems to detest. The essence of Wolff's point is simply this, then: An historically informed, critical politics doesn't need culture jamming to be effective, but the reverse will never be true.

Notes

1. P. D. Cate and M. Shaw, eds., *The Spirit of Montmartre: Cabarets, Humor, and the Avant-Garde, 1875–1905* (New Brunswick: Rutgers, 1996).

2. L. Hyde, *Trickster Makes This World: Mischief, Myth, and Art* (New York: Farrar, Straus & Giroux, 1998).

3. Robert W. McChesney, *Rich Media, Poor Democracy: Communication Politics in Dubious Times* (New York: New Press, 2000).

4. Kalle Lasn, *Culture Jam: The Uncooling of America*™ (New York: Eagle Brook/William Morrow, 1999).

5. Rick Poynor, "Kalle Lasn: Ad Buster," *Graphis* 325 (2000), 96–101. See also Rick Poynor, "First Things Next," in Poynor, *Obey the Giant: Life in the Image World* (August/Birkhauser, 2001), 141–150.

6. Naomi Klein, *No logo: Taking Aim at the Brand Bullies* (New York: Picador, 2000), 280.

7. Ibid., 291.

8. A. Rebensdorf, "Capitalizing on the Anti-Capitalist Movement," *Alternet*, August 7, 2001 (*www.alternet.org*).

9. Klein, 297.

10. Ibid., 295.

11. See note 4 above.

12. Ibid.

13. Janet Wolff, *The Social Production of Art*, 2nd ed. (New York: New York University Press, 1993), 85, emphasis added.

Teaching as a Subversive Inactivity

The Responsible Design Teacher

Roy R. Behrens

Thirty years ago, as a graduate student, I was stumped by a series of questions about an esoteric research problem. Someone said to ask for help from a certain teacher whom I had never met, because this person was rumored to be one of the smartest people on campus.

Unfortunately, when I found this designer and explained what I was working on, he refused to cooperate. Instead, he looked at me pointblank and said that solving my problems was not his responsibility: "I'm not here to give you the answers," he replied. "I am here to annoy you with questions."

He was partly right. I was undoubtedly annoyed, and I walked away in disbelief. But I did not abandon those questions, and, in the years since, I've never stopped rooting for answers. At the same time, nor have I ever forgotten that single, brief encounter (I never saw this person again, and he later died prematurely), partly because the experience was so frustrating, but also because I have come to believe, as I think he did, that one of the secrets of teaching (whether graphic design or any other subject) is to know when to step back and to act through inactivity—to function less as an authority than as a catalyst.

To provoke action from someone through omission or implicitness is often referred to as *closure*. Presented with unfinished or incomplete patterns, we tend to respond automatically by fretting about it, while filling in the gaps ourselves. In psychology, this phenomenon was investigated in 1927 by Bluma Zeigarnik, a graduate student of the Gestalt psychologists at the Berlin Psychological Institute. In her pioneering experiment, 164 subjects were asked to take on various manual tasks, with instructions that these be completed both accurately and quickly. In half the instances, she interrupted them, leaving their work unfinished, while in the other half they were allowed to go on unimpeded. Afterwards, by interviewing the subjects, she concluded that, by an overwhelming margin, unresolved experiences were remembered far more vividly than completed ones.

This tactic of triggering closure through incompleteness, known now as "Zeigarnik's effect," is commonly used in advertising to ensure that television audiences, for example, will recall a certain product long after they've seen a commercial. And of course this is also one reason why I can still clearly remember my encounter with that uncooperative teacher.

All this is old hat to designers. After all, the ubiquitous motto of modern design is "Less is more," or, as Abram Games once said, as a graphic designer "you wind the spring, and it is released in the mind of the viewer." But it is no less essential in teaching to provoke by playful teasing, and to leave out nonessentials. The ensuing scholastic fandango, which Mihaly Csikszentmihalyi calls "flow" (in a book with the same title) or "optimal experience," results from the constant adjustment between the incompleteness of a teacher's prompting and the capacity of a student to complete it.

Csikszentmihalyi provides an example in a wonderful story about his dog Hussar, who loved to run circles around him during their walks together while daring his master to catch him. "Occasionally I would take a lunge," writes Csikszentmihalyi, "and if I was lucky I got to touch him. Now the interesting part is that whenever I was tired, and moved halfheartedly, Hussar would run much tighter circles, making it relatively easy for me to catch him; on the other hand, if I was in good shape and willing to extend myself, he would enlarge the diameter of his circle. In this way, the difficulty of the game was kept constant."

According to David Lodge (in *Small World*), such gamelike adjustments can also be found in activities as unrelated as watching a striptease and reading: "The dancer teases the audience, as the text teases its readers," he writes, "with the promise of an ultimate revelation that is infinitely postponed. Veil after veil, garment after garment, is removed, but it is the *delay* [my italics] in the stripping that makes it exciting, not the stripping itself; because no sooner has one secret been revealed than we lose interest in it and crave another . . . To read is to surrender oneself to an endless displacement of curiosity and desire from one sentence to another, from one action to another, from one level of the text to another. The text unveils itself before us, but never allows itself to be possessed; and instead of striving to possess it, we should take pleasure in its teasing."

As a teacher, I think I've always been aware of the importance of being implicit, and yet it has never been easy to do. At moments when I am unsure of my abilities as a teacher, I respond instinctively by overcompensating. Knowing that I am responsible for the outcome of my students' work, I lecture too incessantly, intrude when I shouldn't, and use classroom problems that are far too rigid. In part, I may still be rebounding from my experience with the opposite tendency that prevailed in the sixties, in which as a student I was free to indulge in the ambience of "doing my own thing." But it also grows out of the passion with which I want to instill in my students the "truths" I have slowly, painstakingly learned about perception, aesthetics, typography, color, page layout, illustration, problem-solving, and the history of design.

Today, after so many years in the classroom, I still struggle daily to try to become less domineering, to evolve toward a posture of teaching that drifts between the poles of control and acquiescence, between structure and lack of direction. Looking back on my life as a teacher, I am reminded of the porridge tasting in "Goldilocks and the Three Bears" (too hot, too cold, just right), as I seem to have tried on a similar set of teaching philosophies (too loose, too tight, just right).

I am also reminded of a passage in a brilliant book by British psychologist Liam Hudson titled *The Cult of the Fact:* "The teacher who leaves his students' minds open, in a state of promiscuous athleticism, is scarcely a teacher at all. His proper function, in other words, must be an ambiguous one: he must transmit an intellectual tradition with gusto, and instill loyalty to it, but leave open the possibility of gradual or even revolutionary change. And what matters in practice is not so much the teacher's motive, nor even his style, as the elbowroom he allows."

If you truly leave elbowroom, you do not end up with obedient pups. One of the things that most pleases him (and me), said Brother David Steindl-Rast, a Benedictine monk, author, and teacher (when interviewed by Joan Evelyn Ames in *Mastery*), "is a student who doesn't imitate me, a student who takes what's good for her or him and runs with it. I like independent students who can stand on their own feet and not get hung up on me. It's the same quality I like in cats: a certain standoffishness, having their own mind, taking what they want, and leaving the rest behind. You can't train a cat the way you can train a dog. So I like cat-type students rather than dog-type students."

More than a dozen years ago, I was browsing through a book when I ran across the following unattributed maxim: "The secret of teaching is to appear to have known all your life what you learned this afternoon." I stopped and read this over again. And again. This is not a prescription for teaching, I thought, it's a blueprint for seizing and keeping control. In contrast, the aim of a teacher should be the transfer of power, from teacher to student, and the persuasion of each student to accept responsibility for his or her lifelong education—a goal that is often reliably reached by various forms of deliberate provocation, among them intentionally leaving things out.

(Do Not) Go To Jail: Monopoly and Political Protest
Teal Triggs

"May Day Mayhem across the Board," read the April 17, 2001 headline in Britain's national newspaper *The Times*.[1] The story revealed May Day protest organizers' strategies for causing maximum disruption during the 2001 anti-capitalist May Day demonstrations to be held in London. These were to become some of the most notorious the U.K. had ever seen, with thousands of protesters cordoned off by police for up to eight hours in London's West End shopping district. The *board*, in this case, referred to a reimagined anarchist version of Parker Brother's Monopoly game, the defining symbol of these protests. This version of the Monopoly game became more than just a visual motif for protestors as it appropriated the aims and the interactive nature of the original game itself. Why was the Monopoly game adopted in the first instance and in what way did it signal a new visual brand of political protest?

Historically, May Day was a Pagan festival marking the coming of spring, but following the 1886 workers' campaign in Chicago, an attempt to reduce the number of hours in a workday, it soon became recognised as an international workers' day. The Chicago campaign witnessed 80,000 workers on strike, a series of violent demonstrations, criminal convictions, and four subsequent hangings. It inspired America's Federation of Organized Trades and Labor Unions to pass a resolution that constituted eight hours as a legal day's labor "from and after May 1 1886."[2]

According to the British radical leftist newsletter, *SchNEWS*, the tradition of antagonistic May Day marches in the U.K. ended in 1978, when Britain's Labour government declared May Day an official holiday.[3] While workers' celebrations continued internationally, May Day was perceived as a symbolic labor day until 2000, when it was revived in a different form. May Day developed a new momentum with the rise of international global actions, such as those that took place during the anti-globalization demonstrations in London in 1999 and those held during the World Trade Organization summits in Seattle (1999), Prague (2001), and Genoa (2001). As a result, May Day is now promoted by anti-capitalist organizations as a day of "celebration for all those struggling against capitalism and globalization."[4]

During the previous decades, political protest was often identified with the promotion of single causes from organizations ranging from anarchists and socialists to animal rights supporters and environmentalists.[5] Issues that made the news included the poll tax, animal rights, traffic congestion, GM crops, anti-fur trade, and vivisection. It wasn't until the revived May Day events that many of these disparate organizations, including the WOMBLES (White Overall Movement for Building Liberation through Effective Struggle), Reclaim the Streets, and The People's Global Action, were brought together under one unified umbrella. Linking such organizations under the single banner with an anti-capitalist maxim meant a range of positions could be tolerated. This tactic of staging a unified mass demonstration gave rise to a critical mass of supporters and guaranteed maximum disruption in the city. In turn, this produced much sought after international press coverage as a vehicle for raising the public profile for different causes.

Community participation is an important strategy for bringing together and involving as many people as possible in a political event. The organization, Reclaim the Streets, for example, initiates illegal street parties in an effort to "reclaim the streets" against the domination of the car. The street party is simultaneously a social and political event. As George McKay, a writer and activist, argues in his book, *DiY Culture: Party & Protest in Nineties Britain*, "Social criticism is combined with cultural creativity in what's both a utopian gesture and a practical display of resistance."[6] For May Day 2000, organizers who instigated Guerrilla Gardening fused party and protest in the way protestors communally dug up the green space in front of the British Parliament and planted trees in a symbolic act to make the environment better. One protestor quoted in a national newspaper explained, "The gardening action is about everyone participating. It's an experiment in taking back urban land and using it freely—as a meeting space, as a provider of food."[7] The aftermath of this action was summed up by one of the more potent media images of the May Day protest: In a nostalgic nod to the history of DiY and punk, protestors strategically placed a clump of green grass in the shape of a punk Mohawk on top of the head of the Winston Churchill statue in front of the nation's Parliament building.

You can contact us in the following ways:

post	BM Mayday London WC1N 3XX
e-mail:	
enquiries	mayday2001@hushmail.com
discussion list	mayday-monopoly@egroups.com
website	www.freespeech.org/mayday2k
telephone	07989 451 096

Mayday Monopoly is conceived as a celebration of Mayday in London. Whilst we welcome people from outside the capital, we would also welcome events that celebrate Mayday in other areas. There are Monopoly games based on many other cities in the UK and around the world! We will publicise any events organised along libertarian lines.
This leaflet contains a few ways to get involved. It is not meant to cover everything, so feel free to contribute to Mayday Monopoly in any way you want.

ADVANCE TO MAY 1...

WHY NOT START THE DAY WITH A CRITICAL MASS BIKE RIDE?
Meet 7.30am at Marylebone Station (off Marylebone Road)or else at Liverpool Street Station, converging at Kings Cross for a late Breakfast. Continuing during the day to link up with and support various actions around the Monopoly board.

An invitation to play ...

MAYDAY MONOPOLY
disOwn it all™

COMMUNITY NEWS
EXTRA!
Millions Phone In Sick Today.
Scandal!

Tuesday 1 May 2001

The most remarkable image for the May Day protest the following year (2001) was in the form of the Monopoly game, whose strong graphic identity provided a unifying visual style for the protestors.[8] The game is licensed in over eighty countries, thereby "making it the most popular proprietary board game in the world." The aim of the original game dealt with the promotion of land monopolism, and for May Day protestors provided a fitting vehicle for their concerns with global profitability and power. As one May Day spokesperson reflected:

... when many of us were kids growing up this was the game that we related to. *The Monopoly Game* directly relates to the economy, workers, and users. Our intent [for the May Day protests] was to use it as a symbol which could be subverted.[9]

From its origins, the game itself grew out of a sensitive political climate at the height of the Great Depression. Although Charles Darrow is credited with the invention of Monopoly in 1930, many game historians suggest that a similar game was developed much earlier, in 1903, by Lizzie J. Magie, a young Quaker woman living in Virginia. Magie, who was a follower of the single tax movement, had applied to the U.S. Patent Office for her game called *The Landlord's Game* (1904), which was meant to be "an easy, fun-filled method of teaching the evils of land monopolism." Although Magie approached Parker Brothers in 1924 with her game, it was turned down and deemed as too political. However, in 1934, when Charles Darrow brought Monopoly to the attention of the game company Parker Brothers, the game was accepted. Similarly, Darrow proposed a game that was based upon the manipulation of large sums of money by engaging with "complex negotiations to acquire valuable blocks of property."[10] The goal was to eventually bankrupt all the other players with the winner emerging solvent. In the original board game, Darrow modeled his house and hotel properties on the street names found in the popular resort of Atlantic City located on the Jersey shore. These included the Boardwalk, Park Place, and Marvin Gardens, three railroads that carried "wealthy vacationers to the resort and the utility companies that serviced them."[11] The London version of Monopoly replaced the Atlantic City properties with names more familiar to a British audience. For example, Boardwalk becomes Mayfair and Park Place becomes Park Lane.

The original playing pieces of the Monopoly game were common household items, such as buttons, and were supplied by the players themselves—later game pawns were crafted from wood. However, by 1937, tokens were cast from metal and continue to represent domestic items such as a flatiron, thimble, and shoe. Later tokens included the racecar, top hat, battleship, and from the early 1950s, Scotty the dog, wheelbarrow, and horse and rider. The most recent token to emerge in 1988 was, appropriately, a full sack of money. The playing cards represented land title deeds, while community chest and chance card options helped to direct the player's actions. For the May Day activists, the tokens and playing cards were also game elements that became symbolically charged:

We liked the idea because we didn't have to explain why *Monopoly*. Different groups could do stickers, pamphlets, which were based upon the six tokens, each of which represented themes for them. For example, the dog equals animal rights.[12]

The Monopoly game established a unified and accessible "readymade" graphic identity and, at the same time, the interactive element of the game was cultivated in order to encourage more individuals to become grassroots activists. The game also presented a unique format for engaging political participation and organizers used the game's property-led board as an instrument for staging diversions in a "real-life game of Monopoly."[13] While the original intent of the Monopoly game was

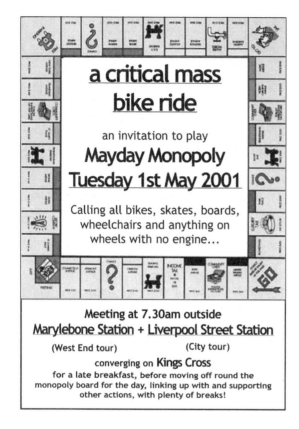

a critical mass
bike ride

an invitation to play
Mayday Monopoly
Tuesday 1st May 2001

Calling all bikes, skates, boards,
wheelchairs and anything on
wheels with no engine...

Meeting at 7.30am outside
Marylebone Station + Liverpool Street Station
(West End tour)   (City tour)
converging on Kings Cross
for a late breakfast, before moving off round the
monopoly board for the day, linking up with and supporting
other actions, with plenty of breaks!

to utilize specific property locations in which players could buy and sell property in order to accumulate wealth, protestors were encouraged to select a famous landmark or street from the board of the London version of the game that related to their cause and to stage a demonstration at that location. Protesters were able to target specific issues, while maintaining a unique coherency as a "cumulative action." Adopting the format of the game provided May Day activists with an opportunity to create "numerous autonomous actions" while still centered in locations found around the Monopoly board.[14] For example, anti-fur-trade activists could choose to target the fashion houses of Mayfair, anti-monarchists on the Mall, protestors against cars in the city at Trafalgar Square, whereas critics of Third World debt met on the Strand, and so forth. Stickers mimicked the game's graphic style, replacing title deeds with slogans such as "Homes Not Hotels," "It's Only Monopoly Money Reject It All," and "Capitalism Is Death: Play for Life." Public Utility and Railroad Company title deeds were replaced with "Abolish Commodity Create Community" and "Phone in Sick, Call a Strike, Take the Day Off." The "Go To Jail" card was replaced with "Refuse £200 Do Not Go to Jail," and, conversely, "GET OUT OF JAIL FREE" cards were circulated including legal information—the phone number of a solicitor's office and what to do if you were arrested.

Organizers encouraged direct action through the playing of a "live" version of the game. Spreading out the protest locations was intended to further stretch police resources on the day. Even before May Day, concerns were raised about the effectiveness of such a campaign might have. The metropolitan police prepared a pre–May Day press release warning London's business community that the game would encourage "groups of protestors to create action at a venue shown on the monopoly board . . . [with] the aim to bring the centre of London to a standstill and disrupt business and other normal working day activities."[15] In an accompanying booklet for the protest titled "May Day Monopoly: Game Guide," its authors provide a rundown of properties associated with each district. Oxford Circus, for example, is located in the middle of London's bustling shopping district. It was chosen to become the main focal point for protestors in a mass gathering planned for the evening rush hour, as its High Street shops and restaurants—such as the Body Shop, McDonald's, The Gap, and Starbucks—represented for protesters the worst of global capitalism and consumer culture. The guide states that "Oxford Street is now the jugular vein of consumer capitalism in central London and an epicentre of exploitation." With each property, the guide lists alleged wrongdoings by each corporation, which ranged from sweatshop labor to unfair working conditions.

The way in which the Monopoly game was designed provided an easily reproducible graphic template for individuals who wanted to create their own May Day protest stickers, posters, or badges. A template could be downloaded from the May Day Web site, printed out, and then cut-and-pasted to fit as required by the size of the sticker, badge, or poster. Although protesters adopted a do-it-yourself approach to the production of their visuals, organizers avoided any stylistic reference to the punk DiY aesthetic. This in itself signaled a significant shift away from the aesthetic traditions that had heretofore permeated grassroots British activism. The punk aesthetic reflected a sense of immediacy and accessibility in early political activist graphics, but an overabundance of photocopied leaflets, pamphlets, posters, etc., prompted concerns that suggested DiY culture had developed its own clique and, as a result, "a certain style which one must conform to."[16] The development of what might be deemed as a more "sophisticated" graphic style represented perceived changes in the nature of contemporary activism itself. As one May Day activist concluded:

> Most [activist] work is heavily influenced by punk and counter-culture materials. It fetishizes the lack of resources and the lack of organisation. We were organised and were involved in technology (like the Web site) so we wanted to present that aspect, to make it glossy and attractive. We need to get out of the ghetto that activists are seen to be in.[17]

Following May Day 2001, the London Metropolitan Police press office stated, "The event was a policing challenge," claiming their tactics to be "successful in neutralizing the threat of anti-capitalist rioters." At the final count, one hundred arrests and 59 convictions were made.[18] No official comment was forthcoming on the May Day Monopoly Game. As for the protestors themselves, the sheer size of the protest was seen as a success and the game as an integral part of that. They maintain that only a very small proportion of their number were "rioters" and that similar protests would continue until such time as, to quote the words of the May Day Monopoly Game Guide, "we bring . . . the whole game to an end!"

Notes

1. Daniel McGrory, "May Day Mayhem across the Board," *The Times,* 17 April 2001, n.p.

2. Mark Steel, "May Day May Day," *The Independent,* 27 April 2001, n.p.

3. Various authors, "Maypoles & Beanstalks," *SchNEWS Squall Yearbook 2001* (Brighton: Justice?), 27.

4. For the history of May Day 2001, see *www.maydaymonopoly.net*.

5. Natasha Walter, "From Seattle to guerrilla gardeners on May Day, the activists are learning to do joined-up protest," *The Independent*, 22 April 2000.

6. George McKay, ed., *DiY Culture: Party & Protest in Nineties Britain* (London: Verso, 1998), 27.

7. Op cite.

8. The original idea to use the Monopoly game came from not any advertising agency, but one activist who attended the preliminary organizational meetings.

9. "Peter" (no second name), interview with author, London, 2001.

10. Maxine Brady, *The Monopoly Book, Strategy and Tactics of the World's Most Popular Game* (New York: David McKay Company Inc., 1974). See also Burton H. Wolfe, "The Monopolization of *Monopoly*," *The San Francisco Bay Guardian*, 1976. For these articles and other articles on the history of the Monopoly game see also *www.adena.com/adena/mo/*.

11. Ibid.

12. "Peter" (no second name), interview with author.

13. Daniel McGrory, n.p.

14. London May Day Collective, "May Day Monopoly: Game Guide" (London: London May Day Collective, 2001), 3.

15. "Metropolitan Police May Day 2001 Business Briefing 9:30 A.M. Thursday 26 April 2001," republished by UK Independent Media Centre, *www.uk.indymedia.org*.

16. George McKay, 26.

17. "Peter" (no second name), interview with author.

18. Press Officer, the London Metropolitan Police, interview with author, 17 January 2002.

He Might Be Giant: Shepard Fairey

Michael Dooley

Shepard Fairy barely breaks stride as he slaps a sticker on an electrical box. Then another one on a newspaper rack. A street sign. A bus bench.

A few people who recognize the slightly built Fairey warmly greet and cheer him as though he were a celebrity. But most of the passersby in Silver Lake, a hip but seedy neighborhood that separates Hollywood from downtown Los Angeles, barely pay any attention. It's only afterward that his small, glossy one- and two-color graphics catch their eye. The most striking has the word "obey" in heavy capital letters beside a tightly cropped face with a vacant, but ominous, stare.

The face is a stark, flat, stylized image rendered in sinewy blobs with the symmetry and flavor of a Rorschach blot. And, in fact, it's intended to be open to individual, often conflicting, interpretations. It could be taken as an Orwellian threat, an underground cult, or a sneaky sales ploy. Anyone who recognizes the face as that of the late Andre the Giant, a seven-foot-four, 520-pound pro wrestler, might think it has something to do with the recent upsurge in popularity of the World Wrestling Federation. But the actual meaning has been evolving for over a decade, even for its creator.

Fairey, twenty-nine, knocked out his first version of the "Giant" sticker in five minutes at a Kinko's back in 1989 when he was attending the Rhode Island School of Design. The black-and-white artwork, smaller than three inches, was a grungy photocopy swiped from a newspaper ad. The hastily scrawled text read, "Andre Has a Posse." Fairey was poking fun at his fellow skateboarders, who travel in cliques called posses and unthinkingly decorate their boards with corporate logos. As the crude little stickers increasingly appeared around Providence, they began to capture the imagination of a wider audience.

By taking something with no intrinsic value, like the image of an athlete from a bogus white-trash sport, and elevating it into an icon, Fairey feels he's exposing and subverting consumer culture's susceptibility to propaganda. He prefers using an oblique approach because "I hate stuff that's too self-righteous." Rather than subject people to sloganeering, he wants them to have their own epiphanies.

The closest he's come to didacticism is a manifesto he wrote in 1990 and has since posted on his Web site. He equated his work to the philosopher Heidegger's concept of phenomenology, "the process of letting things manifest themselves." Although he believes "Giant" is something people should grasp intuitively, he came up with a bunch of big words to convince the "intellectual assholes" who require an explanation that there's some legitimacy behind what he's doing. He also thinks it makes them feel they're part of an exclusive clique with access to privileged information.

What began as an inside joke has become for Fairey a single-minded obsession. Every weekend he sets out from San Diego, his Honda Civic packed with stickers, hand-cut stencils, posters, and wheat paste. Nowhere near as large as Andre, he also brings along a sixteen-foot fold-up ladder to allow him access to pole tops, roofs of abandoned buildings, and other hard-to-reach spots that provide dramatic exposure for his larger pieces. Billboards are a favorite location. He once hijacked a dozen Sprite "Obey Your Thirst" boards up and down the California coast, obliterating everything but "obey" and turning them into "Giant" boards. For him, "any unadorned surface that isn't going to lower property value" is fair game.

Fairey usually works alone, but he's pulled off several huge installations that involve elaborate planning sessions and accomplices with walkie-talkies on the alert for cops. He also mails his stickers and posters, which now include hundreds of variations with figures as diverse as Jimi Hendrix, Joseph Stalin, and Ming the Merciless, to legions of kindred spirits. Thanks to his own global volunteer posse, there have been "Giant" sightings in Singapore, Russia, and on the Paris gravesite of Doors singer Jim Morrison. Supporters consider him a courageous street activist, a contemporary Dadaist or Situationist, or a postgraffitist who uses the print medium instead of the spray can for tagging.

Along with "Giant," Fairey himself has unwittingly become an urban legend famous for being obscure. But he finds it "totally ironic" that people think he's cool. "I'm a dork. I'm a loser. I'm not cool at all. Everybody just projects their idea of what's cool on me. I'm boring. I never go out. I don't know what's hip in music right now or anything."

The self-proclaimed loser has been the subject of a documentary short, *Andre the Giant Has a Posse*, that's screened at New York's Museum of Modern Art as well as Sundance and other festivals. His own work is now being shown at galleries around the world. And he says his obeygiant.com Web site gets 15,000 hits daily.

Frequent targeting of Los Angeles has also gained him the attention of the entertainment media. As a result, his handiwork occasionally pops up in the background on MTV and HBO shows and can also be glimpsed in movies like *Gone in Sixty Seconds*, *The Devil's Own*, and *8mm*. He claims the one in *Batman Forever* was digitally inserted without official approval by a fan working on the film.

Not everyone is a devotee, though. Some people find him naïve and delusional about the ability of his graphics to affect change. Most critics simply consider him a vandal. And, in fact, he's willfully engaged in civil disobedience, reclaiming pockets of public space already glutted with establishment propaganda. Consequently, he's been busted five times and continues to risk imprisonment. But he remains unfazed, saying he doesn't care whether people love him or hate him, as long as they respond to what he's doing.

The roots of Fairey's style are diverse. His visual minimalism was inspired by skateboard graphics, which have to jump off the wall in stores to compete with all of the others on display. His appropriation of preprinted source material and his handcrafted production methods grew out of the do-it-yourself punk music aesthetic. His humorous use of mass-media characters is akin to the Church of the SubGenius, a satirical mock-religion that anointed a 1950s clip-art drawing of a pipe-smoking dad as their divine savior. And like Andy Warhol, Fairey has an affinity for high-contrast visuals and for elevating the mundane to the iconic. Covering large surfaces with multiple posters also evokes the pop artist's style, but the repetition motif is based on necessity rather than homage.

Fairey's strongest early influence was L.A.-based guerrilla postermaker Robbie Conal. He says when he saw Conal's 1987 yellow-and-black "Contra Diction" poster, an attack on President Reagan's public lies and obfuscations regarding covert government operations in Iran, "I thought it was so powerful. He had this really unflattering portrait that was a great painting, well executed, but with clever, bold type. I just thought it was a beautiful way to combine art and politics. I loved it." Since then, Fairey and Conal have participated in joint exhibitions.

And like Conal, Fairey has run afoul of the law. He believes his harassment is largely based on community fear of copycat defacements, and suggests that he's being unfairly singled out. "If there's anything that's going to overrun the city, it's movie posters. They're coming down on me for my stuff when it's mostly Universal Pictures or Warner Bros. Records that are paying these snipers to go out and do it. And they're probably a lot easier to track down than I am." He says he's stopped canvassing his home base of San Diego because the city found him out and threatened his company with a lawsuit.

That company is Black Market Inc., which he started with partners Dave Kinsey and Philip DeWolff shortly after his 1996 move from Providence to the West Coast. Hidden in a building on the outskirts of downtown San Diego, Black Market is a ten-person visual communications agency that proclaims itself an anomaly. They conduct "guerrilla marketing on a corporate scale" that operates in the gap between underground subculture and the public at large. Specializing in "the development of high-impact marketing campaigns," they number Pepsi, Hasbro, Netscape, NBC, and GTE, as well as film studios and record labels, among their clientele. They're sought out by corporations, staffed by, as Fairey puts it, "a bunch of fifty-year-old schmucks who don't know what's going on," who want to achieve credibility with the youth-culture crowd, the ones who resent and resist typical corporate sales strategies. He now finds himself in a position of designing Mountain Dew graphics during the work week, while liberating Sprite billboards in his free time.

Fairey recently created two-color illustrations of bad-boy comedian Andy Kaufman and his alter ego, Tony Clifton, for Universal's *Man on the Moon* biopic. It was a secondary, supplemental campaign that deviated from the traditional broad-based mainstream ads. Vibrant, harshly colored stickers, stencils, and posters with the words "Andy Lives" were rolled out to fifteen major cities as a way of stimulating curiosity and creating pre-release buzz. He also helped put up some of the posters.

DeeDee Gordon, copresident of Look-Look, the marketing and trend analysis firm that assigned the project, said Fairey was hired "because his style of art resonates with youth. He's created his own grassroots following. People seek out his posters and collect them." She commends Fairey for doing an effective job driving major traffic to the AndyLives.org Web site. As for the unauthorized use of public display space, she has no comment.

Fairey spent only a few hours on the Kaufman drawings. He's managed to streamline his way of creating images to the point where he's pretty fast. "There are a lot of illustrators and painters who do beautiful work that I either don't have the skill or the patience to do," he says. "But you don't have to be God's gift to art to be effective. My technique is not that noteworthy. Anybody can steal images and refine them with a little practice. But for me, it's all about impact, and an illustration that's well crafted but doesn't capture somebody's attention is not serving its purpose.

"It seems to me there's more visual stuff than ever out there, more billboards, more ads, more everything. It's gnarlier than ever, and there just isn't as much room for time-consuming illustration. I look at everything commercially. Supply and demand. If people aren't willing to pay for it, how do you justify the time?"

These days, Fairey's personal project is funded with Black Market profits. "I don't even think about 'Giant' as making money, ever. I only think that the more money I make from it, the more stuff I can put out there." He recently agreed to let Listen.com, a music Web site, create 3,500 posters and 60,000 stickers with "Giant" as its centerpiece. He figures it's another way to mess with people's minds, to have them wonder if "Giant" has just been a ten-year teaser campaign. He also says he was well-compensated in the deal.

Fairey is ambivalent about his role in capitalizing on the capitalists. "I want to encourage people to do not just posters but anything creative that is contrary to being spoon-fed your culture by MTV and all the über-hip companies. So it's kind of ironic that I'm doing work for those companies. But *somebody's* going to do it. There are a few different forces battling here, and I'm just to the point where I don't have a problem with the contradictions. The world is full of contradictions."

In a 1996 *Wired* magazine article, Fairey was quoted as saying, "I don't like advertising." He now claims his remark was taken out of context. "I was never trying to say advertising in and of itself is wrong. What I was saying was, I don't like the way advertising tries to manipulate, to make people insecure. It's very, very competitive psychological warfare with no rules of combat. It's definitely fair game for vandalizing and critiquing, especially the national campaigns. But everybody makes their own decisions. Nobody twists your arm to smoke or drink. Nobody's making you puke your lunch up to be like women in fashion magazines."

Once upon a time, "Giant" was anti-advertising, a silent spokesperson without a product. Now it's become its own brand, with Fairey negotiating licensing deals for T-shirts, hats, and backpacks. He figures it still has enough street credibility to last a while longer. When he began his project he fantasized it could be taken pretty far, but he never imagined it would be as big as it is now.

Reflecting on the trajectory of his own life, he recalls his childhood in the conservative, old-money section of Charleston, South Carolina, as being very repressed, fraught with frustrations and insecurities. His family discouraged his involvement in punk rock, skateboarding, and other rebellious behavior. "Finally in eighth grade, I had to take a stand for myself and stop fading into the woodwork, even though I risked getting persecuted by my parents and teachers and friends. But I'm glad it happened. I think a lot of people, even if they're unhappy, spend all their lives following the path of least resistance. They're just very meek and obedient."

When asked about the extent his youthful anxieties contribute to his prolonged preoccupation with "Giant," Fairey pauses, then declares, "All the stuff I criticize I'm totally guilty of. Which is why I feel I can comment on it so effectively. I have made, and am still making, the mistakes I'm ridiculing.

"If you had to sum up who I am, 'Giant' is like a mirror to me. It totally reflects my need to get my imprint out there, to satisfy my adrenaline craving, and my artistic craving. You can really understand me quickly just by looking at 'Giant.' There's not much more to it."

When the time comes to canvass another area of town, Fairey climbs into his Civic and drives off, continuing to obey his inner "Giant."

Originally published in PRINT *LIV:III, May/June 2000.*

Guerrilla Street Postering

Civil Disobedience in Los Angeles

Robbie Conal

Guerrilla street postering—"sniping"—is the most direct, unmediated form of public expression available to pictorial artists. It's also narcotic. And illegal. But if you're a pissed-off painter with a gripe against your government's abrogation of civil rights in the name of "Homeland Security" (and color-coded national alerts, whatever they are) and you want to reach the Public, with a capital *P,* there's nothing like a little late-night urban art attack to get your freak on. Consider it a form of minor civil disobedience: misdemeanors perpetrated to protest higher crimes. What really freaks me out is that John Ashcroft, our Attorney General (the man responsible for *justice* in America, for Christ's sake!—oops, that's another subject), believes that surveillance is safer than civil liberties.

A few words about unmediated: this is a distribution issue, like how you do or don't get whatever it is you do *seen* by a lot of people. Instead of just your mom and your friends. How to communicate your concerns about important public issues to the Public. You could show art in an art gallery—but you have to make a business deal with a gallery owner.

Mostly, they'll show your art if it will sell. That pretty much leaves out ugly little black-and-white portraits of ugly old white men in suits and ties who've abused their power in the name of representative democracy.

How about illustrations in periodicals and books that have major distribution: newspapers, magazines, even free weeklies (*Village Voice, LA Weekly*)? You've got to get your art through an art director, an arts editor, an executive editor, and a publisher. (That's true of even this book, right, Steve?) A veritable gauntlet of mediation. Forget TV (unless you make news breaking the law, getting arrested for vandalism, or worse, talking back to the police, which is another story).

Of course if you're rich you could buy . . . forget that too, it don't apply. So we have running the streets in the middle of the night with a highly irregular army of guerrilla volunteers, hanging paper.

My hot issues are democracy, global capitalism, televangelism, and the environment—so far. When I reach the boiling point, I draw or paint adversarial portraits of the perpetrators and add a couple of satirical, punning words. Colloquial American English is the most subversive form of communication on the planet, and humor helps. It's the only way to stand (in both senses of the word) and deliver what's going on.

Then we digitize and fiddle around in Photoshop (we, because it isn't like I do this alone). It takes a bunch of people to make the posters. Photographer, designer, computer graphics wunderkinds, friends who work for free. Somehow we spit out a combination of image and text that could pass for "infotainment." Funny, but not nice. Critical, but not slanderous. On the edge. Just enough to tickle people on their way to work in the morning into thinking along with us about issues that make me gag. This isn't just art about politics, it is politics. Audience receptivity is important. As David Lynch would say, "Stick your finger into the zeitgeist." You have to figure your angle of penetration. Then slip it to 'em.

Then I make a deal with a friendly offset litho printer: pay $100 a month for the rest of my life to get a few thousand posters now. The Wimpy and the hamburger scenario.

Time for some guerrilla wrangling. It's surprising how many people are up for running the streets to perpetrate a little mischief in the most dangerous urban areas in the universe. It's sexy, a great date, if you're into mutual municipal code violation. Besides, no artist makes art for any audience without the "heh-heh" factor. As in, "Wait 'til they see this; it's gonna look so cool." Yeah, nasty portraits of politicians and bureaucrats up all over the streets is gonna blow their minds. Well, you have to at least think it's gonna be a gas, because there's almost no other reason to do it.

Trust me, it's a total loss. Making art with the intention of changing people's minds about issues that are important to them is hubris. Personal catharsis works for me. Participating in the national debate in a "trickle up" way figures into it—lots of people see the posters (if we do it right), whether they want to or not. But getting the guerrillas together in an all-night coffee shop—in LA we meet at Canter's Deli on Fairfax— feeling the buzz of the multi-culti crowd, not to mention the matzo ball soup and strawberry milkshakes—wow! Then I get high driving around town, doing the deed, with downloaded CDs blaring guerrillas' greatest hits. In walkable cities like New York, San Francisco, and Chicago, we have crews with headphones, rollerblades, whatnot. The action is addictive. We have liftoff.

How Low Can You Go?
The Stupid Awards
David Vogler (with a little help from his friends)

Remember the concept of "Desert Island Disks?" That was the parlor game where you'd be asked to imagine living on a deserted island and be forced to select your ten favorite record albums to take with you. I guess the thought was that, instead of choosing actual life-sustaining material (like food and water, for example), you'd be better off endlessly listening to a collection of personal oldies.

Or how about that other idiot conversation-starter where you'd be asked to select two people from history you'd most want to have dinner with? The uppity Lincoln Center crowd would almost always select the likes of "Gandhi and Jesus." Of course, the smarty-pants youngsters would respond with something unoriginal like, "I dunno, definitely not Hannibal Lechter!" and then burst into self-satisfying laughter.

Well, here's a new twist on an old favorite.

Late last August, my wife and I hosted a party in our loft and invited a bunch of our friends and co-workers. (It's probably relevant to note this was just days before September 11 and was the last carefree gathering I attended before the end of America's "Age of Innocence.") In attendance was a diverse group of folks that represented a variety of design disciplines from the worlds of fashion, industrial, new media, and graphic design. At one point, someone jokingly started a list of "Hi

Lites" and "Low Lites" of design. Considering the melting pot of aesthetic backgrounds and the excessive consumption of Guinness, I suppose this was inevitable.

The final result was the following non sequitor list of dubious design milestones from the past thirty years. In a way, it reminded me of that "Cheers and Jeers" column I've read in *TV Guide* while killing time at the grocery store checkout line. Only this list has no "Cheers." I'm afraid the party favorites were the absurd designs that were flat out irresponsible. *"Those designers should have known better!"*

They say that you grow from making mistakes. What can we learn from this? Whether they realize it or not, today's designers wield a mighty powerful sword. Let me state the obvious: Smart design permeates every aspect of our lives and regulates pop culture. The flip side to the coin is that dumb design can be equally powerful. At this point in time, we're all still prisoners of biology and our brutish primal needs. We still breathe, eat, fuck, and die the same way our flea-bitten, chimpy ancestors did millions of years ago. We're the same barbarians, just better deodorized and dressed a little nicer. Instead of rooting up an insect in the jungle, we're shopping for brightly colored plastic nonsense at Moss and the MOMA gift shop. Not much has changed. But that's where designers come in. Little by little the work of today's designer contributes to the long-term picture. For better or worse.

Who knows? Maybe years from now the design solutions we place on a pedestal today will be the fodder for drunken party humor tomorrow. Time will tell. But for now, please allow me to humbly present in no particular order, the top twenty-five examples of design irresponsibility. And please don't shoot the messenger.

Chrysler's PT Cruiser

This new mass-market car was designed to appeal to the aging boomer who wants a vehicle that feels "cool" but still has enough practical utility to cart their whiney kids to soccer practice. The PT Cruiser is an odd duck. It's a cross between the retro car driven by ZZ Top in their music videos and a classic Al Capone gangster mobile. I'm not quite sure what that says about Middle America, but apparently consumers have fallen in love with it.

The Original Interface for Prodigy

Back in the late 1980s, the Internet was in its Jurassic period. IBM and Sears teamed up to launch a proprietary online service called "Prodigy." The interface featured astoundingly poor vector graphics that was not unlike the crude DOS text lines of an airport monitor's display. In their defense, they did the best they could considering they had to work with 8-bit RGB colors running on computers no smarter than today's average Palm Pilot. It looked awful, worked only on Windows, and had the chutzpah to actually contain *a paid advertisement* at the bottom of every screen! Say what you will, but Prodigy pioneered "radical" concepts that would later be the building blocks for many of today's legitimate Web sites, online business models, and virtual communities.

NYPD Blue's Camera Work

This wildly popular ABC cop drama pioneered the "shaky cam" technique when it premiered ten years ago. (It also was the first network to show a brief glimpse of Dennis Franz's naked, cellulite-riddled ass in primetime, but that's another story). This "eyewitness" camera technique was fresh at first and fooled the viewer into thinking they were seeing "raw," unrehearsed footage. In the context of *NYPD Blue* it contributed to the story. But soon Madison Avenue started using it everywhere. When this calculated camera technique started showing up in commercials for Eggo Waffles it became laughable and distracting.

Color Photography in the New York Times

"What the hell is the world coming to if the sacred 'Grey Lady' starts running color photos?" To many die-hard readers, the idea of modern color printing in the *Times* was nothing short of blasphemy. I'm sure they're over it by now.

The Round iMac Mouse

When anyone does a review of the best industrial design, Apple computer always scores big time. As well it should. The Macintosh single-handedly changed the course of personal computing and has become the gold standard. Apple's brilliant marriage of hardware and software produced the best user experience in the industry. But their biggest boner had to be the 1998 iMac mouse. This round "puck" looked gorgeous in photo shoots, but was ergonomically annoying. This was an instance where function followed form. Luckily Apple redeemed themselves in the summer of 2000 by replacing this flawed mouse with a superior optical version in the shape of an egg.

Ronald Reagan's 1984 Campaign Ads

Depending on whom you talk to, the design effort to re-elect President Ronald Reagan was either a high or a low point. The ad campaign was made famous by the tag line "It's Morning In America," and featured folksy voice-over prose with emotional images of majestic Californian sunrises. Many of the cynical liberals at the time referred to the spots as *"Mourning in America!"*

Dumb-Ass Digital Type

I'm no prude. Heck, I like typographic experimentation as much as the next guy. But that whole mid-1980s nutty-type era was getting a little out of hand. For a period of time it seemed that every designer coming out of art school would collage together multiple overlapping headlines and try to pass it off as meaningful communication. Baloney. A lot of this illegible layered look was the result of a designer's ability to gratuitously manipulate computer fonts, rather than produce an intelligent message. Computer typesetting has caused as much harm as it has good. The biggest typographic casualty has been the art of quotations. Some of the sexiest letterforms in any font set are the quotes, commas, and apostrophes. However, more often than not, today's designers blindly hit the keyboard producing "spikes" or inch marks in place of real quotes. The tragedy is that most of these folks either never had the education to notice the difference or simply aren't anal enough to use the hidden keyboard commands to change the "dumb straight quotes" into proper "smart curly quotes." Sure, maybe I'm splitting hairs, but God is in the details. And all the type purists I know cringe when they see grand movie credits roll up the big screen littered with these easily corrected typographic errors.

Joe Camel

The birth of big tobacco's kid-friendly icon represents the most blatant and loathsome marketing device from corporate America. Shame on them! How did the illustrator who painted those images sleep at night? Further, more than a few women pointed out to me that Joe's elongated, uncamel-like face was suspiciously phallic looking as well. I bet that's no accident.

Bill Shatner

One could argue that Paramount's multibillion-dollar *Star Trek* franchise owes its success to Mr. William Shatner, the actor who played the ubiquitous Captain Kirk. His over-acting, dime-store hairpiece, and poorly concealed belly truss may not have been what you'd expect in a starship captain. But despite being the target of easy jokes, Shatner/Kirk is a beloved hero. The producers who wrote, cast, and "designed" the character of Captain Kirk positively influenced many generations of fans, but often at the expense of subtlety.

New Coke

On April 23, 1985, the Coca-Cola Company introduced "New Coke" and expected a huge hit. The internal marketing geniuses at the company secretly tested the new formula in more than 200,000 blind taste tests and it always came up a winner. The new Coke recipe also used fructose corn syrup instead of cane sugar, therefore making it cheaper to manufacture. Driven by greed and their maniacal quest to crush their Pepsi competitor, Coca-Cola simultaneously discontinued the old formula when they switched to the new-version Coke. The public went nuts. In the eyes of the audience, Coke was an American institution that could not be tampered with. The controversy produced scores of crabby editorials, public debates, and violent protests. At one point a mad rush to horde the "old" Coke became popular. Even Andy Warhol went on record against New Coke and was rumored to have stockpiled many cases of the old stuff. Coca-Cola finally buckled under negative public opinion and brought back the original formula less than three months later on

July 11, 1985. The return of "classic" Coke was so important that ABC actually interrupted *General Hospital* to break the news. The Coca-Cola Company hedged its bets by selling New Coke and Classic alongside each other, but the damage was irreversible. By 1986 New Coke had only a 3 percent market share. In 1990 it was halfheartedly relaunched as "Coke II," and was finally put out of its misery.

Breast Implants

Honestly, are they really necessary? Excessive tattoos, tongue piercings, and fake breasts are generally bad news. You'll regret it later in life. But kids, if you must have the procedure done, my contacts at *Screw* magazine tell me the best tit jobs go in through the armpit and under the pecs to subtly elevate the whole area, as opposed to the antiquated process of entering the underside, which leaves telltale wrinkled bags immediately under the skin. Mammoriffic!

Any Product from the Creepy Amway Corporation

Do you know anyone who actually buys Amway products? Neither do I. Yet the cult-like nuts who run the company rake in millions. Based in Grand Rapids, Michigan, Amway sells third-rate junk through a suspicious person-to-person direct marketing gimmick. Amway recruits desperate sad sacks looking for an easy "get-rich-quick" ticket out of the trailer park. This sort of hoodwinking amounts to nothing short of a global pyramid scheme. Trust me on this one, if anyone ever approaches you boasting about "a business opportunity as an Amway distributor" run like hell.

1970s American Automobiles

The Pacer, the Pinto, and, of course, the K-Car. Without question, these products represent the very best examples of the very worst design.

That "Heimlich Maneuver" Poster

You know the one I'm talking about. The poster is laid out on a peculiar 30-degree angle and illustrated with the kind of disturbing line-art figures usually reserved for airplane-crash-procedure warning cards. According to law, this odd two-color poster is supposed to be publicly displayed at all eating establishments. However, I've only seen them taped up in greasy-spoon diners. I've yet to see this garish warning boldly hung in one of David Bouley's joints.

The NBC N Logo Debacle

For years the icon of the NBC television network was the colorful peacock. But in 1976 they paid big bucks to kill the bird and replace it with a fresh, new logo. With great fanfare they unveiled a cold corporate mark in the shape of an abstract *N*. It was met with almost universal disgust. To make matters worse, after the *N* was plastered all over the airways they discovered the designers and marketers hadn't done their homework. A rinky-dink local station in Nebraska already had a logo that was identical. It seemed no one had done a search before committing to the new NBC *N*. With great embarrassment, NBC quickly paid the little station to clam up and allow them to use the *N*. In the end, it didn't much matter. The public missed the peacock and it was soon brought back anyway.

Space Food Sticks

During the Apollo program, NASA did what was virtually impossible: In record time they sent a man to the Moon and successfully returned him safely to the Earth. Advertisers seized the moment to create new products with a "space" theme based on actual NASA foodstuffs. Kraft gave us "Tang," which was essentially an orange Kool Aid–like powder that was mixed with tap water. But Pillsbury came out with "Space Food Sticks." The package described them as a *"non-frozen balanced energy snack in rod form containing nutritionally balanced amounts of carbohydrate, fat, and protein."* Whatever. They were nothing more than a moist Tootsie Roll wrapped in high-tech foil to give them a futuristic look. Shortly after they went on sale, the public lost interest in the space race, and Pillsbury unceremoniously discontinued the snack.

Obnoxious, Fat, Daytime Talk-Show Hosts

Mindless daytime talk shows are nothing new. But in recent years a new genre has emerged. I'm talking about Rosie, Oprah, and Roseanne. I can't imagine anything more unpleasant than watching these insufferable women pushing their agendas by chatting with washed-up movie stars and quack therapists. Oprah's forced geniality and rehearsed gestures of compassion are legendary. Rosie's brassy, personal politics polluted every show. And Roseanne is, well, Roseanne. But there may be hope yet. As of this writing, Oprah's ratings are dropping, 2002 is Rosie's last season, and Roseanne's syndicated flop has quickly been cancelled.

NYC's Conversational Signage

Here in New York, the streets are clogged with signs blurting out traffic demands such as "DON'T BLOCK THE BOX!" Yet at the same time there are many signs that try to enforce civic compliance with a more relaxed, conversational approach. The most notable signs are the ones that actually say, "Don't even think of parking here!" and "Littering is selfish and filthy, so don't do it." Who writes this copy? I imagine these were designed by some exhausted, nebbishy municipal worker at the end of his rope.

The Verizon Logo

Everyone unanimously agreed that the Verizon logo is one of the worst pieces of corporate identity in the past fifty years. The logo breaks all the rules they taught you in art school: It doesn't reduce very well, it lacks a clear conceptual idea, and it's astonishingly amateur in execution. If you've had the misfortune of having to work with it, you know what I'm talking about. Its awkward shape is astoundingly ill conceived. Either the designers were asleep at the wheel or the corporate heads of Verizon bullied them into delivering this graphic stinker. I suspect the final solution was the result of too many cooks spoiling the broth. A good logo should embody the qualities of the company it represents. In this case the Verizon logo succeeds. It captures everything the company is known for: ineptitude, lack of aesthetics, and bureaucratic decisions made by committee.

The Sneaker Phone

Years after Maxwell Smart made the nation guffaw with his kooky secret agent shoe-as-a-phone routine, the *Sports Illustrated* people actually offered a working telephone in the shape of a sneaker for those willing to buy a subscription.

The New "Less Gay" Mr. Clean

One of Procter & Gamble's most popular and profitable cleaning products is "Mr. Clean." For years the poster boy for this lemony liquid was a beloved beefy, bald man wearing a single questionable gold earring. Mr. Clean dressed in a skin-tight white muscle T-shirt and always appeared flexing his biceps while promoting a tidy home. I don't know about you, but that sounds like the attributes of a Chelsea gay guy to me. When the Mr. Clean icon was recently updated, the illustrators attempted to temper his "Village People quotient" by making him look more like a benevolent muscular dentist. Perhaps they went a little too far to the right. The modern Mr. Clean now has bushy white eyebrows and a deviant smirk that reminds us of Aryan inmate Vern Schillinger from HBO's gritty prison drama, *OZ*.

The Marshmallow Peep

The disturbing Peep has delighted children for decades. What could be wrong with a mysterious blob of sugary marshmallow in the pseudo-shape of an innocent yellow "chick?" As far as I'm concerned, this is the real meaning of Easter.

The Usurping of Public Space

I was once in a movie theatre and in the middle of the film a teenage punk's cell phone went off. What was worse, *he actually took the call!* This discourteous fucker actually talked for ten minutes before realizing he had pissed off an entire

1,000-seat movie house. Today's technology and design has contributed to the invasion of public space. Or rather, the notion of private space is now an endangered species. Cell phones make every place a place for private conversations. Under this trend, 4,000-square-foot pre-fab suburban McMansions clog the suburbs and zillions of gas-guzzling SUVs are akin to taking the living room out on the road. Have we not learned anything?

The "Poop-ifiying" of America

The Farrelly Brothers, *South Park*, Jim Carrey, teen-sex farce summer movies, *Beavis and Butthead*, the list goes on and on. It smells like the last half of the recent decade was giddy with what I like to call "poop culture." Enough already. (Full disclosure: I deserve my fair share of the blame. As a creative director for Nickelodeon, I spent years inventing juvenile fart humor for a living.)

Michael Jackson's Face

If the self-proclaimed "King of Pop" had spent more time recording new hit songs rather than abusing his face, maybe his career would still be a success. After a great run in the 1980s, poor Michael Jackson soon dropped out of the spotlight and was engulfed with child-abuse lawsuits and excessive plastic surgery. In the abstract, let this be a lesson to us all. Sometimes it takes more courage and creativity to know when to stop and just leave well enough alone. *What were his surgeons thinking?* Didn't they have the professionalism and common sense to simply turn down Michael's requests for repeated procedures? They say plastic surgery is a design art form. In a crazy, surreal way, perhaps Michael Jackson's face is the best modern example of when designers act irresponsibly.

Adbuster

Véronique Vienne Interviews Kalle Lasn

Kalle Lasn's documentaries have been broadcast on PBS, on CBC, and around the world. He is the publisher of *Adbusters* magazine and founder of the Adbusters Media Foundation and Powershift Advertising Agency. He has dedicated himself to launching social marketing campaigns like Buy Nothing Day and TV Turnoff Week.

VV: What do you think about AIGA's new code of ethics? Don't you think it's a step in the right direction in terms of responsibility?

Kalle Lasn: Yes, AIGA has finally come up with a code of ethics to back up its longstanding talk of professional standards. But is this the best AIGA can do? A list of rules about fees and decorum? There's a need for ethical standards, but in this age surely ethics must take a much longer view. I'd like to suggest a more timely and straightforward code: the code of true-cost design.

"True cost" simply means that before designers begin work on a new product, they consider the ecological and psychological consequences of what they do. In other words, they plan to minimize the damage before they maximize the cool.

VV: What would be your guidelines for finding the true cost of a product?

KL: Well, let's say you're designing a leaf blower. The little two-stroke engine you plan for the thing probably has a life of a few thousand hours. Each one of those hours will produce a bit of stress and annoyance and pollution for everyone who is forced to listen to the machine and to breathe its fumes.

So before you start work, you do the math. You decide how much per hour that aggravation and pollution costs society (for the sake of example, say one cent per hour). You multiply that by the 3,000-hour lifespan of this tool. The result is a rough estimate of the ecological and psychological cost of your leaf blower over its lifetime: thirty dollars.

Now you have a decision to make. If the true-cost figure seems unacceptably high, and you do not feel you can make it lower, then you should turn down the job. Or you can try to design a leaf blower that's quieter and cleaner. Or maybe you decide instead to design a better rake, or a leaf composter.

VV: True cost is a theoretical exercise, isn't it? There is no way to know for sure what is the true cost of a product. So designers should think of true cost as a personal and professional discipline.

KL: I don't think of it as a theoretical exercise. Of course, this whole area is very subjective right now. There are few objective criteria for deciding what the true cost of a product is. But we cannot simply throw up our hands and walk away. Bit by bit, we must learn how to calculate these costs, because if we don't, we are effectively calculating them as zero—which is the worst thing we can do. If the AIGA code of ethics said, "designers do no harm" and asked us to estimate, as rigorously as possible, the true cost of the products we design, then we, and future generations of designers, would be nudged into a whole new way of thinking about our work. Bit by bit, over the years, I think we would then turn what is now a largely theoretical exercise into something much more precise and scientific.

VV: I think what's intriguing is to try to consider the psychological cost as well as the ecological cost of a product.

KL: Yes, it's fascinating. You know the mental environment is a new idea and what is becoming clearer is that there are often quite severe psychological costs associated with the design and marketing of products. Right now our culture is suffering an epidemic of mental illness. A recent study by Myra Weissman at Columbia University showed that young people today are three times (300 percent) more likely to suffer from a mood disorder, or an anxiety attack, or a bout of depression compared to people in their fifties and sixties. Half of all North Americans will visit a mental health professional or take some kind of psychoactive drug like Prozac sometime in their life. Many researchers believe that mass-media clutter and the thousands of marketing messages our brains absorb every day, are partially to blame for this epidemic of mental dysfunction.

I think we designers have to question our role in all this. We have to confront both the ecological and the psychological harms we do.

You know there are two kinds of products. First, the kind that sits on the table: it's beautiful, it's got nice form, a cool feel. You pick it up, turn it around in your hands and say, "Wow! what a wonderful product—the client will love it and it will sell well in the marketplace."

Then there is a second kind of product, the one that doesn't sit on a table to be admired, but is in the customer's hands every day—to brush his teeth, shave his beard, drive him to work, or whatever. I think we designers have to pay more attention to that second kind of product—the one that, for years, maybe decades, maybe centuries will delight, ease, charm. It will be shared, cursed, repaired, and will ultimately sit in a landfill long after the designer is food for worms.

If we thought more about the psychological dimensions of products in use, I think we could do all kinds of weird and wonderful things. We could design a hot-water tap to be used less. We could design a lawnmower to be shared by all the residents of a city block.

We could design a "carbonometer" that sits on the dashboard of a car and tells the driver how much carbon he is pumping out of his tailpipe. The possibilities explode as soon as you break out of the commercial design box.

VV: Can you also take into account the positive benefits of a product? If a beautifully designed object is soothing psychologically, how does this effect your true-cost analysis?

KL: Yes, in time, I think we can learn how to value things like the health benefits, the stress-reduction power, and perhaps even the aesthetic pleasure of the products we design. But first we have to make sure our products do no harm—in other words, that our true-cost analysis yields an acceptable result.

VV: Are you going to explore that idea in the *Adbusters* magazine some more?

KL: Yes, in fact, ever since we put out our "First Things First Manifesto" and "Design Anarchy" issues we've been getting an incredible amount of feedback about design ethics, responsibility, and related issues—especially from young designers. Every day we get e-mails and phone calls from design students and some of them come to visit us in our Vancouver office. They all want to feel that this profession they are getting into is about more than just satisfying a client and making a ton of money.

As the planet degrades, I think a slower, greener, less-cluttered, and less-commercial aesthetic will emerge. We are going to as many schools and conferences as we can talking about this emerging aesthetic, and about eco-design, bio-mimicry, psycho-design, codes of ethics, and so on.

VV: What is bio-mimicry exactly?

KL: Bio-mimicry is mimicking nature. I think it's one of the key aspects of future product design. It's already popular in architecture and some other professions.

In design, bio-mimicry would involve looking at how nature does the same job as the product you are designing.

Somehow, you'd try to incorporate what you can learn from nature into the design of your product.

VV: Actually, I feel that most clients think that the "greening" of their product is just a good marketing slant. They say, "Yeah, we're responsible," when actually what they're trying to do is to find a new spin.

KL: Yes, this kind of green-washing is very prevalent. Of course, there are companies out there who are serious about sustainability, who believe in the values we've been talking about, and who consider the ecological cost of their products from cradle to grave. They like to have the feeling that their products are not harming future generations, not harming the planet in any way. But such companies are few and far between.

By and large, especially for large corporations, green thinking is mostly about negotiating a better relationship with the public. For them, it's all about putting a prominent green symbol on their packaging: our product is green, our packaging is green. It's not a serious attempt to be responsible. That is why we cannot rely on our clients to set ethical standards. That's why it is so important for our profession to come up with its own codes.

VV: In Europe, of course, they are much more advanced in that way of thinking—but are they really leaders in the field? European companies, I think German companies in particular, are environmentally and psychologically conscious.

KL: Yes, many European companies are well ahead of us here in North America. But I wouldn't call them leaders, I would say they are ahead by a few years. They have yet to come up with the big-picture solutions toward a truly sustainable global economy. What I am talking about is the idea of an across-the-board, true-cost marketplace, in which the cost of every product tells the ecological truth. This would mean that the ecological damage caused by a "bad" product—like, for example, the gasoline-powered automobile—is internalized right into the market price of the product. Such broad-based, market-reform thinking is still in its infancy, even in Europe.

VV: Finally, there are those who would question the whole notion of designers evaluating true costs. Any parting words for them?

KL: We designers are in the unique position—design being so new—of still being able to shape our culture as it grows. We can carve out a soul for it beyond its current commercial masturbation. I think true cost is something we can live by, explain to our kids, put into our professional code of ethics. It's something we can hang our profession on.

Last Word

In a Continuous State of Becoming
Design Responsibility Tomorrow

Véronique Vienne

We are about to redefine the very nature of design. A decade or two from now, we will shake our head in disbelief when considering how far we've come. Products designed for novel appeal and short-term use will seem as obsolete to us as Leonard da Vinci's flying machine and Philippe Starck's chrome-plated, three-legged lemon squeezer.

In the near future, as a matter of course, we will take cradle-to-grave responsibility for the objects we design. Our conscience will demand it, our environment will require it, and—can you believe it—our clients will insist on it.

So morose by today's standards, the word "sustainable" will replace the word "modern" in everyday language. When talking about a new electronic gadget, a new car, a new pair of sneakers, or a new skiing resort, people will say: "Right! It's awesome—and *totally* sustainable."

Most exciting perhaps will be the way we look at things: not as isolated objects anymore, but as dynamic components of a living macrocosm that includes all the befores and afters of the manufacturing process.

Designers will question where a specific food chain starts and where it ends; whether the projects they work on are part of an ecosystem that's solar-powered or fossil-fueled; how far back they can trace the genesis of the materials they use; and how practical it will be to dismantle the products they design in order to remanufacture them once they have outlived their present function.

Still a novelty, this momentous change is a hot topic in journalistic circles. In the press, some of the most arresting stories published in the last few years turn out to be fascinating epics describing lengthy recycling odysseys. George Packer, a *New York Times* reporter, followed an old T-shirt donated to a Manhattan charity all the way to Uganda, where it was bought for $1.20 by a toothless old man who has four wives and thirty-two children.

Michael Pollan, also from the *New York Times*, bought an eight-month-old calf in North Dakota for $598 dollars in order to follow its "highly unnatural journey" into steakdom—and "learn how the meat industry really works."

Victor Chu, a "fashion technologist," told *BusinessWeek* how he is developing a biodegradable casing for prepaid cell phones that contains flower seeds that can be planted once the phone runs out of credit.

Paul Glader, a staff reporter at the *Wall Street Journal,* investigated the whereabouts of mangled steel columns from the World Trade Center that ended up at a smelting plant in Newark specializing in refrigerator coils and construction nails.

Some stories are uplifting, others are disturbing. Japanese waste management companies mine discarded cell phones to extract precious metals like silver, copper, and gold.

Each month, "end-of-life process managers" at Hewlett-Packard reclaim 200,000 pounds of plastics from discarded computers and printers.

Old television sets, circuit boards, and copying machines, shipped to China, India, and Pakistan for recycling, release their toxic pollutants in the environment of these developing countries.

In Kabul, Afghans recycle bricks from decade-old ruins to rebuild their city with traditional materials rather than put up cheap aluminum structures.

In Baltimore, an inspired bibliophile created a small charity in order to collect and distribute for free thousands of unwanted used books—and dispatch them down the food-for-thought chain.

But recycling, a twentieth-century concept from the 1970s, can no longer encompass the kind of eco-consciousness that's needed today to solve the garbage glut that's choking landfills. It is often too costly to collect, transport, sort, and clean discarded products for traditional reclamation methods. Companies are forced to explore novel solutions to deal with their waste-management issues. New solutions tend toward "remanufacturing"—the making of brand new products from previously assembled parts.

Practically, for designers, it comes down to designing products that are easy to assemble—and easy to dismantle. To make reusing safer, faster, and thus more cost-effective, plastic and metal components should be stamped with codes indicating their provenance and their chemical composition. And the pricing of products should reflect their environmental impact, their cost to public health, their psychological benefits, their social merits, and their geo-political implications.

The age of sustainability will give designers a chance to spread their wings at last. No longer relegated to making products merely profitable and appealing, they'll be inspired to imagine the future. Like Leonardo da Vinci. Or like these contemporary pioneers who are designing architectural units with fog-catching sails for water collecting, developing creature-like robots with flexible sensors that control "muscles," and experimenting with advanced composting techniques to protect crops from droughts.

No longer "durable" goods, the things we design and use should be renamed "timely" goods to celebrate the fact that the best stuff in life is "of-the-moment," "in-the-now"—in a continuous state of becoming.

Originally published in Graphis *343, January/February 2003.*

Biographies

Hugh Aldersey-Williams is an author and journalist with interests in design and science. He is the author of books on American and international design for Rizzoli, and of *The Most Beautiful Molecule* (Wiley, 1995), which relates the discovery of the Nobel Prize–winning third form of the element carbon, buckminster-fullerene. Most recently, he curated the "animal/house" exhibition at London's Victoria & Albert Museum, which documented architecture's new turn to nature.

Julie Baugnet is an associate professor of design at St. Cloud State University in Minnesota. Most of her freelance design work is for nonprofit organizations.

Leslie Becker is chair of graphic design at the California College of Arts and Crafts. She has served as consultant to NASA on the interior of the manned space station, on the Board of the AIGA/SF, and does pro bono work for Kelsey St. Press, an award-winning, nationally recognized women's press. She has presented papers at AIGA National Conferences, AICAD Conferences, written for *Print* magazine, *SFDC* magazine, *Graphis New Talent*, and *Design Book Review*.

Roy R. Behrens is a professor of art at the University of Northern Iowa, where he teaches graphic design, illustration, and design history. He edits *Ballast Quarterly Review*, art directs the *North American Review*, and is a contributing editor of *Print*. His most recent book is *False Colors: Art, Design and Modern Camouflage* (Bobolink Books, 2002).

Nancy Bernard has worked in visual communications for twenty-five years. Until 1996, she was an illustrator, project manager, and packaging designer. From 1996 to 2001, she was managing editor of *Critique*, the magazine of graphic design thinking. She is now director of collaboration for the Palo Alto branding firm, Neutron LLC.

J. D. Biersdorfer writes about technology and pop culture—and sometimes about the collision between the two—for the *New York Times* and other publications.

Anne Bush is the chairperson of the graphic design program at the University of Hawaii. Her essays on design have appeared in *Visible Language, Emigre,* the *American Center for Design Journal, Design Issues,* the *AIGA Journal,* and *Visual Communication.*

Robbie Conal grew up as an "art brat" in New York City. He got psychedelicized at San Francisco State University in the sixties and professionalized at Stanford University in the seventies. In the eighties, encroaching adulthood forced him to get his art and social concerns together and make pictures about subjects that were important: politics, power, and the abuses of both. Four or five times a year he turns them into thousands of street posters and, with a very irregular guerrilla army, puts them up in major cities around the U.S.

Michael Dooley is a Los Angeles–based designer whose work was recently featured in the updated edition of *Graphic Wit: The Art of Humor in Design.* An educator, magazine writer, and *Print* contributing editor, his articles have also appeared in several books including *Graphic Design History, Looking Closer: Critical Writings on Graphic Design, Sex Appeal: The Art of Allure in Graphic and Advertising Design,* and *Graphic Design USA.*

Stuart Ewen is distinguished professor of film and media studies at Hunter College, also in the Ph.D. programs in history, sociology, and American studies at the Graduate Center of the City University of New York. His books include: *PR! A Social History of Spin, All Consuming Images: The Politics of Style in Contemporary Culture, Captains of Consciousness: Advertising and the Social Roots of the Consumer Culture,* and, with Elizabeth Ewen, *Channels of Desire: Mass Images and the Shaping of American Consciousness.* Again with Elizabeth Ewen, he is presently at work on a three-century history of stereotyping, tentatively entitled *Typecasting: On the Arts & Sciences of Human Inequality.*

Thomas Frank is the editor of *The Baffler* magazine and the author of the books *One Market Under God* and *The Conquest of Cool.*

Ken Garland was art director of *Design* magazine (London) from 1956–62, when he left to establish his own graphic design studio as Ken Garland and Associates. He has contributed many articles to design periodicals in the United Kingdom, United States, and Europe. His own publications include "First Things First" (1964), "Mr Beck's Underground Map" (1994), "A Word in Your Eye" (1996), and

"Metaphors: A Portfolio of Text and Image" (2001). He has lectured widely in the United Kingdom, United States, and Canada, and is currently visiting professor in information design at the Universidad de las Américas, Mexico.

Peter Hall is a contributing editor for *Metropolis* magazine and research fellow for the Design Institute at the University of Minnesota, where he edits the online conference review, Knowledge Circuit. He also teaches a seminar on design theory at Yale School of Art's MFA graphic design program. He wrote and co-edited the books *Tibor Kalman: Perverse Optimist and Sagmeister: Made You Look*, and co-authored *Pause: 59 Minutes of Motion Graphics*.

Steven Heller is the art director of the *New York Times Book Review* and co-chair of the MFA Design program at the School of Visual Arts. He is author of over eighty books on graphic design, popular culture, and illustration, including *Merz to Émigré and Beyond: Avant Garde Magazine Design of the Twentieth Century* (Phaidon Press), *Cuba Style: Graphic Design from the Golden Age* (Princeton Architectural Press), and *The Graphic Design Reader* (Allworth Press).

Mr. Keedy is a designer, writer, type designer, and educator who has been teaching in the graphic design program at the California Institute of the Arts since 1985. His designs and essays have been published in *Eye, I.D., Emigre, Critique, Idea, Looking Closer 1, 2,* and *4, Faces on the Edge: Type in the Digital Age, New Design: Los Angeles,* and *The Education of a Graphic Designer.*

Maud Lavin is the author of *Clean New World: Culture, Politics, and Graphic Design* (MIT) and a monograph on the photomontages of *Hannah Hoech, Cut with the Kitchen Knife* (Yale). She is an associate professor of visual and critical studies and art history, theory, and criticism at the School of the Art Institute of Chicago.

Victor Margolin is associate professor of design history at the University of Illinois, Chicago. His most recent book is *The Politics of the Artificial: Essays on Design and Design Studies.*

Carolyn McCarron is a senior art director at Gillespie/McCann Erickson in Princeton, New Jersey. She previously worked for Waters Design in New York and Houghton Mifflin Company in Boston. She has written articles for *Communication Arts, Adobe Magazine,* and the *AIGA Journal of Graphic Design.*

Katherine McCoy is a senior lecturer at Illinois Institute of Technology's Institute of Design in Chicago, after co-chairing the department of design at Cranbrook Academy of Art for twenty-four years. A 1999 Medallist of the AIGA and elected member of the Alliance Graphique Internationale, she consults in communications design and design marketing, writes on design criticism and history, and organizes continuing professional education programs through High Ground Tools and Strategies for Design.

David Reinfurt runs a graphic design practice in New York City called O-R-G and teaches in the Interactive Telecommunications Program at New York. See also *www.o-r-g.com*.

Chris Riley has been a researcher and advertising strategist since 1982. He has worked in nearly every market in the world over the course of twenty years. The last eleven years was as head of strategic planning at multinational ad agency Wieden + Kennedy. He has worked with some of the world's best brands—Nike, Coca Cola, and Microsoft—in Europe, Asia, Latin America, and the USA. He opened Studioriley in June 2002 as a place to create healthy brands through good strategic design. He has spoken on environmentalism, education, and the arts at conferences in the U.S., Europe, and Latin America. He was a founding director of the Portland Institute of Contemporary Art.

Chase A. Rogers founded her design studio, FuelFactor, as a means to express her many interests in the form of innovative design techniques. Academically trained as writer, artist, and designer, Chase iterates that in this global community we share everything, for better or worse, and that we need to begin acting on that premise to create programs of change toward pragmatic social ethics. We are obligated to healing ourselves and the natural environment.

Michael Schmidt is an associate professor teaching undergraduate and graduate graphic design courses at the University of Memphis. He volunteers at the Mid-South Peace and Justice Center's Global Goods store, selling fair trade items made in developing nations.

Judith Schwartz is a designer in New York City.

Matt Soar's articles and essays on visual culture have most recently appeared in the *AIGA Journal of Graphic Design, Cultural Studies,* and the edited collections *Looking Closer 4* (Allworth Press) and *Image Ethics in the Digital Age* (forthcoming from University of Minnesota Press). He recently completed a major research project on the cultural politics of graphic design, centering on issues of social responsibility. Matt is currently visiting assistant professor of video and and media studies at Hampshire College.

Gunnar Swanson is a graphic designer, media designer, writer, and educator. He has taught at the Otis College of Art and Design and the University of California Davis, headed the graphic design program at the University of Minnesota Duluth, and directed the multimedia program at California Lutheran University. He is the editor and designer of the Allworth Press book *Graphic Design and Reading*.

Susan S. Szenasy is chief editor of *Metropolis*, the New York City–based magazine of architecture, culture, and design. She is the author of several books on design, including *The Home and Light*. She holds an MA degree in Modern

European History from Rutgers University and teaches design history and design ethics at New York's Parsons School of Design. She is the co-founder of R.Dot (Rebuild Downtown Our Town), a coalition of New York City organizations and individuals that came together after the 9/11 tragedies to contribute their expertise to building the twenty-first-century metropolis at the site of the former World Trade Center.

Teal Triggs is director of postgraduate studies, faculty of art, design and music, Kingston University, United Kingdom. Her writings on graphic design, typography, education, feminism, and politics have appeared in numerous design publications and books internationally. She is also co-editor with Roger Sabin of *'Below Critical Radar': Fanzines and Alternative Comics from 1976 to Now* (Slab-O-Concrete, 2000).

Tucker Viemeister is President of Springtime-USA (a partnership with the young Dutch industrial design company famous for their "Roodrunner" delivery bike for the Dutch PTTPost). The New York studio focuses on opportunities in product, new media, branding, space, mobility, and social strategy—projects that leverage Tucker's special talents and experience creating lots of comfortable, practical, profitable, and fun stuff like OXO Good Grips. He is serving on the Board of the Architectural League of New York and is a Fellow of the Industrial Designers Society of America.

Véronique Vienne is the author of *The Art of Doing Nothing* and *The Art of Imperfection* (Clarkson Potter), as well as *Something to be Desired,* a collection of essays on design (*Graphis*). She is also working on a book on Chip Kidd (Laurence King Publishing). A frequent contributor to *Graphis* and *Metropolis* magazines, she writes about design and cultural trends for a number of mainstream publications. Born and raised in France, Véronique lives in New York, where she teaches a course called "The Integrated Studio" at the School of Visual Arts (SVA) in the Graphic Design MFA program.

David Vogler is a rogue, a rascal, and a raconteur. After spending fifteen years working for The Man at various corporations such as Disney, MTV, and Nickelodeon, he opened his own practice focusing on design and product development.

Cheryl Towler Weese, with her partner Kathy Fredrickson, runs Studio Blue in Chicago, a firm that develops and designs books, environmental design, identities, and a range of Web and printed matter.

Index

Books from Allworth Press

Citizen Brand: 10 Commandments for Transforming Brands in a Consumer Democracy by Marc Gobé (hardcover, 5½ × 8½, 256 pages, $24.95)

Emotional Branding: The New Paradigm for Connecting Brands to People by Marc Gobé (hardcover, 256 pages, $24.95)

Design Issues: How Graphic Design Informs Society edited by DK Holland (paperback, 6¾ × 9⅞, 288 pages, $21.95)

Looking Closer 4: Critical Writings on Graphic Design edited by Michael Bierut, William Drenttel, and Steven Heller (paperback, 6¾ × 9⅞, 304 pages, $21.95)

Inside the Business of Graphic Design: 60 Leaders Share Their Secrets of Success by Catharine Fishel (paperback, 6 × 9, 288 pages, $19.95)

Design Humor: The Art of Graphic Wit by Steven Heller (paperback, 6¾ × 9⅞, 224 pages, $21.95)

The Graphic Design Reader by Steven Heller (paperback with flaps, 5½ × 8½, 320 pages, $19.95)

The Education of a Design Entrepreneur edited by Steven Heller (paperback, 6¾ × 9⅞, 288 pages, $21.95)

The Education of an E-Designer edited by Steven Heller (paperback, 6¾ × 9⅞, 352 pages, $21.95)

The Education of a Graphic Designer edited by Steven Heller (paperback, 6¾ × 9⅞, 288 pages, $18.95)

Graphic Design History edited by Steven Heller and Georgette Balance, 6¾ × 9⅞, 352 pages, $21.95)

The Elements of Graphic Design: Space, Unity, Page Architecture, and Type by Alex W. White (paperback, 6⅛ × 9¼, 160 pages, $24.95)

AIGA Professional Practices in Graphic Design: The American Institute of Graphic Arts edited by Tad Crawford (paperback, 6¾ × 9⅞, 320 pages, $24.95)

Business and Legal Forms for Graphic Designers, Third Edition by Tad Crawford and Eva Doman Bruck (paperback, 8½ × 11, 208 pages, includes CD-ROM, $29.95)

Careers By Design: A Business Guide for Graphic Designers, Third Edition by Roz Goldfarb (paperback, 6 × 9, 232 pages, $19.95)

Please write to request our free catalog. To order by credit card, call 1-800-491-2808 or send a check or money order to Allworth Press, 10 East 23rd Street, Suite 510, New York, NY 10010. Include $5 for shipping and handling for the first book ordered and $1 for each additional book. Ten dollars plus $1 for each additional book if ordering from Canada. New York State residents must add sales tax.

To see our complete catalog on the World Wide Web, or to order online, you can find us at *www.allworth.com*.